Full Out Fiend

Copyright © 2022 by Abby Millsaps

All rights reserved.

eBook ISBN: 9798986018065
Paperback ISBN: 9798990077003

No portion of this book may be reproduced, distributed, or transmitted in any form without written permission from the author, except by a reviewer who may quote brief passages in a book review.

This book is a work of fiction. Any resemblance to any person, living or dead, or any events or occurrences, is purely coincidental. The characters and story lines are created by the author's imagination and are used fictitiously.

Developmental Editing by Melanie Yu, Made Me Blush Books
Line Editing, Copyediting, and Proofreading by VB Edits
Cover Design © Silver at Bitter Sage Designs

To Mel and Beth—
This book exists because of you. Thank you for seeing Fielding's potential and for encouraging me to write what I love.

Content Warning

Full Out Fiend is a full-length romance novel that contains content some may find triggering, including offensive language, substance abuse, failed contraception, discussion of state and federal abortion laws in the United States, and emotional abuse/gaslighting from a parent toward an adult child. It is a dual POV story featuring characters in their mid-to-late twenties. It ends with a happily ever after.

Chapter 1

Fielding

"You're killing us," Jake mutters before lining up another twelve shot glasses. "I'm gonna start making you pour these yourself if you keep this shit up."

My focus jumps to his face, and I anxiously search for genuine hostility behind his jibe. The logical part of my brain knows he's joking, but there's still a residual uncertainty on my end when we interact.

He finally looks my way and casts me a reassuring eye roll.

I exhale a breath I didn't know I was holding before finding my voice. "Don't pretend like you don't love it. Admit it, man. I'm good for business." I sit a little straighter and puff out my chest.

He smirks and mutters under his breath about being good for something.

I fight back my own smile, reveling in how amazing it is to be in his good graces once again, then take a sip of the beer I've been nursing for the last hour as I scope out the scene on the dance floor.

The Oak is packed, the vibe downright jovial. Nineties pop blares through the speakers, and there are more asses shaking to the beat than filling up the seats. Jake can bitch all he wants about the extra work I create when I buy rounds of shots for the bachelorette parties that frequent his bar most weekends, but he freaking loves this.

Besides, who am I to deny the ladies of Hampton when they're out on the town, celebrating a bride's last hurrah? I like to think of my generosity as contributing to the greater good.

They drink for free.

The Oak maintains its status as the place to be each and every weekend.

And more often than not, I land myself a distraction for the night in the form of someone who isn't spoken for.

There was a time when happily married was just my type.

I silently jeer at the self-deprecating thought. It's going to be hard enough to push down memories a la Victoria Thompson over the next two weeks. No point reliving that shit now.

Volunteering at Camp New Hope may not be the best idea I've ever had, but I need the clinical hours to meet the conditional requirements of my acceptance into medical school. And the camp needed a volunteer to run the first aid tent.

It's not like she'll be there. I cleared that with the director before I committed.

But still.

I drain my beer, then watch Cole line up the shots on a tray.

"You coming?" he asks with a smirk.

"Nah. You know I like to sit back and watch the magic unfold."

He shakes his head and chuckles before he navigates through the crowd of gyrating bodies on a path to the closest bridal party. Mere seconds pass before their squeals of delight rise above the cacophony of the whole bar belting out a Britney song. I can't resist raising my phone and snapping a selfie to send to my brother.

Fielding: Don't worry, bro. The ladies of Hampton won't go thirsty tonight. Upholding the Haas family tradition at The Oak in your honor.

When my phone vibrates a few seconds later, I expect to see a response from my brother, but it's his girlfriend.

Little Wheeler: BEHAVE, Fielding. Dem and I are supposed to be having a relaxing weekend before my classes start back up. Do NOT give him shit to worry about right now.

Fielding: Every party has a pooper...

Little Wheeler: Guilty. I'd rather shit on your parade than have to clean up a mess from California. Love youuuu

"Hmph." I scoff at her preemptive scolding, but I can't really judge her for jumping to conclusions. I have a solid record of creating or finding myself in situations that require my brother to save my sorry ass.

Cole shifts back behind the bar, still balancing the tray in one hand. He sets it down gingerly, then looks up and juts his chin in my direction.

"One left," he declares. As if I can't see the lone shot with my own eyes. "You want it?"

I glower at the shot glass mocking me from where it's centered on the tray. I'm done for tonight. I have to be up early tomorrow. But I didn't miscount. And Jake didn't overpour.

"Which party?" I challenge.

"That group right there." Another jut of his chin toward a rowdy gaggle of women across the bar.

I snatch the shot off the tray, hop off the barstool, and turn on my heel to rectify the situation.

Chapter 2

Daphne

As a little girl, I believed in fairy tales.

Prince Charming saving the princess. The promise of a better life. The magic of happily ever after.

But I'm pretty sure Sleeping Beauty never woke up to a text message from Prince Charming's brother, informing her that they'd both been granted "free passes" for the weekend of their bachelor and bachelorette parties.

A free pass. My fiancé, Anthony, wanted a free pass. One last chance to—what? Sleep with someone else? Pick up an STD a few weeks before our wedding?

As if Vegas isn't dirty enough. My fiancé is currently two thousand miles away, seeking out pleasure in a stranger. While I'm in our hometown, surrounded by people I don't really like, pretending this night is everything I always dreamed it would be.

I don't know why, but this of all things is what finally broke me. I'm wrecked. Drained. Running on fumes when I should be brimming with excitement about my upcoming nuptials.

Striding out of the stall, I push down a fresh wave of tears along with the self-blame that bubbles just below the surface. I didn't do this. I didn't make him do this. But no matter how many times I remind myself that Anthony's an adult and he's responsible for his own decisions, I can't help but worry that I could have—should have—done *something* to prevent our demise.

Life has been nonstop for months. All our time together has been spent going over wedding details and arguing about the budget. That, and I moved in with my parents at the beginning of summer since my lease was up. We haven't had much time alone to really connect.

Anthony agreed that staying with my parents temporarily was the right decision—that we didn't need to rush moving in together. He wanted to wait until after the wedding so he'd have time to clean out his apartment and make space. I didn't think to question it at the time.

Now I'm questioning everything.

I turn on the tap and ignore the women beside me reapplying lip gloss and gushing about each other's outfits. That should be me. This night was supposed to be fun. Okay, maybe not fun—a girls' night in with my BFF and my little sister would have been more my speed—but I shouldn't be struggling to get through my own bachelorette party. I don't let the thought linger, though. If I do, I'm bound to cry. Again.

I still when a perfectly manicured hand reaches across and shuts off the sink. When I look in the mirror, my best friend's gaze is reflected back at me.

Serena's the only one who knows what's really going on. What Anthony did—how he did it—and what I plan to do next. Honestly, it was easier to get dressed up and come out tonight than it would have been to cancel with no explanation.

I'm calling off my wedding.

But even though he's the one who shut his phone off and made himself unreachable, I need to talk to Anthony first.

So here I am: a jilted bride, dressed in white, hoping my bridesmaids are too drunk to notice that I'm even more quiet than usual tonight.

"You good?" Serena asks, handing me a paper towel and helping me go through the motions. I'm grateful she didn't ask if I'm okay. She knows I'm not. I'm tired of being disregarded. Disregarded and underestimated.

"Good," I confirm with as much confidence as I can muster, meeting my best friend's gaze once more and giving her an assured nod.

"Melissa texted. Some guy bought us all shots. Duty calls. See you out there."

Serena has just as much love for my bridal party as I do. Aside from her, everyone in the group is related to Anthony in some way. His cousins and his brother's girlfriend are a special breed of handful—I'm pretty sure every one of them is already wasted. I wouldn't be surprised if they got into an actual bar brawl tonight.

Tucking my thick, curly hair behind my ears, I give myself one more assessment in the mirror.

I can do this. I *am* doing this. It's time to do what's best for me without worrying about what everyone else thinks or how they might react. I owe it to myself to turn back now before I'm so far in that I don't even recognize my own reflection.

I spent all day trying to make sense of Anthony's actions. I just keep circling back to the same conclusion: he did it because he could. Because he thought I'd take it. That I wouldn't cause a fuss.

But he's wrong. He just doesn't know it yet.

Chapter 3

Fielding

I'm stopped three times on my way over: once by someone Dempsey and I went to high school with at Archway Prep, then twice by patrons who mistake me for my identical twin. After exchanging niceties for the third time, I've had enough. I move through the bar like a panther stalking its prey, the crowd shifting as the scene blurs around me. If someone calls out or tries to stop me, I don't hear them. I'm solely focused on my target.

That target just so happens to be a cluster of scantily clad women wrapped in tight black dresses and gathered around a tiny high-top table.

The group parts instinctively as I approach, although none of them pay me any mind. They're too caught up in side-eyeing each other and cackling at everything and nothing.

I scan the group and try to catch someone's attention. They're all essentially clones of each other. Midtwenties. Perfectly arched brows. Faces painted with heavy makeup. Fake smiles, revealing blindingly white teeth.

All of them, that is, except one.

Her gaze settles on me an instant after I spot her, and I feel a physical tug in my core.

She's a stunner. Naturally beautiful, with thick curves and distinct features. Her makeup is lighter than that of her friends. Her body is softer.

Her eyes meet mine, and when I return her stare, she boldly refuses to look away. Even in the dark lighting of the bar, I can tell her irises are the lightest shade of blue, almost gray. She has this ethereal glow that shines from the inside.

She's also the one wearing white: the bride-to-be.

I look away and try to focus on anything or anyone but her. I can't let myself fall under the spell of someone who's unavailable. I'm done chasing after what can never be mine.

When no one else looks my way, I focus back on the angel in white. She's still staring, and something about her unabashed attention lights up my insides. It's like we're the only two people in the room. Like we could have an entire conversation without exchanging a word.

Tilting my head and giving her a pointed look, I hold up the unclaimed shot in question. Her cheeks redden, the heat moving down her neck and flushing her perfectly pale skin in the most alluring way.

I intended to tease the person who refused the shot. No one is better at making a scene than me. But the look on her face and the tension in her shoulders tells me she's the culprit, and there's no way in hell I can give her a hard time now.

I take a few more seconds to examine the scene. She's not engaged with any of the other women. They're all existing around her, and she's in her own world. Everything about her body language screams *I want to be anywhere but here*. How the hell has no one in the group noticed her discomfort? Or maybe they have noticed, and they just don't care.

My flirtatious intent transforms into defensiveness on her behalf as I piece together what's happening. She doesn't need a sleazeball fuckboy pushing a drink on her. If anything, she needs a friend.

"How are we doing tonight, ladies?"

That gets their attention.

Multiple heads spin in my direction, loose, voluptuous curls bouncing. Suddenly, twelve pairs of eyes are giving me their full attention.

"Hi," the woman closest to me croons as she places her hand on my arm.

"What's your name?" another one giggles.

I don't take my eyes off the bride.

"What are we celebrating?" I try again. I need more context—and I really want to hear her speak.

"It's Daphne's bachelorette party!" a clearly intoxicated redhead exclaims.

"Yeah," one of the blondes chimes in. "But she's the ultimate party pooper, so it's not exactly a wild time."

I cringe at the lack of filter. That shit wasn't even passive aggressive. The bride-to-be—Daphne—is standing *right there*.

"Is a wild time a requirement for a bachelorette party?" I challenge. "I mean, I've never been invited to one myself, so I don't know what's expected. Did it say 'wild time guaranteed' on the invitation?"

The women break into fits of giggles, each one talking over the other, trying to get my attention.

Their attempts are futile. I can't look anywhere but at her.

Apparently, she can't take her eyes off me, either. We're in a stalemate—a sexy, intimate, how-far-can-we-push-this stalemate. It's rare for a person to actually maintain eye contact when stared at the way I'm homed in on her. This woman really is different from every Jen, Kelly, Caitlen, Nikki, and Jessi in this place.

"We need more shots!" the redhead declares.

I lower my hand and angle my body to hide the single shot I'm still holding. The last thing we need is for these women to connect the dots about who supplied round one. Especially now that I realize it's the last thing the angel in white—*Daphne*—wants.

A high-pitched chant of "shots! Shots! Shots!" breaks out as Daphne rolls her eyes. I waggle my brows in reply, fully invested in seeing how this plays out. The smallest hint of a smile teases at the corners of her mouth. My brain instantly goes haywire when I focus on the perfect pink outline of her lips.

"Come *onnn*, Daph. You're supposed to be living it up! Let's get wasted!" The redhead pulls on Daphne's arm, disregarding any semblance of boundaries or personal space.

"I'm good. You guys go. I'll save the table."

She speaks. Even her voice is angelic—soft and a little raspy. My heart stutters.

"*Daph*," the redhead whines.

"I said I'm good," she insists. The flush of her cheeks deepens, crawling down her neck and painting her chest crimson.

I force myself to look away from the flushed skin along the neckline of her dress.

The redhead stomps one foot as she crosses her arms over her chest. "You're such a spoil-sport. Just come up to the bar! We're more likely to get free drinks if the bride is with us."

I've heard enough.

"No means no, Red."

With a scowl on her face, she opens her mouth, but I whip out my secret weapon before she can argue, smoothly sliding the shot I've been harboring under the table to her.

"Here. Drink that, then head up to the bar and tell Jake that I said the next round's on me, too."

The redhead doesn't question a thing—just accepts the random drink from a stranger before biting her bottom lip salaciously and throwing it back

"And who should I say is buying?"

I look back at Daphne, who's still considering me, before I reply.

"My name's Fielding. Fielding Haas."

Chapter 4

Fielding

The group scatters—most of them literally abandoning the bride now that free drinks are up for grabs. One girl lingers for a few seconds before Daphne gives her a subtle nod. Within seconds, she and I are standing at the high-top alone.

Awkwardness settles around us.

I should take the hint. A better man would leave her alone. But there's something about her I can't turn away from. And I never claimed to be a good man.

"Smoke break?" I joke, tilting my head in question.

"I don't smoke," she murmurs, looking away for the first time and tucking her thick dark hair behind her ear.

"I don't, either. Do you trust me?"

She doesn't reply. But she doesn't object. I take her teetering at face value. What do I have to lose?

Reaching for her hand, I smirk in satisfaction when she lets me pull her away from the table. "Come on," I insist as I navigate through the crowd and out the front door.

I hold on to her until we're rounding the corner, ducking into the narrow alley between The Oak and Clinton's, the restaurant next door.

Most people don't even realize this alley exists. It connects downtown to the back parking lot, and it's just wide enough to pass as a cut through.

I drop her hand, then rest my back against the cool bricks and squint through the darkness.

Mirroring my position, she settles against the opposite wall, staring past my shoulder for a moment before she closes her eyes and blows out a long breath.

She's almost a foot shorter than me. Ideal, really, for appreciating the full, gorgeous tits straining against the white fabric of her dress. I watch as she inhales with eyes still closed, her chest rising in a way that has me holding back a groan.

She's got this pale, luminous skin framed with a flowing halo of dark curly hair. Her dress fits nicely, but it's a more modest cut than any other girl in the bar is wearing tonight, which drives me a little insane. A few inches shorter or just a bit tighter and I could get a better idea of every soft, luscious secret she's hiding.

I'm standing across from an angel in the middle of an alley: the kind of woman who looks like she was custom made for me.

She's a ten. But she's curvy as hell with an ass that's literally two handfuls. So she's a twelve. I have to clench my fists at my sides to quell the urge to reach out and pull her into me.

We're close enough that I can see her pulse thrumming in her neck. She must feel my eyes on her, but she doesn't step away. Doesn't fidget under my examination. I force myself to look away, granting her a few moments of peace I'm sure she needs if she's been dealing with pushy bridesmaids all night.

I blow out a long breath as I remind myself that she's wearing white for a reason.

She's the bride. More than spoken for. So off limits I should be stalking down this alley without a backward glance.

But instead, I'll stand here and revel in this little slice of purgatory, then gladly accept my ticket to hell if it means I can be near her for just a little longer.

She breaks the silence first.

"This would be less awkward if one of us actually smoked."

It's the dry delivery that confirms this girl is so much more than meets the eye.

"It seemed like you could use a break," I retort.

Her lips press together in a slight grimace. "Maybe that's what it looked like to you, but I'm not a damsel in distress who needs saving. I've been dealing with that group of women for almost a decade. I had it under control."

So tonight wasn't an awkward one-off encounter? Yikes.

"Okay, fine. Maybe *I* needed a break and wanted company," I quip. Turning it back on me is probably a safer angle than questioning her shitty choice in friends.

She lifts her impossibly pale blue eyes, squinting at me as if she's deciding whether to call me on my bullshit.

"My name's Fielding, by the way. I know I already introduced myself in there, but yeah..."

It's not the smoothest line. But I want her to trust me. She just followed a stranger into a dark alley. I don't want to spook her before we even have a chance to properly introduce ourselves.

She nods once, accepting my reintroduction without challenge. "I'm Daphne."

I offer her my biggest smile, turning so my shoulder pushes off the bricks before I take a microstep forward. "It's nice to meet you, Daphne. Do you live around here?"

"Hampton born and raised, although I moved to Chagrin Falls after high school. What about you?"

"I grew up in New York, but my family moved here when my brother and I started high school. I've been here ever since."

"So you're a townie?"

I grasp at my chest in mock outrage. Sure, I've lived in Hampton for fifteen years, but I don't quite meet the qualifications of a townie. I didn't grow up here. I didn't attend the public schools. But I'm not about to offend this woman if that's her vibe.

"I don't consider myself your typical townie. But I probably don't have time to tell you my life story. I'm sure your friends will be texting or calling any second, if they haven't already."

Daphne scoffs and turns her head to glance in the direction of the bar. "Joke's on them. My phone's off."

"Really?" I challenge in surprise. Sometimes I forget my phone even has the ability to power off. "Why?"

She looks up, and I swear she inches closer. The alley is dark, but not so dark that I can't see the way she's assessing me. It doesn't feel sexual or like she's checking me out. Her head is tilted, her thoughtful expression morphing into bewilderment when I don't turn away from her appraisal. I feel completely exposed to her in this moment, but I don't hate it. It's like she's probing my integrity and analyzing who I am on the inside.

She's trying to figure me out. Eventually, I shudder involuntarily under the intensity of her stare.

A few breaths pass, then something shifts between us. It feels like a decision has been made. When she speaks, her voice is soft and vulnerable.

"This morning, my fiancé got on a plane to Vegas for his bachelor party. Before takeoff, he had his brother text me. He wanted me to know we both had "free passes" this weekend. By the time I read the text, Anthony had already turned his phone off, and I had no way to reach him."

What the actual fuck?

"I've put up with a lot over the years... we've been together since I was a sophomore in high school. But I won't stand for this. I'm done."

She clears her throat and pulls her shoulders back before she speaks again.

"I'm calling off the wedding. He just doesn't know it yet."

The resolve in her declaration is poignant. And hot as hell. She doesn't say anything else—instead, she leans back against the bricks on her side of the alley and blows out another long breath that transforms into a sigh.

I gulp down the discomfort that's lodged in my throat. I don't know where to even start after that confession, so I jump to the most obvious question. I think I already know the answer, but I'm still compelled to ask.

"All those girls in there with you..." I trail off, hoping she gets my drift.

"They know nothing. Only my best friend Serena knows what actually happened... and what I'm going to do. I'm just here playing a part. Most of my bridal party consists of Anthony's cousins and friends, so I couldn't very well cancel tonight without them coming up with their own theories."

Holy. Shit.

"Damn, angel. This really isn't your night."

"It wasn't. But then you showed up, and now I'm thinking it could be?" she counters without missing a beat.

My body snaps to attention as I search her face. She's looking up at me with those gorgeous pale eyes through dark, thick lashes, biting on her lower lip in clear invitation.

Fuck me.

I would take this woman home in a heartbeat. Let her wrap those thighs around my head until I had properly suffocated, died, and gone to heaven. Or hell. Either option works if it means I get to spend a night with her.

But I'm not exactly a catch. Most of my conquests these days are consensual but intoxicated encounters to pass the time. I am, without a doubt, the most emotionally unavailable human at this bar. Probably in the whole fucking city. I'm still not over a relationship that never even existed, for fuck's sake.

But right now, I'm sober and peering down at an insanely attractive woman who's made me feel more in the last ten minutes than I have in the last two years.

There's something here. And if she feels it, too—who am I to deny her?

This girl is clearly looking for an outlet and trying to get over someone she thought she loved. We're both broken. Maybe we could be enough for each other for tonight.

"So what do you say, Fielding? *Is* tonight going to be my night?"

It's an offer. A challenge. A moment of truth. Lucky for her, my personal version of truth has never bent in an arc of morality and justice. My version of truth takes what it wants, consequences be damned.

"I think it is," I confirm with a smirk.

Chapter 5

Fielding

It takes less than two strides to close the space between us. My hand instinctively weaves into the hair at her nape, fingers curling into the thick mane and tilting her head up.

I bend.

She rises.

We're inches apart, dancing around the possibility of everything this night could be. As I stare into her eyes, I realize she's holding her breath—from anticipation or worry, I'm not sure.

"I'm not going to kiss you," I murmur reassuringly. "Not here. Not yet. Not where anyone can see. I'm good at keeping secrets."

She nods, her face relaxing as I move to tuck a loose strand of hair behind her ear.

"I promise I'll make up for it later. If we're doing this, we're going to do this right. As soon as we're alone, I'm going to kiss you here"—I run the pad of my thumb along her lower lip—"and here"—I brush the tips of my fingers down her neck—"and definitely here," I declare, tracing the sweetheart neckline of her white dress.

She shudders under my touch before grinning up at me with an eagerness I feel in my bones.

"I'm going to make a fucking feast out of your tits, angel." I caress down the side of her body, grabbing a handful of ass and squeezing.

"Then I'm going to dig in and eat this ass for dessert."

A whimper escapes her lips in response to my words.

"You're sure you want to do this?" I confirm.

She's the freaking bride-to-be. But I've always had a thing for off limits.

"Pretty sure."

"Pretty sure won't cut it, Daphne. We have to be on the same page about what's happening here. One night. No strings. You don't ever have to hear from me again. I'm going out of town tomorrow, then I'm starting med school in Cleveland a few weeks after that."

She cocks her head and narrows her eyes, worrying her bottom lip, thinking this through. Good. I have no problem playing my part. But she has to be all in.

"Really sure," she finally declares.

I straighten up and put space between us. If I don't, there's no way we'll leave this alley anytime soon.

"What do you need to do before you can get out of here?"

I'd almost forgotten that there are a dozen drunk bridesmaids inside The Oak. Based on what I've observed, they probably haven't even noticed she's gone. But she'll no doubt still have to jump through a few logistical hoops before she can make a clean getaway.

"I just need to find my friend Serena. She'll cover for me."

"Are we going to yours or mine?" I wonder out loud.

Daphne scoffs as if the answer is obvious.

I cock one eyebrow in question.

"I'm temporarily back with my parents," she admits, "and they live next door to Anthony's parents." She stares at the ground, tracing a crack in the cement with the toe of her high heel. She huffs out an exasperated sigh before asking, "If we go to your house, are you going to kidnap me and tie me to the bed?"

Her question is in jest. I think. I take it as my opportunity to lighten the mood.

"Do you *want* me to tie you to my bed?"

Her head snaps up and her eyes blow out, the black of her pupils dominating her light gray irises. There's more shock in her reaction than desire—*noted*.

I have no problem taking this angel home and stripping her out of her pure white dress and vanilla expectations. Maybe I can even add some flavor to her repertoire.

I clear my throat to get my head out of the gutter.

"I live on the edge of town, down 303 toward the Cuyahoga Valley National Park. I'll give you my address and phone number, and you can give them to your friend." Hopefully, my transparency will put her at ease.

"Not necessary," she declares. She smiles once more before stepping forward to head toward The Oak.

I reach for her on instinct.

"Hey..."

She freezes, letting me take her hand without hesitation, just like she did when we came out here.

"If you change your mind—" I start.

"I'm not going to change my mind," she interrupts.

Good.

But just in case...

"If you change your mind at any point," I pause and give her a pointed look for emphasis, "I can drive you back into town or take you home. Standing offer."

She squints through the darkness, like she's still trying to figure me out. I meet her gaze head-on, just like when we locked eyes in the bar. The energy that thrums between us is almost audible it's so damn strong.

"Why are you doing this, Fielding? What's in it for you?"

Is that a hypothetical question?

From her gorgeous legs up to her thick thighs... from the curve of her hips to those luscious tits I'm already fantasizing about...

She's gorgeous and soft, feminine and sensual. She's got this luminescent pale skin that will mark up so pretty for me. By the end of the night, she's going to be pink and red all over, and I'll make sure she loves every second of it.

I gently tug on her arm to pull her back into my body, hovering for a breath before bending to whisper in her ear.

"You, angel. I couldn't take my eyes off you from the second I came over to your table. But with all this white"—I skim both hands up the sides of her dress—"I thought I never stood a chance. You're giving me an opening. And I'm fucking taking it.

"You may think I'm a nice guy, but I'm not a good man. I see what's in front of me. I know what I'm getting out of this night. Get in there and tell your friend goodbye. I need to feel those thighs squeezing around my head, and soon."

I give her the smallest nudge in encouragement, then smack her ass when she turns to leave.

She yelps, looks back over her shoulder with wide eyes, and grins.

I don't bother watching her walk away—I refuse to waste another second when I'm so close to having her in my bed. I stride through the alley in the opposite direction toward the back lot so we can officially get this night started.

Chapter 6

Daphne

This isn't me. I've never picked up a stranger in a bar. I've never even had a one-night stand.

Serena's eyes widened in shock when I whispered my plans in her ear, but her surprise quickly transformed into encouragement, just like I knew it would.

She'll cover for me tonight. Then tomorrow she'll help me make sense of everything: how to cancel all the vendors for the wedding and how to break the news to my parents. It's going to be a nightmare to navigate the fallout over the next several weeks, but I don't have to think about that tonight.

Serena has always been on my side. I've known her since our first year of cosmetology school. She's never been a fan of Anthony, and this "free pass" nonsense put the nail in his proverbial coffin in her mind.

In mine, too, I guess.

The worst part is the nagging sense of knowing that teases at the edges of my mind. I've spent nearly a decade making excuses for my almost-ex-fiancé's behavior—telling myself that all relationships have ups and downs or that I was being overly sensitive when he did or said something that didn't land well.

But then I think about the way he'd make comments about female actors when we'd watch a movie. And how he asked me to change outfits before going to his parents' house for dinner last week. Or that time a few years ago when I found a dating app on his phone, but he insisted he was trying to help a friend.

If I'm honest with myself, the inklings were always there. But we grew up together, and over the years, we wove into each other's lives in a way I thought was permanent and inevitable. After three years, then five years, then eight years, all the little things were easier to dismiss than fight about.

We started dating my sophomore year of high school. I was so young now that I look back on it—but I was the last of my friends to have a boyfriend.

As one of the boys next door, Anthony wasn't even on my radar, but he was a year older and had a car. After one particularly bad fight with my mom—she had this protein shake she insisted I try, and I just wanted cereal for breakfast—he found me crying in the side yard between our houses. He was a big guy, even at sixteen—tall and girthy, perfect for playing right guard on the Hampton High football team. He had always teased me when we were younger, so when I saw him there, I quickly dried my eyes and tried to take off toward my house before he could spot me.

I didn't make it inside. But the teasing never came, either.

He offered to drive me to school that morning, and he even stopped at Jersey Bagels on the way. The freedom that came with having a friend with a car—having a way to get to school that wasn't the bus or begging my mom for a ride—was blissfully beautiful.

I took solace in his presence. In the way he'd make me smile when I was on the verge of tears because of something my mom said about my outfit or my hair. He wore too much body spray. His car was cloyingly sweet. It should have been nauseating. But given the alternative, I found comfort in the scent—in his car—in his company.

But was he really that great? Or was he just better than what I was used to?

I didn't like him in any romantic sense at first. But when he asked me to the homecoming dance, I was afraid to say no. I didn't want things to change between us. He was my safe space, my lifeline to and from school, a way to assert my independence.

I agreed to go to the dance with him that fall. Then I let him kiss me before he dropped me off at home. By the winter formal, we were officially dating. And by prom, we were inseparable.

Our relationship progressed slowly, in a way I thought was natural. But in hindsight, I can see that I was going through the motions: checking the boxes and unexpectedly planning a future with someone who was comfortable and convenient.

I'll never forget the first time he brought up the topic of marriage.

He was at his cousin's wedding, and he was drunk off his rocker. He called me that night and told me that he knew I was the one for him. I was only a senior in high school, but the thrill of his words—the thrill of being *wanted*—filled me with so much warmth.

I had never felt cherished like that before. *Valued*.

I'm not sure I've felt that wanted since—until now.

I blow out a deep breath, struggling to muster the excitement—and arousal—that coursed through me in the alley just a few minutes ago.

I never do things like this, but I'm doing it tonight.

I'm doing it with Fielding.

Butterflies of anticipation flutter in my stomach as I think about the man who's had me in a trance for the last half hour.

He's gorgeous. Like ridiculously good looking. Tall—really tall—with a head of messy blond waves and striking blue eyes. Big, strong hands that left a trail of tingles everywhere he touched. A smirk that made all my feminist ideals leach out of my brain and left me swooning.

He's the type of guy I've always thought was out of my league. But he was laying it on thick out in that alley. Every word, every action, even though he was propositioning me, felt sincere.

He likes what he sees—he made that abundantly clear. And I like this version of me, too. Especially tonight. Tonight, I'm taking back control and climbing into the driver's seat of my own life.

I gulp down the familiar flavor of self-consciousness. I've worked too hard to let self-sabotaging thoughts ruin this.

I've already made my decision.

This won't go down in history as the day Anthony cheated on me with a prostitute in Vegas.

This will be the night I finally stood up for myself and took back my power.

Fingers wrapped around the door handle, I glance back at my bridal party one more time. They're hanging off bar stools and making a scene on the dance floor. Not one glanced my way when I came back inside, so I doubt they'll realize I'm gone.

Serena catches my gaze and offers me a mock salute, banishing any lingering hesitation and sending me off with a little boost of courage. I push open the front door of the bar, then stride a few steps to the left and peek around the corner into the alley.

It's empty.

He's gone?

My heart drops for a millisecond before the roar of an engine grows louder on approach. I don't even have to look down the street to know it's him.

My legs tingle with adrenaline. My core pulls in anticipation. Seconds later, he drives into view, straddling a motorcycle and looking even hotter than he did in the alley.

He swings into the open parking spot in front of me but leaves the bike running.

I try to hide my shock as I gawk at him, those impossibly long legs straddling all that metal.

"Have you ever ridden a bike, angel?" he calls out over the sound of the engine.

I blush at the pet name he seems set on. I wonder if he plans to use it later tonight. I sort of hope he does.

I shake my head, not trusting my voice to reach him over the rumble of the bike.

A spark of concern flashes on his face, and his eyebrows crease together in the most adorable way, forming a little wrinkle above his nose. Two seconds later, he's dismounting and stalking toward me.

"I'll call us a car then."

That.

That right there.

That attentiveness and concern—it's foreign to me, but I like it. It's like a warm hug. Genuine and real.

That's why I'm doing this with him.

If he can read me this well, I'll be fine. Maybe even more than fine if any of his dirty talk from that alley plays out as promised.

"No way," I object, striding to meet him on the sidewalk. "I want the full Fielding experience. Take me on a ride."

He freezes where he stands, smirks, then holds out his hand in offering. The punchline passes between us silently. I can't help but roll my eyes at the unspoken dirty joke.

I'm not kidding. I want him to take me on a ride tonight.

He's a stranger.

A stranger with a motorcycle.

But something in my gut tells me he's also a good guy. Even if he claimed not to be a good man. I've already decided he's decent. Kind. And if that cocksure attitude is any indication, he's also really good in bed.

I don't need or want a good man right now. Everyone said I *had* a good man—and look where that got me. I just need a good distraction. This motorcycle and the six-foot-two blond holding out a helmet for me will be more than good enough for tonight.

Chapter 7

Daphne

Being on the back of a motorcycle is thrilling. The rumble of the machine under my bare thighs serves as the perfect teaser for the night ahead as we zoom headfirst toward the main event. I don't even blink as we whiz through a construction zone, orange barrels blurring in a visual inferno. I'm done toeing the line and playing it safe. I don't need a warning about what happens next.

Fielding slows the bike as we approach a gated driveway. I dig my nails into his sides like I've done multiple times over the last ten minutes. First I gripped him out of fear; now my touch is all anticipation.

The bike comes to a smooth stop, and he punches a passcode into the security box. What in the world...? I don't mean to watch, but I do.

The gate swings open like something out of a movie. Or an episode of *MTV Cribs*.

We coast along the tree-lined driveway as a huge home comes into view.

I guess he forgot to mention that his *place* is a literal mansion.

I school my expression as he rolls the motorcycle into the opening garage bay.

He stops and secures the bike, then swings off with ease. My legs wobble after straddling a vibrating hunk of metal for the last ten minutes, leaving me to contemplate how to approach my dismount.

Within seconds, he's offering me his hand and murmuring, "Offer stands, angel. Say the word and I'll take you home."

I scoff at his presumption. "I'm not going anywhere but into that enormous house."

He bites down on his lip, then hits me with a dazzling smile. Hand in hand, he leads me through the dimly lit garage.

I hold on tight as he guides me through a door. A few low lights illuminate our path down a long hallway, but he doesn't bother flicking on more.

Suddenly, I feel off balance, trailing after a stranger in a foreign place. I didn't even think about whether anyone else would be here. Does he have roommates? A family?

"We have the whole place to ourselves," he whispers, as if he can read my mind. "Do you know what that means?"

I let silence serve as my answer before he continues.

"I want to hear you scream at the top of your lungs every time I make you come tonight, angel."

My cheeks flush in the dark. We just met. I'm all in with this one-night stand business, but I have little confidence that I'll be able to finish with a stranger.

It only happened about half the time with Anthony—and only when I really focused. But that's not something I want to share with a man I just met, whom I'll likely never see again.

I steel my spine as Fielding guides me through the dark house. This night is *mine*. No expectations. No judgment, either. If this guy wants to step up to the plate and try to make me orgasm, who am I to stop him?

I didn't set out to pick someone up. I didn't set out for any of this to happen. Yet here we are...

Fielding approached me. He saw what no one other than Serena bothered to see. When he looks at me... *shit*...

At that exact second, he glances over his shoulder and pulls two water bottles out of the fridge.

When this man looks at me...

My insides turn to goo. My brain sort of does, too. All I feel is lust: a carnal urge that makes our connection feel natural and instinctual, like a needy, heady electric current running between us.

When he looks at me, he looks like he wants to eat me alive.

I want to let him. Almost as much as I want him.

Chapter 8

Daphne

I expected things to feel awkward. I expected my body to tense up when the reality of what I'm doing sank in. I expected my brain to kick into overdrive, my anxiety to spike, my mind to overanalyze each word, every move.

But as we weave through the dark maze of this mansion Fielding calls home, eagerness dominates all other sensibilities.

Now we're in a room that smells like him: salt and musk, with a hint of crisp apple.

The lights are low. There's an enormous bed positioned against one wall; French doors that lead onto a patio or balcony along another. The space is neat; tidier than I'd expect for a motorcycle-driving, bachelorette-party-targeting, one-night-stand kind of guy.

I've given up trying to think with any logical part of my brain. I'm giving in to this moment and this man. It's like I'm drunk on lust, inebriated with desire. Letting the animal inside me make decisions is an almost foreign sensation—to act on impulse without applying logic and reason—but it's also freeing, and it feels really freaking good.

He guides me over to the far side of his room instead of the bed—I follow. Obediently. Hungrily.

He smirks before pushing me against the wall, bringing his lips to mine, and moaning on contact.

His kiss is demanding. Dominating and hungry. His tongue dips into my mouth with force before he pulls back, peppers me with pecks, and leaves me panting for more.

I kiss him back—*finally*—pushing down stray thoughts about how different this kiss is to any I've experienced before. I sink into the eagerness of his mouth on mine. The taste of him consumes me as blatant, unfettered desire courses between us.

Everywhere he touches heats up. Even when he runs his hand down my stomach, or squeezes the width of my hips, I don't shy away. He so clearly wants me—all of me, just like this—every doubt and self-conscious thought melts away, one by one, with each graze.

I'm breathing heavily by the time he moves his mouth away from my lips, skimming down the sensitive skin of my neck. He nips at my ear before demanding, "Take this dress off before I rip it from your body."

Emboldened by his directness, I reply with sass I don't normally assert.

"Take it off yourself if you're so eager."

He's tall—I noticed it in the alley, then really registered the difference when I had to wrap my arms around his waist on the back of the motorcycle. But craning back to look up at him now reaffirms how foreboding he really is.

He holds my gaze for one second, then another. Heat builds in my core as he stares into the depths of my desire. Finally, he grasps me by the shoulders, spins me in place, and pins me to the wall.

He brushes my hair to one shoulder, inspiring goosebumps along my back. The warmth of his breath tickles my skin before he dusts feather-light kisses on my neck.

His fingertips trace the back of my neckline in a slow, drawn-out gesture. He's not hesitating. But he's clearly in no rush.

The dress tightens, stretching across my chest as he gathers the fabric, then grips the zipper.

The pull of the fabric is as tight as the tension coiling in my belly, his unhurried pace creating the most delicious anticipation in my core.

This man will be my undoing.

I've never been more eager to come undone.

The zipper travels down—down, down, down—the sound of the slow slide and the release of the straining fabric consuming me. Every inch of my exposed skin is greeted by his hands, then his lips. He's kissing down my spine. Then he's dropping to his knees.

I roll my shoulders to shuck off my dress as he unhooks my bra, the fabric fluttering down my body and pooling at my feet.

Fielding's touch disappears for a fraction of a second as I stand there, nearly naked, pressed against his bedroom wall, desperate for him to make his next move.

I gasp when his fingertips brush against my ankles and physically shudder when his lips meet the crease of my pressed-together thighs.

With his hands hooked under the lace of my thong, he peels it down and discards it at my feet in one swift movement.

I'm bare. Naked, exposed, and so damn needy to feel him anywhere. No. not anywhere—*everywhere*.

Both his hands knead into the fleshy part of my ass, his breath still hot on the apex of my thighs.

"Fuck, angel. It's even better than I imagined."

I gulp at his praise, a tiny part of me wishing he'd stand back up before he notices the cellulite on my legs.

As if reading my mind and choosing to do the *exact opposite*, he doubles down, nips at the right cheek, then growls like a feral animal.

"This ass. These hips. You're the whole damn package, Daphne. I could stay on my knees worshipping your backside all night. But I really want to taste your cunt."

I have to brace my palms against the wall to stop my knees from buckling.

"Will you let me do that?" he murmurs, his nose probing my ass as he nudges me against the wall. "Can I fuck you with my tongue and suck on your clit until you come all over my face?"

Fuck. Me.

Literally.

My cheeks are so hot they feel sunburnt.

I'm more grateful than ever to be pressed up against the wall. If he had said that to my face, I might die. There's that ever-present tingling of insecurity nudging at my conscious and reminding me that he could be making fun of me in this moment.

But he's not.

I can feel his sincerity. His *lust*. In the way he touches, in his tone.

I quiet the voice of self-doubt in my head and reply as confidently as I can muster.

"Yes," I agree on an exhale. "But only if you promise to fuck me senseless when you're done."

One hand cracks against my ass cheek.

"Deal, angel. Get up on the bed. I want you to sit on my face."

Chapter 9

Daphne

He removes his shirt and pants, simultaneously chasing after me and swatting playfully at my backside as we cross the room. I don't even have a chance to worry about how my behind looks because he hasn't taken his hands off me.

I climb onto the bed and kneel as he props up against the headboard and arranges the pillows the way he wants them.

"Come here," he murmurs in a low growl that sends a fresh surge of moisture trickling down my legs.

I crawl toward him, then straddle his torso awkwardly, uncertain about how exactly this is supposed to work.

"Up," he instructs without hesitation, jutting his chin.

Is he serious? I shift forward and straddle his chest, but I stop when my knees meet his shoulders.

This feels... unbearably awkward. And maybe even physically impossible?

"Hey, Daphne," he murmurs, running his enormous hands up my thighs as my muscles twitch from the awkwardness of the position.

When our eyes meet, he's got that cocksure smirk on his face.

"When I said sit, I meant sit. You can't expect to enjoy the ride if you aren't securely locked in place."

He grips my legs in encouragement, massaging where my thighs meet my ass as I scoot up farther.

"There ya go," he encourages when my center is finally hovering above his mouth. It's easier to straddle his head, but I'm still off-kilter and confused about how the hell this is supposed to work. What if he passes out from lack of oxygen? Should I ask if he has a safe word?

"You can put your hands on the headboard or in my hair. Now *sit*," he commands.

He tickles the backs of my knees then, making it impossible to hold my own weight as I careen back from his touch. I plop down not-so-gracefully onto his mouth, then suck in a ragged breath when his tongue darts out to greet me.

He chuckles against my folds, the feeling both unfamiliar and thrilling, before he speaks again.

"I figured you might be ticklish. If you want to get me back later, my weakness is my armpits."

And then he stops talking altogether and makes much better use of his smart mouth.

The first few licks are tentative and exploratory, like he's getting acquainted and purposely holding back.

It's exquisite.

But when the flat of his tongue runs from my ass up along my entire slit, then presses hard against my clit, I'm done for. I whimper at the sensation. He grips my thighs in response.

I should be worrying about crushing him, but then he does that hard, delicious stroke again... and *again*... and my hips start to move in rhythm to the symphony he's composing between my thighs.

Emboldened by his eagerness, I grip the headboard and use it to bear down, notching up the pressure of his mouth on my pussy. He growls in what I assume is pleasure or approval, the vibrations reverberating deep in my core.

He's holding my hips so tight there will no doubt be blue and purple fingerprints in the morning, grinding me against his face with so much force I cry out again and again. The sheer power of him has me singularly focused on wringing out every ounce of satisfaction he's willing to give me.

And, fuck, does this man know how to give.

This is exactly how I like it. It's how I do it when I'm alone. Forget gentle touches and soft caresses—I live for hard, steady pressure on my clit, just like this.

A euphoric sense of confidence blossoms in my chest as I moan my pleasure.

My thigh muscles tingle from the position, but it's nothing compared to the delicious heat warming my veins and percolating low in my belly.

Is this really happening? He's already figured me out. This man and his mouth are going to bring me to orgasm. This is *actually* going to work.

Fielding holds me down on his face as the tip of his tongue flicks rapidly over my clit. It's almost too much—*too good*—before he switches it up and sucks me into his mouth.

The sensation is overwhelming and all-consuming. If I wasn't already sitting firmly on his face, I would have been toppling over right about now. Just when I think I can't take another second of his sucking on my clit, he bites my aching nub, the sting jolting my hips forward before it transforms into deep, rolling pleasure.

"Again," I pant without thinking.

He bites more of me. Harder this time—my clit and the lips of my pussy stinging from the raw, delicious sensation of teeth on delicate flesh.

Fuck. *Fuck*. The tingle starts in my toes as I glance down to see him staring up at me.

"Please," I beg, and I swear to God, even though my thighs are covering half his face, he smirks. "Please do that again. It feels so fucking good."

He doesn't hesitate. He nips at my clit, bites hard on my pussy, and sucks on my folds in rapid succession as waves of pleasure detonate and travel to every nerve ending in my body.

He feasts as I spiral, drawing pleasure from my body and prolonging my release until I'm breathless and lightheaded and so fucking satisfied.

Chapter 10

Fielding

"You have two minutes to recover before I need access to that pussy again," I murmur, tracing the length of her spine with one finger as she pants softly beside me.

I may like calling her angel, but there's a little devil inside her who's more than capable of handling everything I have to give.

I reach over to the bedside table to snag one of the waters and a condom.

"Here," I urge, cracking open the plastic cap and holding it in front of her face. "Drink this."

She scoffs before peering up through hooded lids. Her cheeks and neck are flushed, and there's a light sheen of sweat along her forehead, creating a halo of little curls that cling to her face. I can't help but feel a surge of smugness at her totally blissed-out state.

"You give me one orgasm, and now you think you can tell me what to do?" she teases, rolling to her side and taking a tiny sip of water before glancing over with raised brows.

"I just made you come so hard you almost passed out, angel. I need you hydrated and primed now that I know you like it that rough."

She locks eyes with me for another second before tipping the bottle back and greedily sucking down half of it in two gulps. She's adorable. And feisty. A firecracker in my bed. A fucking feast for the taking.

I can't wait to kiss her again. Or to feel her tight little pussy clinging to me as I rail into her. And if she begs in the heat of the moment? I hold back a groan just thinking about the word *please* coming out of her mouth moments ago.

I'm rock hard from eating her out and watching her revel in her post-release ecstasy, but I want more.

No, not want. *Need* better describes the ravenous hunger coursing through me.

My desire for her—the need to satisfy her and make her come again and fuck her hard and fast as I chase my own release—is so much stronger than I expected.

Everything about tonight is more than I imagined it could be. More intense. More fun. More intimate. More satisfying. I can't wait another second to taste her.

I roll over and frame her in with my arms, pressing my forehead into hers in a move that might be a touch too intimate.

She wraps her arms around my neck and holds me tight, deepening the moment as our lips meet and our bodies glide against each other, acquainting themselves.

I want to touch her everywhere. Learn every curve, unlock every pleasure point. She's so soft and kissable.

So that's what I focus on. Kissing the shit out of this gorgeous, glowing angel who landed in my bed for the night.

I push my tongue into her mouth as I caress the length of her body. I'm hard as hell, and every stroke of her tongue against mine goes straight to my dick. I'm trying my damnedest to take my time, but she's insatiable.

Her hips tilt up in an inviting rhythm, her bare, wet core grazing against my boxers in a provocative dance that I know isn't giving her enough pressure. She's teasing herself as much as she's teasing me.

I jolt when she reaches into my underwear and wraps her fingers around my length.

"I want you," she murmurs against my lips, yanking on my dick while simultaneously pushing down the elastic of my boxers.

I hum with pleasure, moving my mouth to kiss the delicate skin of her neck before whispering, "So have me. Anything you want tonight—it's yours."

I sink my teeth into the tender flesh of her neck, and the noise she makes almost has me blowing my load in her palm.

I work my way down her body—kissing, sucking, biting every inch of pale, luscious skin. I pause when I reach her chest—two mounds of ample gorgeousness topped with dark pink peaks that look like they're desperate to be plucked and teased.

"Fucking perfect," I mutter before cupping both tits and running the pads of my thumbs across her nipples.

Daphne mewls in response—arching her back, then tilting her hips up to meet mine again. As if I need the encouragement.

I take one nipple in my mouth, lavishing it thoroughly, while my other hand wanders down her stomach.

When I reach the apex of her thighs, I grin—she's so wet and warm. She's beyond ready for me.

I roll her nipple between my teeth once more before switching sides, giving just as much attention to her other perfect tit while my fingers stroke her core.

"Fuck... Fielding. Please," she whimpers.

I hold back a groan. The way she begs is such a turn-on.

"What do you need, angel? I'll give you anything you want," I murmur, toying with her clit as I suck her nipple harder into my mouth.

"You. I need you. Hard and fast. Now. Please..."

Without conscious thought, I react to her plea, my body instinctively taking control. I pop off her nipple, lean back on my knees, rip open the condom wrapper with my teeth, and suit up.

"I got you," I promise, eyeing her gorgeous, writhing form as I line myself up with her entrance. "I know just what you need," I whisper before I slam into her perfect cunt.

Shock waves ripple through me. Intense pleasure spikes up and down my spine.

Her eyes fly open, growing as big as saucers, homing in on me and holding me in a trance. The connection is instant and exquisite.

Hovering over her body, I give us both a moment to get used to the sensation while her pussy flutters around my cock and she stares right into my soul.

I can't look away. She's cast a spell, completely enchanting me. I don't even feel compelled to move as energy and emotion zap between us. I just hold her gaze, stunned by the intensity of this moment.

She lifts her hands, cups my face, and softly begs, "Please."

That one little word spurs me to action. She's dripping wet with pleasure, so I don't bother building her up before assuming full speed. My hips piston forward, hard and fast, just how she asked for it, my dick slamming in and out of her tight, molten channel.

I give her what she wants. How she wants it. Full out.

Every thrust is hard enough to reverberate through her whole body. Her tits bounce as I fuck her, her hips tilting up and angling in a way that tells me I need to adjust our position.

I grab a pillow without breaking pace and shove it under her ass so fast I don't think she even realizes what I've done.

But the loud, drawn-out moan she gives up on the next thrust tells me she more than appreciates the effort.

I have no other motive in this moment than to fuck her senseless and send her careening off the cliff into another orgasm. Her need for pleasure—her desperation for release—makes me so damn eager to make this good for her.

She's given me the facts. I know my role in all this. I'm the easy lay: the one-night stand she'll hopefully never forget. I'm determined to make her feel good, to be the perfect distraction.

When she chants "yes, yes, yes," under her breath, like she's close, I go out on a limb and see how far she'll let me push.

"Daphne."

Her eyes fly open as if I've startled her, almost like she forgot where she was or who she was with. I keep pounding into her—refusing to let her lose what I'm certain is building pleasure in her core.

"Do you trust me?"

She replies with a dazed smile and an eager nod, throwing her hands above her head and pressing into the headboard to bear down as I thrust into her perfect cunt.

I move one hand up her body, slowly and methodically so she feels the path of my palm before I close my fingers around the curve of her neck.

Her eyes widen in response to my grip, but she doesn't pull back or panic. In fact, she moans louder, challenging me to tighten my hold and really let her feel it.

I squeeze her neck in time with my thrusts as her pulse dances under my fingertips.

Balancing on my knees, I flatten my other hand across her hips, low on her pelvis, pressing down and matching the pressure I apply to her throat.

Held down and at my mercy, she goes fucking wild, trying to rock her hips and match my rhythm, screaming her encouragement as she races toward the finish line.

I push harder on her pelvis, letting the force drive her higher. I squeeze her neck, drawing out a moan that transforms into a scream as she gets closer.

"Come on, angel. Prove to me you like it hard and fast. I want to feel you come all over my cock."

She clenches around me as she cries out. The tightness is exquisite—her perfect cunt choking my dick so hard I see stars. It only takes two more thrusts for me to join her, toppling over the edge and spilling into the condom with a ferocity I've never felt in my life.

Lightheadedness sweeps over me, reminding me to loosen my grip on her throat and slow my thrusts as we ride out the aftershock of coming together.

I collapse forward, making sure not to crush her as I ease out of her body. Our foreheads touch, and we lock eyes. I can't *not* look at her. I've never wanted to just stare at someone like this before.

We're both slick with sweat, flushed, and grinning. And even though this is supposed to be a one-night stand, I can't help but cup her face in my hands, tilt her chin up, and kiss her over and over again.

Chapter 11

Daphne

Lips to lips. Hands to face. Legs wrapped around each other. Every part of my body craves his touch. We haven't stopped touching since we collapsed back into bed.

His tongue sweeps into my mouth again before he trails a path of kisses along my jaw and down my neck. I'm totally spent—I barely made it to the bathroom, but Fielding insisted—and I'm seconds away from dozing off in his arms.

But he won't stop kissing me. And I can't get enough of it.

I've never had a one-night stand before, but I'm pretty sure it's not supposed to feel like *this*.

The sex was phenomenal—hard and fast, with no excuses and one goal in mind—but this cuddling? These soft touches and little sighs we keep passing back and forth between the sheets? This is heaven. I'll let him call me angel all damn night if he promises not to stop.

He rearranges himself, then shifts me up higher on the mattress so he can throw one leg over me and make me his little spoon. He keeps doing things like that—moving me and molding my body to fit into his, lifting me and positioning me like I weigh nothing at all.

I revel in the feeling of his large hand cupping my bare hip while his other arm snakes under my neck and he plays with my hair.

After we both came, I briefly considered getting up and getting on with it—grabbing my clothes and calling a rideshare or asking Serena to come pick me up. But then he hummed serenely into my neck. And something deep in my chest was instantly settled by the sound of his contentedness.

Plus, this bed is insanely comfortable. My body and my mind are yearning for sleep. And this man—who was a literal stranger hours ago, but who now possesses intimate knowledge about what I like and what makes me tick—is holding me like he doesn't want to let me go.

Tomorrow, I'll have to face the reality of what my life has become. I'll have to deal with the fallout; I'll have a million calls to make, an entire wedding to cancel.

But none of that is a concern right now. My misery will keep. These moments of being cherished and worshipped won't. So I'll stay in this bed, in this man's arms, and let myself have this night before I have to face the wretched reality of my tomorrow.

I jolt awake, panting and parched, desperate to calm my racing heart. I force my eyes wide open, willing myself to stay conscious and not slip back into the nightmare that was playing out in my mind.

I take in the room around me, the light of the moon streaming through the open blinds granting me a sense of peace as I scan the foreign surroundings.

I remember where I am. Why I'm here. Who I'm with.

Once I remember, I feel calm. Or at least calmer than I did a minute ago when I was trapped in the horrors of my own mind.

That wasn't the first wedding dream I've grappled with. But this one felt suffocatingly scary. Terrifying enough that the crush of adrenaline still lights up my nerves. The saddest part is that the dream wasn't even outlandish: nothing crazy happened to inspire this sense of dread.

It was my wedding day. Anthony was at the end of the aisle. Everything was going exactly as planned.

That's the problem—had my future played out as planned, I would have been trapped in a living, breathing nightmare. My reality—what I almost went through with; what I'll have to call off and navigate in the coming weeks—that's the real nightmare now.

I blow out a long breath, rolling to my side and trying to get comfortable.

Fielding stirs behind me. He reaches around my front with one arm, hooking under my hips and pulling me back until I'm flush with his body.

I wiggle my ass playfully as he cuddles me close.

He bites my shoulder in response, eliciting a whimper I would be embarrassed by if I were with anyone else. But not him. Not tonight.

"Settle down and go back to sleep or get ready for round three, angel," he whispers, his voice husky with sleep.

I still at his words, but not because I have any intention of settling down. There's no way I'll fall back to sleep anytime soon after the dream I just woke from.

"Round three is an option?" I muse, reaching behind me and gliding my hand down the valleys of his abdomen to find him fully erect. I tease my fingertips up the length of his shaft, then run my palm over the crown, making him moan in response to my touch.

"Abso-fucking-lutely."

He grabs my waist and hauls me up with him as he rolls flat on his back, positioning me on top as he rearranges himself beneath me.

We're both naked. I'm either *still* or *once again* damp between the thighs. I usually hate being on top. I never know where to put my hands, I worry about the dreaded double-chin effect, and I hate having to suck in my stomach—but those thoughts don't even exist in my mind thanks to the perfect distraction of Fielding's hands on my tits and his abs contracting beneath my thighs.

His fingers map my body, pinching and tickling in all the right places as he gazes up at me through half-closed eyes with a dazzling smile plastered on his face.

"You're a fucking dream," he murmurs as he palms both my breasts.

I swivel my hips in response, then bring my hands up to his, encouraging his fingers to clamp down harder on my nipples. He catches on quick, squeezing and pulling simultaneously as I moan my appreciation.

"How the fuck did your dumbass fiancé want a free pass for the weekend? I'm trying to figure out how to sign up for a monthly membership. Your body is incredible, Daphne. You feel so fucking good in my hands."

I grip his erect dick in one hand and roll my hips forward, rubbing my sensitive nub with his cock. I whimper as he grunts, both of us lost to the sensation of our bodies coming together.

I work myself up and down his length, holding his cock firmly against my core and creating the most delicious fire against my clit.

"Fuck, I love that. Use me, angel. Show me how hard you like it."

His words spur me on. I've never felt this uninhibited during sex. I don't worry about riding him too hard or about crushing him. Fielding makes it so easy to get lost in the moment. All I do is *feel*.

He moves his hands down my body until we're a tangle of fingers: me gripping and grinding on his dick, and him caressing and pulling on my pussy lips, spreading me open and running his fingers through my slick arousal.

"So fucking gorgeous," he murmurs, gazing up at me with the most earnest expression. "All of you. Every fucking inch. You're beautiful, Daphne. I can't believe I get to make this pussy come again tonight."

I release his dick, placing my hands on the tops of his thighs behind me and arching back to give him even more access to my most intimate places.

"Look at you. You love showing off for me, don't you?"

He uses both hands to spread me open. Every fingertip is an individual spark that sets my core on fire.

"You're so wet," he purrs, making the observation sound like the sexiest compliment. "So wet and ready. Your body knows what it wants now, doesn't it angel? Your body knows exactly what it's about to get from me."

He lifts one hand to his mouth, licking the tips of his fingers before bringing them back down to my clit. I moan on contact—I can't help it. I'm so turned on by his words, his praise, the way he's looking at me, and the promises he's making to my body.

He uses his whole hand to cast slow, hard circles against my clit, his attention flicking from my face to my pussy, then back up again.

"I can't wait to slam into you. I can't wait to hear you scream when I make you come a third time."

Apparently, I can't wait either, because a second later, I pounce. Leaning forward, I practically attack his chest with kisses, then grip his dick and line him up at my entrance.

A firm hand on my wrist freezes me in place.

"Condom, angel," he murmurs, sweeping a lock of hair behind my ear tenderly and tilting his head toward the bedside table. "They're in that drawer."

I gulp down the lump in my throat. Did I really almost ride him raw—a man I met hours ago, a guy who's made it clear this is just a one-night thing? I'll blame it on still being shaken by that nightmare.

Fielding must realize I'm trapped in my own head, because he sits up, his abs tensing beneath me, and reaches over to the nightstand.

"You good?" he asks cautiously, opening the condom wrapper in slow motion, almost as if he's giving me a chance to change my mind.

"So good," I reply, mustering up the confidence of the woman I was two minutes ago. The woman who was practically using his dick as her own personal dildo. The woman who almost came just hearing the dirty talk he dished out while he played with her tits.

Fielding rolls on the rubber, and not two seconds later, I'm impaling myself on his cock. I roll my hips forward once, closing my eyes and relishing the thickness of him filling me up so completely. Before I can move again, he cups my chin, forcing me to meet his gaze.

"Put your feet flat, Daphne."

His words are authoritative, and I don't even question it, just follow his command, awkwardly maneuvering my legs so I'm squatting over his hips with my feet planted on the mattress.

When I sink onto his length this time, he firmly grips my sides, supporting my ass and pushing me down harder—*deliciously harder*—before lifting me up and slamming me back down.

"You feel so fucking good," he grunts—whether in pleasure or from effort, I don't know. Together we find a fast, brutal pace. He uses his strength to drive me up and down on his dick while I succumb to nothing but everything.

Because that's what this is.

His support. His dominance. The way he's transformed this night into this intimate, inimitable experience. It's everything.

He lifts and lowers my body over and over again, the warmth in my core crawling up my stomach, heating my neck, flushing my face.

"Fuck," he grunts a minute later. "I can't keep this up."

I freeze, prickles of embarrassment poking at the bubble of bliss that's inflated inside me.

"I'm already close. You feel way too good, angel. We've gotta switch things up."

Relief—and another wave of arousal—courses through me.

"Why don't you turn around and let me watch that ass bounce while you ride me?" he grunts, huffing out a breath and shaking his head like he's trying to clear his mind.

I eagerly climb off, turn, straddle him again, and sink onto his dick. We groan in unison, and he grabs my waist, squeezing my hips and kneading his fingers into my ass.

"Daphne," he murmurs.

I glance over my shoulder without hesitation.

"Straddle just one of my legs and grind on me, angel. I can't reach your clit in this position."

Oh. Yes. That *is* important.

I pull one leg in, keeping him buried inside me as he bends his knee and pulls his thigh closer to where our bodies connect.

As soon as we make contact, I'm home.

"Fuck, yes. Oh fuck. That feels amazing."

I can't help the words that tumble out of my mouth—shock, awe, praise.

"Fuck. Shit. Yes."

Even in reverse cowgirl, he makes sure to maintain our electric connection. His hands are all over. I sense his eyes on my backside. He runs one palm down my spine; digs his fingers into the thickness of my ass. He even teases his fingertips against my back door as I ride him, inspiring all sorts of ideas for what we could do if we make it to round four. Or five. Six? Seven? There's no quantitative cap on the lust I feel in this moment. The limit does not exist.

I'm close—every cell in my body hums—and Fielding knows it, too. He spanks me hard before jacking up into me, his perfect dick and solid thigh muscle driving me higher and higher.

"There ya go, angel. Take it. Take it all. Ride me hard and grind that clit until your pussy gives me everything."

I come undone a moment later.

My orgasm is an unstoppable freight train—the strength of a tsunami clashing with the g-forces of a rocket blasting off. My clit throbs with pleasure as my pussy pulses.

I come, and I keep coming. I'm soaking Fielding's lap, but I have no control over my body's reaction to this experience—over my visceral, primal reaction to *him*.

I come harder than I've ever come in my life. I feel freer than I ever knew I could.

When I finally descend back to reality, he's grunting through his own release, our bodies attuned and in sync yet again.

I can't see his expression, but reverence and satisfaction thrum between us. He smooths his palms down either side of my spine, squeezing the tension in my shoulders as he repeats the pattern and massages my wrung-out muscles. When I'm sure he's totally spent, I try to dismount, only to be caught under the armpits and dragged backward into his arms.

"Come here, you," he demands playfully, tucking me in to the little-spoon position once again and tickling my neck with the stubble on his jaw.

He holds me. He kisses me. He pets me and caresses every inch of skin he can find, all the while whispering praise and adoration directly in my ear.

His words send tingles to my sated, thoroughly drained core. They don't stop there. They wrap me in a shroud of comfort and peace. A few of them reach even deeper, singing into the fiber of my being and finding a home in the fabric of my soul.

I know without a shadow of a doubt that I'll leave this night a different person. What's happening between us is changing me—breaking me down and building me up—propelling me forward into a future so much brighter than anything I've ever imagined for myself.

Chapter 12

Fielding

I spill my load in a daze. What a fucking wake-up call.

I'm shocked I even felt her stir beside me—I can fall asleep anywhere and sleep through anything. But as soon as she wiggled that ass into my crotch, it was game on.

Why things feel this fucking good with her defies all reason. But they do.

I kiss her closed eyelids, and she smiles. I don't want to let her go. I don't want this night to end. Even if we stayed up all damn night, it wouldn't be enough.

I'm getting ahead of myself here. Typical. I don't know how to half-ass anything. I only play full out.

But fuck. I can't remember the last time I felt like this.

Except that's not true. Because how could I forget? Her memory festers in my rotten, broken heart. Her smile is permanently etched in the darkest corners of my mind. I don't let myself cling to those memories anymore. Most days I can convince myself Tori was never even here.

Right now, someone *is* here. An angel who just woke me up for middle-of-the-night sex after a mind-blowing fuckfest. She's everything in this moment. Everything I want and everything I need.

I was serious when I said I might need a monthly membership to the Daphne Fan Club. But no—monthly wouldn't be nearly enough. I want an annual pass to that pussy.

It's not just her needy cunt and perfect tits that have me in a trance. Everything she does thrills me. I get the impression she doesn't even know how sexy, powerful, and attractive she is on the inside and out.

Within hours, she's latched on to something inside me. I feel achingly vulnerable and indulgent with her: like it's a privilege to be in her presence, and like I want her to see the real me. More than anything, I don't want her to walk out the door tomorrow and forget I exist.

I can't help but smile at the sleeping beauty in my arms. Her hair's a mess—a gorgeous, dark halo fanning out around her face. She looks peaceful with her mouth slightly parted, her kissable lips turned up in the tiniest smile.

I fight back the urge to kiss her again. Or to wake her for round four. We've fucked more than we've slept so far tonight. She needs rest.

But damn—I hate the thought of wasting even a second of our limited time together.

Maybe I can talk her into staying for breakfast. I know we said this was just for the night, but maybe If I get up before her, I could make waffles. Waffles... bacon... homemade whipped cream. There's no way she'll pass on round four if homemade whipped cream is involved.

I puff out my cheeks and steady my breathing, reluctantly rising up to head to the bathroom.

My feet falter, just slightly, as I stretch my legs and take tentative steps across the room. There's a legit possibility I'll be sore in the morning. This woman's got insane stamina.

Yawning, I flick on the vanity light above the sink and make my way to the toilet, moving to take care of the condom before I take a piss.

As soon as I feel it, I know.

The sensation of ick followed by stomach-dropping dread is an unmistakable combination.

I quietly groan as I shift into the glow of light from the vanity, then glance down to confirm my suspicions.

Goddammit.

There's a significant tear in the condom dangling off my half-mast dick. The whole thing's a mess.

There goes my dream of a good night's sleep, breakfast in bed, and more sex.

I curse under my breath and hop into the shower, not bothering to let it warm up as I scrub myself clean. My brain goes into damage control mode. My blood pressure ramps up by the second.

I try to calm my breathing as I towel off and mentally prepare for the inevitable freak-out I'm about to submit Daphne to.

Part of me wants to freak out, too. But that impulse is eclipsed by the urge to remain calm and make this as painless as possible for her. She's been through more than enough this weekend. I refuse to let this speed bump decimate what we've shared.

I'll tell her what happened and soothe her if I can. I'll encourage her to go back to bed, then we'll go to the drugstore first thing for the morning-after pill.

While she sleeps, I'll look up side effects and figure out what else I can do to help.

I can handle this.

It'll be okay.

I towel off quickly, then hit the light switch, casting the bathroom into darkness. Taking one more fortifying breath, I straighten my spine and walk back to the bedroom.

As soon as my feet move from the cool tiled floor to the plush carpeting of the room, my nerves fire off.

Something's not right.

Beyond the one thing that just went really, really wrong—something else is off, too.

I make my way to the side of the bed and tap the lamp on my bedside table, casting a soft, low light around the room.

The actual fuck?

My bed's empty.

The whole damn room is empty.

I give myself whiplash, jerking my head from side to side as reality sinks in.

Daphne isn't here. And neither is any of her stuff.

She left—*she fucking left*—and I don't even know her full name or her phone number or how the hell I'm supposed to find her if she doesn't want to be found.

I scrub my hand through my hair, then pinch the wrinkle above my nose.

Think, asshole. Think.

I was in the bathroom for less than ten minutes.

She couldn't have gotten far.

I snatch my pants off the ground and pull them up haphazardly as I hop from one foot to the other. I dig my phone out of the pocket and pull up the security feeds for the house.

Bullseye.

She's striding up the driveway with her phone glued to her ear. She's very clearly trying to get away.

I sprint out of my room and down the corridor of my wing of the house, silently cursing that it's one of the farther points from the garage.

I glance back down at my device as I reach the kitchen. She's approaching the gate. I'm never going to make it. I can do nothing but watch in horror as it swings open automatically to let her through.

I'm not even to the garage when a car pulls up. Then she climbs in, and she's gone.

Chapter 13

Daphne

I press the phone to my ear as I approach the wrought-iron gate at the end of the driveway. I think I remember the passcode from last night—earlier tonight, I guess—but miraculously, I don't need it; the gates swing open on their own.

"Did you get the pin I sent?"

I exhale when she confirms she's only two minutes away.

"Okay, good. I need to turn my phone off now."

I end the call and power down my device without saying goodbye.

This is a literal nightmare. I would rather close my eyes and dive back into a lucid, never-ending dream about my own pathetic relationship than have to endure this.

The worst part of it all? I knew better. I freaking knew better.

But after that third orgasm... and the way he kissed me and held me in his arms... I was delirious. Drunk on lust. Incapacitated, reveling in a satisfied, blissed-out state.

I rose out of bed automatically. My feet moved across the room of their own volition. I found my dress, dug the phone out of my pocket, and powered it on without thinking.

As soon as it came to life, a shrill tone blared through the speaker, like an alarm jettisoning me back to reality.

It took several seconds of staring, dumbfounded, for me to realize what was happening. Someone had initiated the lost phone technology and was pinging the location of my device.

In an instant, a flurry of texts and missed calls filled the screen. The notifications came in faster than I could read them.

I stood there, naked, trying to make sense of it all.

I clicked open the thread of messages from Serena—I knew I could count on her to help me navigate this—as the phone pinged almost nonstop in my hand. A quick scan of her dozen or so texts clued me in that I needed to get out of Fielding's house ASAP.

Anthony's very drunk cousin—and my bridesmaid—Melissa, didn't believe Serena when she said I headed home for the night. Rather than being cool about it, Melissa worked the whole damn bridal party into a tizzy, saying I ran off or had been taken or something.

By the time they left the bar, not only had Melissa called my parents, but my parents had tried to call me, and then somehow, miraculously, someone had gotten a hold of Anthony.

Anthony, who supposedly turned his phone off to sleep with a hooker.

Anthony, my ex-fiancé who doesn't know he's my ex-fiancé yet.

Serena tried to do damage control.

But Anthony blew a gasket. And pinged my phone, apparently.

So much for my indulgent, secret one-night stand.

I had no choice but to grab my clothes and hightail it out of Fielding's house. I left without saying goodbye—I was crunched for time, and after what we had just shared, there was no way he'd let me take off so easily. A clean break was my only escape.

I hate that he'll come out of the bathroom and think I ran off on him. But not as much as I hate the idea of Anthony tracking this location and sending someone to get me.

Because he would.

Alleged free pass or not, my ex-fiancé would take shit to the extreme. My parents and all our friends are already involved, and that's embarrassing enough. I refuse to let him shame me or make me feel like I did something wrong.

I lift my fingertips to my lips, then brush them along the hollow of my throat, remembering. Squeezing my thighs together, I savor the ache that's already blossomed there. I regret nothing. But I don't want this experienced to be tainted in any way.

Anthony doesn't get a say in what happened tonight—what I do is no longer his business. Now I just have to work up the courage to let him know that.

Approaching headlights bring me back to reality. Serena slows her car to a stop at the end of the driveway and rolls down the passenger side window, smirking with her tongue in her cheek as she assesses me.

"Was it worth it?" she asks as I slide into the car. She puts her SUV in drive before I even get the door closed.

"So damn worth it," I admit, bewilderment and an emotion that feels a lot like joy washing over me as I sink into the leather seat and remember all the little things that made this night one of the best of my life.

Chapter 14

Fielding

"Okay, super Keegan. Whatcha got for me tonight?"

The eight-year-old grins—is it still a grin if half the teeth are missing from the smile?—before syncing the iPad to his continuous glucose monitor.

He scrunches up his nose as he stares at the device.

"One-twenty-one and steady," he declares triumphantly, flipping the device around to show me the screen. I update his chart and high five him before he skips away.

"Next!" I holler, even though there's only one other child hovering by the door of the first aid cabin.

She shuffles into the room, shoulders slumped, then plops onto the cot with an exasperated sigh.

Sophie Meadows. She's been in here every day, sometimes more than once. I mindlessly grab for her chart, which I keep on my desk instead of refiling each night. I fight back a smile as she sighs again, louder this time.

"I have thirty-seven mosquito bites, and my whole body feels like it has a heartbeat!"

"Hold up. Did you say thirty-seven? Like three-seven?"

Her eyes go wide as she nods.

"Oh *no*. You're just three bites shy of the legal limit, kid. The maximum number of mosquito bites a kid can have at any given time is—hold on, let me double-check my research"—I hold up a random pad of paper from my desk—"forty. Yep. I knew it. You're practically an outlaw."

"What do I do?" she whispers frantically.

"Our options are limited, I'm afraid." I let out a long sigh as I scan her chart and shake my head. She's a third-year camper—a frequent flyer in the first aid tent—with artificial red dye listed as her only allergy. I didn't even know such an allergy existed until I started this job—but I've got three kids with dye allergies, one of which also has a diagnosis for ADHD and a strongly worded email from their mom about the grave consequences we face if her child eats anything containing Red 40.

"First things first. Let's clean and treat the bug bites. Then tomorrow you have to promise me you'll use the bug spray your"—another quick scan of her chart—"grandma packed for you."

The number one rule at Camp New Hope has nothing to do with actual camping. It was drilled into our heads over and over again at volunteer training: never assume you know a child's family situation, and double-check, then triple-check before you mention their parents.

Easy enough to remember, honestly. I'm a twenty-nine-year-old man-child with an emotionally absent father and a dead mom. I don't want anyone asking about my parents, either.

When I turn my attention back to Sophie, she's pouting and hasn't actually responded.

"Can you promise me that, kiddo?" I prompt.

"The bug spray my grandma packed is *so* stinky. I hate it. She *never* buys the right kind."

Rule number two at Camp New Hope: all feelings are valid, and outbursts are rarely about the topic at hand.

"Have you ever used a bug spray you do like?" I try.

She nods, but keeps her eyes cast down on my Crocs. They're bright yellow, and I've put all sorts of stupid emoji charms in the holes. I figured if I was going to perform the role of camp nurse for two whole weeks, I needed the proper footwear. Next year, I'm going to buy these suckers in every color.

"What did that one smell like?"

"Coconut," she replies instantly. "Coconut and pineapple. My dad always used it when we went to the beach to keep the no-see-ums away."

"I see..."

I tap my pen on my notepad, racking my brain for some sort of workaround. I know I can't "fix" everything for the kids that come to Camp New Hope, but the whole point of a bereavement camp is to let them be kids while they're here. If there's something I can do to ease the burden of grief, even just for the week...

"Oh! I know just what we need!"

Her eyes track my movement as I sort through the various bottles and tubes in one of the first aid kits.

"*This*," I declare triumphantly. "Okay, here's the deal, kiddo." I grab my rolly stool and bring it over to her, lowering it all the way so we're almost eye-to-eye.

"We're going to clean all these bug bites, then apply anti-itch cream. I'll give you dye-free Benadryl tonight so you don't scratch. Then you have to promise me you'll use the bug spray your grandma packed."

"But—"

"Ah, ah, ah! Promise me, Sophie. Even if it's stinky! We *have* to keep you under the legal limit." I cup one side of my mouth, then whisper, "My job's on the line here, kid. If someone finds out I let you get this close to forty bug bites…" I shudder dramatically. "I don't want to be sent home for not being a good nurse."

She eyes me skeptically for all of three seconds before she nods seriously.

"Once you've got the bug spray situation handled, come see me tomorrow. You can use a little of this on your arms and neck to get rid of the stinkies."

I pop the lid off the container of solid coconut oil and hold it up so she can take a whiff.

She inhales and smiles. "It smells like coconut!"

"So do we have a deal?"

She holds out a small hand—there's dried paint along her knuckles, dirt under her nails, and at least five inflamed bug bites—and I shake it before reaching for my gloves and the anti-itch cream.

--

A swift knock draws my attention away from my phone. The volunteer coordinator, Maggie Clark, sticks her head around the doorframe for her nightly check in.

"You need anything? More food? A night off?"

I'm off the clock each night at eight, but I haven't left the campgrounds since I arrived ten days ago. I have a private room—a single unit at the end of the boys' lodge—and I'm committed to staying here for the duration of camp, even though my legs are about six inches too long for the bottom bunk.

I don't trust myself to be on call if I left. I can sleep anywhere, and I rarely wake to the sound of my phone going off. I'd be too worried to fall asleep at home, afraid I'd miss a call.

"I'm good," I insist through a yawn. "My notes are updated, and everyone's set for tonight."

Maggie nods once and smiles.

"You're doing a great job, Fielding. The kids love you, and we've never had a full-time first aid person willing to stay for the duration of camp. I hope you don't have any intention of being a one-hit wonder around here. I know this is a condition for med school, but it'd be great to not have to worry about filling this position next year."

I inwardly preen but school my expression so she doesn't know the compliment went to my head.

"You're asking for an early commitment for next season?"

"Yeah." She smirks. "I guess I am."

"Count me in. You couldn't keep me away."

She pulls my door closed, and I pick up my phone again, sighing as I mindlessly scan my messages.

It's a lot of nothing: Updates from my brother and his girlfriend, Maddie. Useless information from my friend Cole, who was at The Oak that night.

I've got them all working to find her—to find *anything* that might lead to her—but it's been almost two weeks since I met Daphne, and so far, we've collectively come up with nothing.

Maddie has run her first name through every social media app that exists. We found two Daphnes in Hampton: one is a sweet older lady who posts pics of her grandkids and inspirational animal memes, and the other looks like she's in middle school.

Maddie can't find any property records, either, which makes sense since Daphne told me she lives with her parents.

I don't know her last name. I don't know her former fiancé's name. I assume she's a few years younger than me—meaning she's a few years older than Maddie—putting her at that sweet spot where none of us crossed paths with her at Archway Prep or Hampton High.

Cole's been cooperative but useless. He doesn't remember running credit cards for anyone in the bridal party that night. I believe him, considering the sizable charge on *my* credit card. Apparently, I bought *all* the drinks for Daphne's bridal party. If I ever see that redhead bridesmaid again, we'll be having words.

Short of hoping I randomly run into Daphne, or that she decides she wants to find me, I'm out of ideas.

Dumpy: Could you just sit at the Oak and hope she walks back in?

Fielding: I could. But she was there for a bachelorette party. I don't think it's her usual scene.

Dumpy: And you know nothing else about her? Her occupation? What car she drives? Anything?

I knock my knuckles against my forehead in frustration. I know a helluva lot about her—so many beautiful, intimate details I never want to forget.

The way her hips curved out and begged me to hold them. The sounds of her breathy whimpers when she liked what I was doing and wanted more. How my nerves lit up with excitement when she begged and whispered "please." The feeling of her thighs tightening around my head right before she came.

I know so many things about her. Yet none of it can help us now.

Fielding: Nothing we can use. I'm starting to think this is hopeless.

Chapter 15

Daphne

"I don't understand. The whole thing is just *off*? You're not getting married at all?"

I plaster on a serene smile as I smooth the warm sugar compound against the grain of hair along my client's bikini line. Unflinchingly, I gather and pull the sugar in a swift downward motion, reveling in a hint of satisfaction when she hisses through her teeth.

"Correct. Our families remain friends"—which is an issue I wasn't expecting to contend with—"but Anthony and I are no longer in a relationship."

Silence stews between us as I pull out another patch of hair along her pubic bone, wincing in sympathy when she yelps this time. That spot really is the worst—even for my nosiest client.

The rest of the appointment is awkward—which is par for the course these days. My wedding was set for this Saturday. I was engaged for nearly two years, and my clients all followed along on the planning journey, asking for updates and gushing about colors and flowers and all the details right along with me at their regular appointments.

It doesn't help that most clients' first questions are whether I'm nervous, excited, or just ready for Saturday. I'm sure none of them expected the types of conversations we've been having when they showed up for their service.

I apply cooling gel and say goodbye to my client, giving her privacy to get dressed so she can check out at the front desk, then I start toward the break room.

Serena catches up with me as she heads the same way to clean out her color supplies.

"Another heartbroken client?" she teases, flipping her thick auburn hair over one shoulder so she can watch me as she washes her bowls and brushes.

"Apparently." I sigh and mindlessly straighten the boxes of color solutions stacked on the shelf in front of me.

"Hey." Serena bumps my hip with hers. "You did the right thing. The right thing, and the brave thing. It'll get easier as the weeks go on."

My eyes prickle with tears I refuse to shed. Serena's encouragement is one of the few things keeping me sane right now.

I knew calling off the wedding would be stressful. Challenging. Heavy. Sad. But I never expected it to be *this* hard.

It's not just the daily, sometimes hourly, reminders when clients ask for wedding updates. It's the sympathy and hesitation in the voices of the vendors when I called to cancel and ask about potential refunds. It's the acid in my stomach that kicks up when I get home from work each day and find a fresh pile of gifts and wedding cards to sort through. And, in a shocking and unexpected twist, it's the onslaught of passive aggressive comments and general disapproval from my own family.

Not only have my parents not accepted that it's over between Anthony and me, but they're actively campaigning for us to get back together.

When Anthony came home from Las Vegas, I told him it was over. I broke the news to my parents that same night, incorrectly assuming they would be on my side and would help me navigate through this.

I couldn't properly explain why I was calling off the wedding without getting into what Anthony chose to do—so I did. I plainly outlined what happened and what he intended to do at his bachelor party.

He hurt me. He destroyed us. He banished the life I thought I wanted—but neither my parents nor anyone related to Anthony seem to think my reaction is warranted.

"You know what they say about Vegas..."

"Boys will be boys."

"Everyone does something stupid at their bachelor party."

"He was about to get married—can you really blame him?"

So much bullshit has been dumped on me over the last two weeks. What does one even say when someone suggests it's okay for a partner to sleep with a hooker a few weeks before their wedding? My limits aren't up for debate. It comes down to morals and self-respect—which I can't really explain without insulting the people who supposedly love me.

"Oh, good. You're back here."

My head snaps up as Marilyn pushes through the break room door and inserts herself between Serena and me.

"These just arrived for you," she declares, unceremoniously dropping a box of chocolates on the counter.

I stare at the box—at the card taped to the front with my name hastily written across the top. "Is he...?"

I don't have the emotional bandwidth to face off with Anthony right now. He's dropped off some sort of gift at the salon every day for the last two weeks. At first, I went out and accepted the gifts—and his attempts at an apology—in person. But it all feels like trauma theater now.

The women in reception *ooh* and *ahh*. Bobbi at the front desk gives me sympathetic but encouraging smiles. And since very few people know the real story about why I won't marry him, I stand there looking like a frigid bitch, unsure of what to even say.

"He's probably still in the parking lot if you wanted to catch him," Marilyn remarks.

I don't. I so desperately don't. But I can't exactly explain that to Marilyn. She's been doing Anthony's mom's hair for the last several years. I am almost certain her loyalties lie with his family.

Just like everyone else's.

"Thanks," I murmur, plopping into one of the break room chairs and tearing off the card taped to the box. I mindlessly open the chocolates and pop one into my mouth, grimacing as the chalky texture coats my tongue. The consistency is off, and the flavor isn't much better. Like biting into one of those wax bottles I liked as a kid.

I open the card, Anthony's chicken scratch handwriting instantly recognizable.

I'm sorry you're upset. I never expected things to happen like this. Please, just forgive me so we can move on. Love, Your Anthony

The lack of remorse is insulting. He's not sorry. He's just sorry this isn't going his way.

I blow out a long breath and place the chocolates on the communal break room table, then quickly scribble a note that they're up for grabs.

I can feel Marilyn watching my every move, but I don't have it in me to care.

I still have fifteen minutes until my next appointment. Maybe I'll go out to my car for a power nap. I'm admittedly exhausted from the logistics of calling it off. Canceling a wedding takes almost as much work as planning one. Everything about this is hard.

But it's still the right call.

Chapter 16

Daphne

I step softly through the side door in a futile attempt to enter the house undetected. Not that it's any use. My parents have been waiting up to greet me (a.k.a. bamboozle me) every night since I called off the wedding.

I toe off my shoes and warily walk through the foyer. I'm almost certain of everyone's location before I even go looking for them.

My parents will be in the living room, my dad reading a book while my mom watches something on TV. My little sister Tahlia is most likely holed up in her room, practicing TikTok dances while she keeps a book propped open on her bed, just in case my parents pop in to check on her.

From the outside, we look like the picture-perfect family.

The reality of life in this home is far more insidious.

"Daphne? Is that you?"

Her tone is sweet, almost caring. The words sound innocent enough. But she has a motion activation security alert on her phone, and I texted her before I left work to let her know I was on my way. She already knows it's me.

"Hi, Mom. Dad," I acknowledge, peeking my head around the corner but purposely not entering the living room.

My dad, Martin, gives a slight nod but doesn't look up from his book. My mom makes a show of pausing the TV and sitting up straighter on the couch, clearly eager to chat.

"The harpist called to confirm things today," she starts.

Thank God. I've had the hardest time getting a hold of her.

"Oh, okay. Did you talk to her, or do I need to call her back?"

She pulls a face, and I know we're in for another spat. I inhale a slow, steady breath and remind myself to keep it together and not let her push my buttons.

"Of course you need to call her back. I don't know what music you've selected for the ceremony!"

I meet her outraged expression with a pointed look.

"Mother..." I sigh.

"Daphne," she snipes.

And here we are, once again. Right where we've been over and over again for the last several weeks. She tries a new angle every other day. Big crocodile tears, guilting me into submission, begging me to reconsider.

The wedding is off. I won't be marrying Anthony.

And yet she's completely disregarding and refusing to accept the truth of the situation.

Thankfully, I have experience dealing with her gaslighting and attempted manipulations. Experience and perspective. I've been out of this house and out of her clutches for years. I've grown. I've healed. I know it's not worth my energy or my peace to argue with this woman. I love her. I always will. But I accepted a long time ago that she's not so great at loving me.

"Did you get a good number where I can reach her?" I ask, rubbing at the tension headache developing between my eyebrows.

"If you cancel all these people, this wedding really won't happen," she hisses through clenched teeth.

I bite my tongue—hard—to stop myself from laughing. Or crying. Or both?

I'm admittedly an emotional mess. It's the week of my now-canceled wedding, and being back in my parents' house is messing with my emotions, too.

"I'm going to eat something, then head to bed," I inform her. "Good night," I add, not wanting to leave things too tense.

As soon as I turn, she's on her feet, following me. "Daphne! We're not done here. You can't just throw away a relationship that spanned a decade over one disagreement!"

And there's the rub.

Whether it's because they not-so-secretly respect Anthony more than me, or because they just don't believe me, my parents have struggled to match my disdain over the situation.

I sigh but continue to the kitchen. I don't have it in me to come up with a new way to defend myself tonight. It's not until I've turned on the lights in the kitchen that she tries a different angle.

"You really shouldn't be eating this late."

I stay silent, refusing to engage. I worked ten hours today. I haven't eaten since breakfast. I'm starving, and I have to be up early tomorrow. I grab a carton of eggs out of the fridge and walk toward the stove.

"Just because you don't have to fit into a wedding dress on Saturday doesn't mean you should just give up entirely."

I dart a glance over my shoulder to make sure we're alone. I may be used to her passive aggressive comments, but I hate the idea of Tahlia listening to this vitriol.

When my eyes land on my mother, her slim frame perched against the kitchen island, one eyebrow raised in challenge, I have no words. I offer her a sad, closed-mouth smile, then turn back to the stove and ignore her completely.

She huffs and hovers but eventually grows tired of watching me wait for the pan to heat up and leaves the room.

Once I'm sure I'm alone, I blink back tears as I fish out my phone.

Daphne: Lucy's back on her bullshit tonight

Serena: Damn. You'd think after two weeks she'd finally take the hint.

Daphne: Wishful thinking. Bobbi told me she still hasn't canceled her updo appointment for this weekend!

Serena: She's delusional. I hate that you're stuck in that house, babe.

I crack three eggs into the pan and season them before I stir.

Daphne: I know. I've got to figure something out.

Serena: My couch is always available! And I don't think Eric has rented your old unit yet. I can talk to him if you want.

I didn't renew the lease on my studio apartment across the hall from Serena at the beginning of summer. Anthony and I agreed that it didn't make sense to pay the month-to-month rate, considering I planned to move into his place after the wedding.

My parents' house was supposed to be a pit stop on the way to happily ever after.

Now it's my own personal version of hell.

Daphne: Maybe. Can I crash at yours on Saturday night? I'm definitely not looking forward to being here all day with them.

Serena: For sure. We'll make a day of it since we're both off. Chin up, babe. The worst is already behind you.

I push the scrambled eggs around the pan and hope to God she's right.

Chapter 17

Fielding

Two Weeks Later

I'm fighting back boredom-induced slumber reading about neural crest cells when my phone vibrates on the coffee table.

I reach for it out of habit but pull back before I can pick it up. Med school officially starts in two weeks, and I'm trying my hardest to establish good study habits. Discipline. Focus. I need to rewire my brain if I'm going to survive the next several years and actually succeed at this.

After forcing myself to finish the page I'm on, I finally close the textbook and glance at my phone.

It's a message from Cole.

Two words. A spark of hope.

Cole: She's here

Fielding: For real? You're sure? Can you ask if her name's Daphne? I'm getting in the car right now if it's her...

I get changed and pace while I wait for his reply—I have half a mind to call the main number at the bar and force him to respond.

Cole: Sorry, we're slammed. It's not actually Daphne. It's the mouthy bridesmaid who insisted you were buying all their drinks that night.

Dammit.

But that's still something.

Fielding: You're sure it's her?Cole: I couldn't forget this redhead if I tried. She's here with another girl. They just sat down.

Fuck. Of course it would be the loud-mouthed one who took full advantage of my credit card that night. Whatever. She's my only lead—I have to get there and try to get Daphne's number.

Fielding: Keep her there. Cole, I'm so serious... whatever it takes... do NOT let her leave.

I grab for my wallet but hesitate when I get to the mudroom. My bike would be faster. But I might need to call my brother on the way.

Frustrated, I grab the keys to my Infiniti and feel my phone vibrate in my back pocket just as I open the door.

Cole: This isn't one of those weird obsessions of yours, is it? Are we about to have another Tori situation on our hands?

I see red.

Not because he's out of line, even though he is. I fucking wish my spiraling, obsessive thoughts would settle and let me leave this girl alone. My motivation is more than a desire to see Daphne again. I have a responsibility to her. Doing the right thing hasn't always been my MO. But with her, it is.

Fielding: Fuck you. I'll be there in 10.

I let myself in through the employee entrance in the back and run my hand over the grates of the liquor cage as I pass it while trying my hardest to calm my nerves.

Navigating through the sea of bodies on the dance floor is a feat, but as soon as I reach the bar, I spot my target.

There's a vacant barstool beside her, so I slide in, rest my chin in my hand, and wait for her to notice me.

Her eyes go demonic, all but bugging out when she looks over and meets my gaze.

"You!"

So she remembers me.

"I need to get a hold of Daphne."

She slaps the bar top and throws her head back with a cackle.

"Oh my god. Seriously? *Seriously*? That's rich. You both disappear the night of her bachelorette party, then she calls her wedding off, and now you want my help reconnecting?"

I glare at her for the less-than-accurate assessment of what went down and how. Before I can put her in her place, she continues.

"I'll do you one better," she declares, smirking as she types out a text. She focuses on her phone for all of twenty seconds before setting it down and doing her best imitation of the Cheshire cat. "All done," she sing-songs.

She turns back to her friend then, effectively ignoring me until her phone vibrates on the bar top. I try to school my expression and not look too eager as she glances at the device.

When I realize she's going to make me work for it, I take the bait.

"So?" I question.

"So what?" she asks innocently.

For fuck's sake.

"Is she coming?" I demand.

"Oh. I didn't text Daphne," the troublemaker informs me, flipping her red hair over her shoulder and fighting back a predatory smile. "I texted my cousin, Anthony. You know. Her fiancé? Or should I say *ex*-fiancé, since she called off her wedding because of you?"

Chapter 18

Daphne

I rest my forehead on the cool, smooth edge of the toilet bowl, willing my stomach to settle as I pull in a shaky breath.

With both hands planted on the floor, I hoist myself up and reach for my toothbrush for the third time tonight.

My throat is raw.

My heart is ravaged.

I can't believe this is happening.

After years of being told it might be hard to conceive because of my heavy, irregular periods—the improbable has actually happened.

I haven't told anyone. I've barely been able to admit it to myself.

But six pregnancy tests—six brands of pregnancy tests—can't all be wrong. And the intense, unshakable nausea I've felt for the last few days is pretty irrefutable evidence.

When I've finish brushing my teeth, I stare at the sallow-cheeked girl in the mirror. My mouth barely curves upward in a pathetic attempt at a smile. The tears I've worked hard to hold back all day gather along my lower lids, and this time I let them fall.

I start my nighttime skincare routine over, careful to avoid applying serum to my neck in case it triggers my nausea again. Thankfully, after I throw up, my stomach seems to settle for a few hours. I should have just enough time to curl up in bed and fall asleep before the next wave of morning sickness hits.

Morning sickness. What a joke of a name. More like *mourning sickness* as I think about the delicious pasta and salad I just flushed down the toilet.

My phone pings from where I left it in my bedroom, but I don't bother rushing to retrieve it.

I was just with Serena—we had dinner after work—and I don't want to deal with anyone else right now. I'm not fit for human interaction. What I need is to get some rest before another full day of clients tomorrow.

I wrap up my routine, using the tips of my fingers to blend my eye cream with the tears that won't stop.

I turn the lock on my bedroom door before making my way over to the bed. It's not that I think anyone will try to come in during the night, but being back in my childhood bedroom does funny things to my sense of self and security.

I pick up my phone to set my alarms, noticing the text that came through while I was in the bathroom. My stomach somersaults when I see the name of the sender.

Melissa: You'll never guess who I just ran into...

I can practically hear her taunting me through the text. But it's the accompanying photo that makes me question whether I need to run back to the bathroom and puke again.

It's an out-of-focus picture of Fielding, a.k.a., the man I ghosted in the midst of a one-night-stand four weekends ago. Memories I once hoped I'd never forget slam into me, every detail about that night, as I study the blurry profile shot.

I hate to blindside him like this. I hate to be dependent on Anthony's menacing cousin to help me. But if she's with Fielding—apparently at the scene of the crime—she's my only viable option.

Daphne: You're at The Oak, right? Can you tell him I need to talk to him? I can be there in thirty minutes.

Melissa: You might as well carpool with Anthony. I already called him, and he's on his way.

Fucking Melissa.

She has *no idea* what kind of trouble she's causing. I'm throwing my hair into a messy bun and reaching for my yoga pants a moment later. Then I grab my purse and dig out my keys, moving faster than I have all week.

Chapter 19

Fielding

I've been sitting at The Oak for half an hour. What I'm waiting for, I don't know. Or maybe I'm just not willing to face the reality of the situation.

Daphne's ex-fiancé is on his way. I have no clue what the fuck I'll say to him. Melissa has already made damn sure he knows who I am—but if she won't contact Daphne for me, this might be my only hope.

Every fiber in my being is saying *GO*. Leave. Forget it.

Yet here I sit. Unmoving. Picking at a napkin and doing everything I can to distract myself from what feels like an inevitable showdown.

Cole checks on me every few minutes, and I'm doing my best to stay calm and reassure him. The last thing I need is for someone to call Jake or interfere with what's about to go down.

I fight back the urge to text Dem. I don't need a lecture right now. My mind is made up. I have to see this through.

Instead of reaching out to my twin, I go for the next best thing and catch up on all the memes and TikToks Maddie sent me throughout the week. I'm chuckling to myself when my skin prickles with awareness.

"Wait, it's this guy? *This* fucking guy?"

On the defense, I crane my neck and shoot a glance at the two men standing next to Melissa. They're in their mid to late twenties with similar features. Both are wearing baseball caps and have their arms crossed in front of their stocky frames in an almost-comical matching stance.

They're on the shorter side—five-nine or five-ten—and the one on the right is smirking, rubbing his chin with his hand, while the one on the left confers with the redhead.

I stare at them awkwardly until the one on the right mutters under his breath to the other. He's got this eerily familiar face, and he's wearing a knowing smirk that tells me I should be able to place him.

"Do I know you?" I try.

"You're about to wish you didn't."

He turns to the guy beside him, who I assume is the ex.

"This fucker's been to our house before, brother. Shown up at parties when he wasn't invited. Created chaos when he wouldn't take no for an answer. Last summer he showed up totally fucked up, then proceeded to convince my boys to circle up and take him on at once, fight-club style."

I feel the blood drain from my face—a sensation I've never actually experienced before—as realization and recognition set in.

Dread churns in my gut.

Regret spreads like wildfire through my veins.

I couldn't place his face. But his voice unlocks a memory buried deep in my brain.

A party. A barn. A lower than low moment.

I choke back bile, my heart hammering double-time as I relive the way the fists pounded on me, unrelenting, unmercifully, before a girl stopped them. A girl who inevitably came home with us that night, and somehow forced herself into my brother's closed-off, frozen, martyr heart.

I couldn't pick this guy out of a crowd. But I've rewatched enough of the videos from that night to easily place the voice.

Fuck that night.

Fuck this noise.

If this guy is who I think he is—and the way he's smirking at me and scrolling through his phone tells me he is—that means Daphne's ex-fiancé is Anthony Adley?

Chapter 20

Daphne

I slip through the front door of The Oak and try to get my bearings. The bar is loud and crowded, but it only takes a few seconds to scan the room and spot him.

It helps that he's six-two with a drool-worthy head of wavy blond hair. He's the best-looking guy in the building. I could spot Fielding anywhere.

Warm recognition floods my gut. But the joy is quickly replaced by prickles of dread.

Fielding's standing near the bar, half on and half off a bar stool, glaring at the people in front of him: Anthony, his younger brother Andy, and Melissa.

My spine goes rigid, and I freeze where I stand.

I desperately want to get to Fielding—to get his attention and talk to him alone. But each face-to-face interaction I've had with Anthony over the last few weeks has been less savory than the last. He and his brother are notorious for riling each other up, and Melissa's already proven she's stirring the pot tonight. There's no way I'm prepared to confront them all together.

I don't trust myself not to break down. Or get physically sick in their presence and give my secret away before I have a chance to tell the one person who needs to know first.

Shuffling farther into the bar, I keep my attention fixed on the group. I maintain my distance, grateful that the shoulder-to-shoulder crowd engulfs me.

I reluctantly turn my back when I reach the bar—if any of them look up and directly across the way, they'll spot me. Thankfully, one of the bartenders catches my eye right away. We do that awkward silent questioning thing. When he tilts his chin in my direction, I let out a breath I didn't know I was holding.

He thinks he knows who I am. I bet he can help me.

I give him the smallest nod, swallowing past the lump in my throat and willing my words not to waver as he leans forward to hear me over the cacophony that surrounds us.

"Hey. This is awkward, but do you know that guy down there? The tall blond. At the end of the bar?"

"Fielding?"

Relief washes over me. "Yes. Fielding. Thank God. Okay, this is going to sound so weird, and I promise I'm not some sort of stalker, but I really need to talk to him. Privately. Anywhere but here."

"You must be Daphne."

Mouth agape, I pause. What am I missing? How does this bartender know my name?

"He's been trying to find you for weeks," he continues. "He rushed here as soon as I told him your redheaded friend was back. Hell, what are the chances you show up, too?"

A small thrill shoots through me, but it's dampened by wariness. I had no expectations of Fielding wanting to contact me or keep in touch. Melissa made damn sure my presence was required tonight.

I'm still lost in thought when the bartender speaks again. "Here, let me give you his number. If you go out the front door and turn left, there's a little alley—"

I cut him off before he can finish his train of thought. "Thank you. Thank you so much," I gush. "You're a lifesaver…"

"Cole," he supplies, his kind smile making his eyes crease as he holds out his phone, Fielding's contact info displayed on the screen. I quickly punch the numbers into my own phone, then send Fielding a text.

Daphne: This is Daphne. Cole just gave me your number. I need to talk to you. Meet me outside in the alley as soon as you can.

I hit send and lift my gaze, desperate for this to work.

Across the room, Fielding fishes out his phone and glances down, the glow from the screen illuminating his enormous, lagoon-blue eyes. A second later, he lifts his head and frantically scans the crowd.

I offer Cole one more appreciative smile, then head out the front door and turn into the narrow brick alley where our worlds collided a month ago.

All I can do now is wait. Wait and try to calm the adrenaline rushing through my veins. Wait and pray there's nothing left in my queasy stomach for me to throw up as I head into an impossibly hard conversation I never expected to have with the one-night stand I never wanted to forget.

Chapter 21

Fielding

It took longer than I hoped to get away. Once Andrew explained to his brother who I was—then proceeded to ignore us all, looking for video footage from the aforementioned incident at his house last summer—I was finally able to mutter "I'm out of here" and slip away toward the back door.

Thank God neither of them tried to take things further.

I already had a strong opinion about Anthony based on what he did to Daphne. Knowing who he's related to only triples the animosity I have toward him.

Out of all the assholes in this goddamn town, why did it have to be an Adley?

So many things about this situation are fucked. Daphne will inevitably find out about the party and the fight. I honestly don't remember many details from that night, but Maddie and my brother have filled in most of the gaps. Along with the videos that still exist on the Internet.

It clearly wasn't my finest moment. But it also wasn't my lowest, either.

None of that matters right now.

What does matter is that the woman I've been desperately looking for found me—and I'm about to see her in person for the first time in almost a month.

I close the employee door behind me, then turn right into the alley.

My body senses her before my eyes adjust to the dark. She's there. Feet away. Waiting for me.

She's facing the opposite direction, probably expecting me to come out the front door. I clear my throat so she doesn't startle.

As soon as she hears me, she spins on her heel, her eyes meeting mine as wave after wave of emotion washes over her gorgeous face.

Surprise. Shock. Timidness. Regret.

What the actual fuck?

I quicken my pace, anxious to close the distance, to be near her again. There's a gravitational pull between us, along with an absurd confidence on my part that if I can get closer—talk to her, touch her—I can somehow make whatever's bothering her better.

Her face smooths into a placid frown, her somberness filling the alley and making me feel like my stomach is full of rocks. But I don't stop. I yearn to be closer. Her eyes are wide, almost glassy. She's very obviously fighting back tears.

This is so different from what I was expecting. I'm doing my best not to get ahead of myself as I read her body language. I clench my hands into fists to try and calm my nerves, but it's no use.

She looks ill—her shoulders are slumped, and she has her arms crossed over her midsection protectively.

I fight back the urge to pull her into my body and soothe her. Instead, I stop a few feet away—close enough to relish our connection, but far enough away to respect her space.

"Daphne—are you okay?"

She turns her head, breaking eye contact and wrapping her arms tighter around herself in the process.

Fuck.

What I wouldn't give to hold her and comfort her right now.

I inch closer, almost involuntarily, leaning forward and willing her to open up to me.

"Talk to me. Are you okay?" I ask again.

"I'm not," she finally whispers.

I don't know what to do with that. But at least she's being honest. I take another small step forward, reaching out a hand and brushing it down her arm. She closes her eyes and shudders on contact.

"I'm so happy to see you. Listen, that night—"

She interrupts me before I even have a chance to get going. "I'm sorry I ran out on you."

"You don't have to apologize. You don't owe me an explanation. But I wish you wouldn't have left the way—"

"No," she insists, cutting me off again. "I do have to apologize, and you deserve an explanation. It wasn't fair of me to do... *what we did*... then sneak out like that. I'm so sorry. I turned my phone on when you went to the bathroom because I wanted to ask for your number. But as soon as it powered on, it blew up with texts and notifications. Anthony was tracking my device. I had to go, and I was worried you'd try to convince me to stay. I didn't want to bring my problems to your doorstep."

I gape in disbelief. That's... *a lot*. And yet there's one tiny detail playing on repeat in my stupid head.

She wanted my number.

"Fuck, angel," I murmur, closing the gap between us so we're standing toe to toe. I smooth one hand up her arm and over her shoulder before working it into the hair at the nape of her neck.

She instinctively leans into my touch, forcing me to fight back a grin.

"I'm so sorry that happened. And that you had to deal with it all alone."

She peers up at me, tears still pooling in her eyes. I want to pull her into a hug. Get her out of this alley, take her somewhere private. I want to insist she come back to my house so we can talk, so I can properly take care of her.

But I still have something to tell her.

Something really fucking awful at that.

I inhale slowly, savoring these last few seconds of peace before I become the bearer of bad news. As much as I want more with her, it has to be on her terms. And she needs to know the truth before I try to propel things further. She deserves to know, even if she gets pissed or never wants to see me again. I hate the idea of losing her—*again*—when I just freaking found her. But staying has to be her choice.

"I have to tell you something," I murmur, gently squeezing the tense muscles between her shoulder and her neck.

She looks up at me, wide-eyed, and pales even more, if that's possible.

"That night? The condom broke."

The weight of my words drops between us and demolishes our connection. All the air is sucked out of the alley. The world stops spinning, and the most selfish, despicable part of me regrets speaking the truth.

She yanks herself out of my hold, stumbling until her back hits the wall of the alley. I watch, aware I'm causing her this pain, as she raises a hand to her mouth and slumps against the bricks.

"I didn't realize it broke until I went to the bathroom, I swear. When I came out to tell you, you were already gone. I tried to find you. Tried to figure out how to get a hold of you. As soon as I got home from camp, I got tested. I'm clean, by the way, and I can show you the results. But you have a right to know, and I didn't want you to think..." I trail off.

"It all makes sense now," she whispers to herself.

"What?" I pry. "What makes sense?"

I move closer to the wall, desperate to hear her, to reignite that spark between us.

"The condom. The condom broke. It all makes sense now."

Fuck. I don't know what else to do or say. I'm confused, but I refuse to push her when she's already in a state of shock and pain.

Except we're sort of on a time crunch here. I don't know how much longer we can count on having privacy in this alley. If only I could convince her to go with me... take her back to my house or somewhere quiet where we could talk...

The silence creeps toward the minute mark as awkwardness churns between us.

I sigh and try to mentally regroup, repeating the question I asked her when I first found her in the alley.

"Are you okay?"

This time, her response comes out loud and clear.

"No. I'm really not okay. Fielding—I'm pregnant."

Chapter 22

Fielding

My back hits the bricks first. My back, then my head. I focus on the way air fills my lungs and the solidness of the alleyway as my chest expands.

I trace the mortar around the bricks behind me with my fingers as all other motor functions and lucid thoughts leach out of my brain.

Maybe if we both just stay out here, pressed up against this wall, we won't have to face the reality of our situation.

Daphne sniffles beside me, and I force myself to clear my throat in response. I need to think. To act. To do *something*.

The condom broke.

She's pregnant.

We're dealing with causation as opposed to correlation here, so that means... *Fuck*. That means...

My brain isn't working. I doubt my voice will, either, even if I could think of something to say.

But I can't just leave her hanging.

I scrape my forearm against the brick wall, seeking her out. She startles when I hook my pinkie with hers—but she lets me hold on. We stand together, barely touching, our backs against the wall as the world spins around us.

No one else on the planet knows what this feels like. No one else but her.

"Say something," she whispers, her words warming my insides and doling out comfort I don't deserve.

"I'd be a shitty dad." I clear my throat after the confession. It's probably not what she wants to hear. But it's my truth. "I'm not mature or wise like my brother. I don't have my life figured out. He'd be so much better at this than me..."

Silence falls between us, but she inches closer. My gut tells me it's the right move, so I risk it: I grasp for more of her hand and hold it completely in my own.

She turns her head and meets my gaze, the weight of the situation sinking in as the sorrow, sadness, and regret I sensed in her starts to make sense.

She offers me a sad smile, and I can't help but turn to her and cup her face with my free hand. "It's okay," I assure her. "It's going to be okay."

An eerie sense of calm washes over me as I stare into her eyes. I don't need to ask. I already know. Something in my gut—instinct, intuition, whatever it's called—is sure that she's carrying *my* child.

But logic dictates that I clarify.

"Is it mine?"

I watch her swallow, then look past my shoulder as she answers.

"I—I think so. The timing makes sense. I went off birth control last year to try to lose weight for the wedding..."

Fury surges through me—why the fuck would she think she needed to lose weight?

"Anthony and I always used condoms anyway. I'm almost positive he and I weren't even together between my last period and... that night."

She looks at me then, searching my face for a reaction, I assume.

"The timing makes sense. And now that I know the condom broke..."

"Fuck. Daphne. I'm so sorry. I'm so fucking sorry."

She leans her head against my shoulder, and I pull her a little closer.

"You don't have to apologize. It's no one's fault. But it happened. And now I have to deal with the consequences."

"We," I correct her automatically. "*We* will deal with the consequences."

"Fielding... I'm... I didn't tell you to trap you."

Her voice is filled with pain. Pain and worry. A hollow loneliness. An edge of uncertainty. I ache to hold her but restrain myself from wrapping her in a hug. We need to make a plan before I can give in to the urge to take care of her.

"Tell me what you want to do, angel. Do you need money? If you want to have an abortion, I'll pay..."

She laughs a sad, muffled cry that echoes through the alley.

"We were together four weeks ago. I'm already six weeks pregnant."

My eyes widen in horror. I know enough from my pre-med classes to know that a woman is usually four or five weeks pregnant by the time she misses her period and finds out she's pregnant. If she's already six weeks... Ohio passed a heartbeat bill a few years ago when Roe v. Wade was overturned, so an abortion is out of the question. At least in this state.

"If that's what you want to do, Daphne, I'll make it happen. We'll go out of state. I'll do the research, arrange the travel plans. Anything you want or need..."

"It's okay. I want to keep it."

I suck in a sharp breath but stop myself from outwardly reacting in any other way. It's her body. It's her choice.

"I—I don't have a logical explanation, exactly, but I always worried I'd have a hard time getting pregnant. And as shocked and dazed as I've felt the last few weeks, I already feel connected to this baby."

"Okay." I nod, pull in a shaky breath, and bury my shock. This is about doing what's best for her and the baby. *Our* baby. "It's your choice. I'll support you in anything you choose. I'm all in. I want to be there for everything."

She squeezes my hand, and I swear the tiny gesture simultaneously tugs on my heart.

"You're the only person who knows," she explains. "I wanted to tell you first, but I won't be able to keep it a secret for long. I'm already so sick... I'm not ashamed, and now that I've told you, I don't want to hide it."

Random medical shit surfaces as my brain works overtime to recall all the information I know about pregnancy. If she's only six weeks along and she's already experiencing morning sickness, her HCG must be really high. Has she made a prenatal appointment yet? Has she started taking vitamins?

I shake my head to calm my racing thoughts. Now is *not* the time to mansplain prenatal care to a pregnant woman.

She opens her mouth to speak, but her words aren't what I hear next.

Him. His voice echoes down the alley, and suddenly, our private moment is not so private.

"Daphne."

Immediately, she drops my hand.

The interruption—especially at a moment like this—is annoying, but the sight of both Adley assholes sauntering toward us makes me livid.

"What are you doing out here?" Anthony demands.

Why the fuck does it sound like he's scolding her?

She heard him, but she's ignoring him. She holds eye contact with me, and as they get closer, she gives me the slightest shake of her head.

No? No what? I can't exactly ask for clarification. She said she hasn't told anyone else yet... so I'll play along as long as she's safe. As long as he doesn't try to pull anything. If he thinks he's going to stalk through this alley and take her away from me, he's got another think coming.

"Is this what I think it is, Daph? Did you think you could call off our wedding, then let this guy lure you into an alley? I guess I didn't need to go all the way to Vegas to find a whore."

Her eyes grow as big as saucers. I clench my jaw and instinctively form a fist.

But neither of us has a chance to react before Andrew interjects.

"This is too good. It's just too good! Fuck, Daph. Are you *with* this guy? You have no idea who this dude is. Wait until you see these videos," he chirps excitedly.

For fuck's sake. These assholes are about to ruin everything.

I know exactly what's on those videos. I know how it looks. I know what I once was. Who I strive every damn day not to be.

I told Daphne I was in. That she could count on me. She smiled at me, that sweet, beautiful smile. She was going to let me in. I almost had a shot this time.

But once she sees those videos...

Fuck.

I ruin everything. I ruin it before it can even begin. I never stood a fucking chance.

"Did you drive yourself here, Daph?"

She doesn't answer him—she hasn't even turned around yet or taken her eyes off me—but when her shoulders slump forward, I know we're officially done.

Anthony doesn't wait for her response before he speaks again. "Say goodbye to your friend. I'll take you home."

Desperate for her to stay, I reach out. But she's already stepping back, stepping toward him, before I can make my case.

I keep my eyes glued to her face—searching for any indication from her that this isn't the end.

But I'm a fool. She's walking away already—and she hasn't even seen the damning evidence that'll keep her away for good.

One of the brothers cracks his knuckles and grunts. These goons might as well be cartoon characters, but I'm still outnumbered. I hadn't considered that there are two of them, and only one of me. I wouldn't put it past them to beat my ass and leave me for dead in this alley.

"Want me to stay back and take care of the trash?" Andrew taunts.

Anthony cackles like a hyena at the jab. "No need, brother. I'd much rather you ride home with us so you can share some of those videos you've got saved on your phone."

Her face is still placid—it's like she's unfazed by the apparent power shift that's just taken place. Why isn't she standing up for herself? Why won't she fight?

I watch in horror as Daphne turns her back to me. Anthony slings a meaty arm around her shoulders, pulling her in to his side, and she doesn't fight it.

It takes all the willpower I possess to keep my feet planted in place. I remind myself to inhale—then exhale—as I stand paralyzed and dumbfounded while she walks away.

She picked him.

She hasn't even seen the videos yet—she knows what kind of man he is, what his intentions were in Vegas, whether he went through with them or not—and yet without a second thought, she let go of me and followed him out of this alley.

I smash my fist into the bricks behind me and let the throb in my hand distract me from the decimation of my heart. This moment. These familiar feelings. This isn't the first time I wasn't someone's final choice. And yet it hurts even fucking worse than it did before.

She. Picked. Him.

I turn and stalk toward the back parking lot, exhaustion washing over me with each step I take. I just want to get home. Get drunk. Pretend this night never happened.

But I learned my lesson last time.

I know myself well enough to know I can't do this alone.

Fielding: Can you come home?

He replies two minutes later.

Dumpy: When?

Fielding: Now. Tomorrow. ASAP.

I'm in my car and fastening my seat belt when his second message comes through.

Dumpy: We're booked on the first flight out tomorrow. We'll be there before lunch.

I glance at the clock on the dash—11:22 pm. That means I've got twelve hours to get blackout drunk, then sober up enough to welcome my brother and his girlfriend back to town.

Challenge fucking accepted.

Chapter 23

Fielding

"Don't baby him like that."

Her nails track through my hair as my stomach churns.

Everything is muffled. Muffled yet resounding. The whole room—*my whole life*—is spinning off its axis.

"I'm not babying him."

It's the word *baby* that wraps me in a chokehold and shoves me toward consciousness.

"I think something's really wrong," she murmurs as she continues to scratch my head. "He wouldn't have asked us to come home otherwise."

He lets out a long, exasperated sigh a few feet away. My eyes are still closed, but I can picture his eyebrows pulling together and that wrinkle forming above his nose. I don't even have to see him to know my twin brother's glaring at me with his stern brunch daddy face.

"Based on the state of the kitchen, I bet he's not even hungover yet—he's probably still drunk."

A body plops onto the bed, and the mattress rebounds. My cheek brushes against stiff, scratchy fabric as a result.

I crack one eye open, smiling up at my brother's girlfriend as she continues to play with my hair.

Rubbing the side of my face against the thigh of her jeans, I tease, "Look at you, Little Wheeler. Now you're the one crawling into bed with me..."

I *umph* when she punches my shoulder, then push up to sit as my head swims with regret.

Fuck.

I scratch at the back of my neck as the ache in my skull crescendos to full-strength. I don't think I'm drunk anymore, as my brother so lovingly assumed, but I'm definitely hungover.

"What'd you do?" my identical twin asks from his perch on the edge of the mattress. He's sitting with his arms crossed, focused on the view of the Cuyahoga Valley National Park through the French doors of my patio instead of looking at me.

My room's on the main level, so the view isn't as spectacular as his on the second floor. But it was safer for our mom to be at ground level, and I was happy to take one of the rooms closest to hers when she was still alive.

Maddie hands me a Gatorade as they wait out my response.

"I found her," I declare, taking my time opening and sipping the sports drink.

"And?" Dempsey pushes.

"*Anddd*," I draw out, annoyed that he's forcing me to come out and say it. Last night's revelations have been pushed to the back of my mind. I haven't let myself dive into the implications—I can't.

"She didn't need me to tell her the condom broke. She's pregnant."

If silence had a sound, it would sound just like this.

"How pregnant?" Maddie demands.

Read: How far along is she? Daphne was in this bed with me exactly four weeks ago. I wish I knew less about the female reproductive cycle than I actually do. But between my pre-med classes and helping Tori through the process of freezing her eggs...

"She's six weeks pregnant."

My brother curses. The consequences of the timing make everything heavier and harder to process. Six weeks pregnant is already *too* pregnant to lawfully seek an abortion in the state of Ohio, and we all know it.

Last night, I offered to take her anywhere, to pay for it all. She shouldn't have to go through this alone, and she should absolutely have a fucking choice.

But none of that matters.

"She wants to keep it," I continue, picking the label off the plastic bottle without looking up. "She wants to keep it, but she's not sure it's mine."

"You told me she was calling her wedding off!" Dempsey exclaims, rising off the bed to pace.

I have to hand it to him. He held off a lot longer than I thought he would.

"She was, and she did. But she was engaged up until the night we met."

My mind flashes back to the foreboding figures stalking down the alley last night. She left with Anthony. I told her I was in, that I wanted to be involved—that she could count on me—and she still left with him.

"Met her ex-fiancé last night, too," I deadpan. "Turns out our old friend Andrew Adley has an older brother."

"*No!*" Maddie gasps, covering her mouth and looking between my brother and me in disbelief. "Fuckity fuck."

"Yep." I swing my legs over the edge of the bed and stand, turning my back to them. I try for nonchalant, but if my brother sees my face, he'll know.

"Anthony and Andrew showed up at The Oak last night. Andrew recognized me immediately. Once he put two and two together..."

"Andrew Adley's not allowed to step foot inside The Oak," my brother gripes, pulling out his phone and shooting off a text.

"Yeah, well. He was there. And she left with them. She told me she was pregnant. I told her I would support her however I could. And she left. She fucking *left*." My voice cracks on the last word—the shame and self-loathing that engulfed me last night washing over me in a fresh wave.

I stomp toward my bathroom, angry with myself for being such a fucking pussy. They both call after me, but I brush them off, slam the door, and lock it for good measure.

I shouldn't give a shit about a one-night stand. I should be grateful Daphne straight up rejected me and left me alone in that alley.

But I'm not relieved. Not even close.

If anything, when she walked away and chose him over me, it further solidified my desire to help her.

What the fuck is wrong with me? I wish I wasn't like this. I'd rather chase after something that might not even be mine than be reasonable about the situation.

It's disgustingly on brand: my most fatal flaw.

If it's off limits, I want it.

If someone tells me to chill, I amp it all the way up.

I don't know how to bide my time. I don't know how to take it easy or hold back.

Dangle the forbidden fruit in front of me, and I'll stop at nothing until I obtain it. I've always been a full out fiend.

Chapter 24

Daphne

Daphne: I'm going to need a ride to work tomorrow. My first client is at 8—sorry.

I sigh and stash my phone. Serena won't give me a hard time about it, but I still hate asking for help.

I curl up in the back seat and let my head rest against the cool glass of the window. For once I'm grateful Andy called shotgun.

They're too worked up to pay me much attention—Andy is busy queuing up video after video of Fielding at a party last summer while Anthony mutters a string of expletives and insults under his breath. They're just egging each other on at this point. I can't wait to get the hell out of here.

Andy insisted I watch the first few videos, but once the shock value wore off, he grew tired of passing his phone back to me. They've been ignoring me for almost ten minutes now. A quick glance out the window confirms we're turning onto Haymarket Street—nearly home.

"Wait 'til you see this one," Andy chirps from the front seat.

I may not be watching the videos anymore, but I still flinch every time the sounds of fists hitting flesh come through the car's speakers. I refuse to let myself spiral or jump to conclusions.

There are two sides—or more—to every story. I was shocked by the first few videos, but I've resolved to not form an opinion or pass judgment until Fielding has a chance to explain.

He'll have that chance soon. I'll make sure of it.

When he locked eyes with me earlier and declared his intention to be involved and help in any way possible, I believed him. I still believe him, despite what's on those videos, and I want to have someone on my side. For the first time in over two weeks, I'm hopeful.

I left with Anthony because I know what he's capable of. Between his big mouth and his brother's hot head, there was no way I could have put my foot down without someone getting punched in the face. That someone likely would have been Fielding.

I left to protect him. I'll text him as soon as I get home. He said he was in. I want to believe him, and this will be his first opportunity to prove he's up for the challenge of what we're facing.

From the moment I saw those two pink lines, I knew that if Fielding was even semi-interested in being involved, I wanted him to be for the sake of my child.

My child.

Our child.

I'm all but certain it's Fielding's. Based on the timing, and the new knowledge that our protection failed. As ridiculous as it sounds, I was almost happy when he told me that the condom broke.

Happy. Hopeful. Relieved.

With my face still pressed against the cool glass of the window, I close my eyes and place my hand low on my belly, imagining a blue-eyed, blond-haired toddler with a toothy grin.

I smile contently and resist the urge to pull my phone out and text Fielding right now. I have to be smart about this and trust that it will work out. It'll all be okay. As soon as Anthony drops me off, I'll text him. Just a few more minutes, and I'll be free.

"Hey, Daph."

The second I walked into The Oak and spotted Anthony, I knew I wasn't getting out of this night without some sort of confrontation. I pull in a cleansing breath and put on my button covers, mentally preparing for what comes next.

"Why don't I drop Andy off at home? Then maybe you and I can go somewhere and talk," he suggests.

We're close enough to our parents' houses now that I feel confident standing my ground.

"I'm not interested in talking. Just drop me off at home, Anthony."

He curses under his breath, slowing the car as we get closer to our destination. He's gearing up to argue, and I wouldn't put it past him to pull a stunt or posture in front of his brother. Instead of waiting for his reply, I cut him off at the pass.

"Me leaving with you tonight doesn't change anything. I was ready to go home. You offered to drive me. I didn't pick you—I just chose not to cause a scene."

As a charged silence fills the car, I hold my breath, waiting to see what sort of angle he's working today or how willing he is to fight.

He clears his throat, and his next words come out soft, almost kind. "I've been staying at my parents' house, ya know."

I exhale, grateful he's taking a more passive approach.

"So when you're ready to talk, I'll be right next door."

He pulls into the driveway and puts the car in park. I unfasten my seatbelt and quietly test my door to make sure it's not locked. Once I'm satisfied he can't physically keep me here, I make my proclamation.

"We had ten years to talk, Anthony. You made your choice. I made mine. I won't be reaching out again. Good night."

Chapter 25

Daphne

He hasn't answered any of my texts. Not the three I sent last night. Or the two I shot off between clients today. Maybe he doesn't check his phone like most people do, but we're not teenagers. I have no interest in playing games. His lack of response over the last eighteen hours has me questioning everything.

Part of me feels stupid. I never even considered that he might chicken out or ghost me—for as fun and carefree as he comes across, he seemed to respect the gravity of the situation last night.

But five unanswered texts?

Five texts. After a hurried and unplanned departure that neither of us was prepared for. We still have so much to discuss—so many things were left unsaid. I thought for sure he'd respond to my first text last night and call me like I asked. But maybe it was foolish to think we could pick up where we left off.

He wouldn't block my number, would he? His friend Cole insisted he'd been trying to get a hold of me. He didn't even *have* my number until last night.

None of this makes sense.

I barely slept, which means I've been even sicker than usual today. I'm exhausted. Restless. Brimming with a mix of anxiety-induced nausea and legit morning sickness.

I tossed and turned most of the night. When I closed my eyes, all I could see were images from the videos Andy showed me. I have so many questions. But I know one thing for sure: the videos didn't have the intended effect. If anything, they had the opposite.

I'm not scared of Fielding. Not in the least. The most vulnerable parts of me know the deepest, most intimate parts of him—that doesn't just come undone because of a few stupid videos without context. I'm not concerned with one side of a story that happened fifteen months ago.

But I do have questions. And I deserve answers. I need to know his side and understand the full story, especially if what he said last night is true.

If he wants to be in the baby's life—in *my* life—I deserve to know who he is, and I want to hear him out. We can figure this out together. But he has to actually talk to me for that to happen.

Which is why I'm once again standing at the end of this ridiculously long driveway, punching in a key code I shouldn't know but accidentally memorized.

The wrought-iron gate swings open slowly, and a wave of nausea hits me. I glance around and spot a perfectly square hedge I'll barf behind if needed. I'm unfazed by the idea, honestly. Nausea has been my near-constant companion for the last week.

I step onto the covered stone porch and inhale before I knock hard on the large, menacing double doors. I knew the house was big when he first led me through the maze to his bedroom, but standing on the porch of this behemoth building, shifting my weight from hip to hip, I can fully appreciate its size and grandeur. In the daylight, every inch of it screams money and privilege.

The door swings open, and a petite, perfectly styled blond woman beams back at me.

"Hi!" she greets enthusiastically. "I'll help you bring everything in." She's sliding sandals onto her feet as her words settle in my mind.

I don't have anything to bring in. My car's not even in the driveway. Embarrassingly, I parked on the street, unsure of how this would go or if I'd even get the gates open.

"Um, I don't, I mean, there's not—"

The blonde searches my face as she steps out onto the patio, then gives me a once-over as her expression morphs from confusion into surprise.

"You're not from Instacart?"

Good grief. Who is this woman? And where's Fielding?

Shit. If he wasn't expecting me... if he actually has blocked me... and now this gorgeous woman is answering his door...

"Is Fielding here?" I manage, bracing my arms across my chest in a half-hearted attempt to shield myself from her answer.

"Oh," she chirps and tilts her head. Then her eyes go wide. "*Oh...*"

What is that all about?

"Yes! Oh my gosh, I'm sorry. I didn't realize who you were! Come in, please. Yes, he's here. He's just inside…"

She pushes through the front door as she talks, not glancing back to confirm I'm following.

I step over the threshold and pull in a steadying breath. In the daylight, this place is so much more foreboding—and our predicament so much more real.

Now that I know we have an audience, all the confidence I've mustered to confront the man I've been trying to reach deflates. And the questions simmering in my mind about who this woman is and how she knows him certainly don't bolster my conviction.

I watch her pretty hair swish behind her as she navigates through the foyer and travels deeper into the house. She obviously knows her way around.

Does Fielding have a sister? She's blond like him, and she's traversing the place with familiarity. Either she's related or…

I shudder at the possibility of *or*.

Finally, she comes to a stop, standing halfway between the kitchen and a sunken great room. The entire eastern wall is made up of floor-to-ceiling windows, offering a breathtaking view of treetops and the first hints of fall foliage.

I freeze in place and scan the massive room, swallowing when I finally spot him on the couch.

Except it's not just him.

It's them.

There are two of them. Lounging on the same couch.

Fielding. And a mirror image of him.

Chapter 26

Fielding

"Um... guys? We have a visitor."

Dem and I move to sit up at the same time, his big stupid head pushing off mine as we smack each other in the process. When I'm finally upright, I seek out Maddie, who's standing in the kitchen. I jump to my feet when I spot Daphne by her side.

"What are you doing here?" I demand.

She cringes, and I instantly regret the way the words came out. I don't want to hurt her, but I sure as hell don't trust her after everything that went down last night.

It's not that I don't want to see her. I've been desperate to get a hold of her for weeks. But last night... when she left... when she picked him...

I steel my spine, remembering the sear of anguish that sliced through me when she walked away. If she's here to twist the knife deeper, I won't survive it.

Swallowing past my concern, I cross my arms over my chest, acutely aware that all eyes are on me.

"I mean, I didn't think I'd see you again after last night," I try again, softer this time, still piercing her with my stare.

My brother grumbles my name under his breath in warning, but I refuse to be reprimanded for keeping my guard up. He knows damn well the kind of power this woman has over me. He's the one who had to book a last-minute flight across the country because of the fallout.

Daphne remains unmoving, staring at me with those big, gray-blue eyes, breathing steadily. My vitriol bounces right off her. Like she expects it. Or she's used to it.

I soften my stance as silent seconds tick by. She looks just as unwell as she did last night—even with her hair styled and her makeup on point, I can tell she doesn't feel good.

She takes a deep breath through her nose, her face scrunching up as one hand brushes against her stomach.

"Shit... Are you about to be sick?" I forget my own emotional stake in the situation and stride toward her on instinct.

She closes her eyes as she blows out a long breath, then she opens them again to peer up at me through her lashes. "I'm okay," she assures me after a few seconds. "It passed."

"Come in and sit down," I insist, cupping her elbow and guiding her into the living room.

She's not even fully seated before Maddie starts in on the introductions. "I'm Maddie—and this is Fielding's brother, Dempsey. Are you staying for dinner? Dem's already been to the butcher, but we bought more than enough food... we're going to grill out. Do you like steak? Please stay. We'd love for you to stay."

I plop down on the couch next to Daphne, careful to keep a healthy amount of space between us. I look from Maddie to Dempsey, then back to Maddie again, who's staring at me with wide eyes. She clearly wants me to say something—so I repeat the invitation. "Would you like to stay for dinner?"

Chapter 27

Daphne

I search Fielding's face and try to read the room. I'm usually pretty adept at picking up on someone's vibe, but I'm completely off-kilter right now. Forget reading the room when the room is a lot more crowded than I expected it to be. I look from Fielding to his brother—Dempsey—then back to Fielding again.

"Sure. I'll stay. I'm Daphne, by the way," I add, trying my best not to let the shock register on my face every time I glance at Fielding's brother, who must be a twin.

"It's a pleasure to meet you," the blonde chirps, before adding, "I'm Dempsey's girlfriend."

Aha. She's his brother's girlfriend. That makes me feel better. I consider making a joke about being Fielding's baby mama, but it might be a little too on-the-nose for where things stand right now.

Fielding's eyes are boring into me. I don't even have to look to know. The intensity is palpable. He's giving off a legitimately hostile vibe that I was *not* expecting. He's done a total one-eighty from last night.

Maybe he got ahead of himself, and regrets what he said now that he's had time to think. Maybe he's *not* all in after all.

I swallow down a fresh wave of nausea. I'm here now—and he invited me to stay for dinner. It's time for an honest conversation about where things stand.

Turning to him, I tuck my hair behind my ear. His proximity unnerves me—he's close enough to touch, yet his demeanor is the complete opposite of what I've come to expect from him. And then to look over and see another one of him staring at me with an even sterner expression? Good grief.

"I texted you as soon as I got home last night. And this morning, too. I only left like that to get Anthony away from you... I know him well enough to know he—"

"Fuck," Fielding mutters under his breath, smacking at his pockets before leaning forward with his elbows on his knees as he shakes his head. "I don't even know where my phone is. I bet I left it in the car. I'm so sorry, angel," he murmurs, cupping my knee. "After you left last night... I—I thought that was it. That you were gone. I completely forgot that we had each other's numbers now."

"I think we'll go outside and give you two some privacy," Maddie announces, grabbing her boyfriend's hand, then dragging him toward a set of glass doors. "Just come out and join us when you're done," she calls over her shoulder.

Something unspoken passes between Fielding and his brother then. It's clear from that look alone that what they share is special. They hold each other's gazes for several seconds before Fielding nods. Then Dempsey is out the door, following his girlfriend.

His hand is still resting on my knee, and I fight down the urge to scoot closer to him on the couch. Something about his touch and being in his presence soothes me.

Or maybe not.

We're alone for all of two seconds before another bout of nausea rises up. "Where's the closest bathroom?" I demand, shooting to my feet and heading toward what I think are the bedrooms.

"Second door on the right," he offers, catching up to me and placing a hand on my low back to guide me.

I beeline for the toilet, and he doesn't bother giving me privacy as he follows me and sinks to his knees. He rubs my back reassuringly as I dry heave into the toilet bowl.

"How many times a day do you get sick?" he murmurs soothingly. I close my eyes and inhale—double-checking that I'm not going to gag again before answering.

"I've only puked two or three times this week. But I gag, dry heave, or spit up bile every few hours."

"When's the last time you ate?"

"Breakfast," I admit. Saturdays are my busiest days. I had back-to-back clients booked from eight until three today, which left no time to stop and eat.

"I wonder if it would help to eat more frequently. Maybe having a little something in your stomach throughout the day would make you less sick."

He manages to keep his suggestion from coming off as condescending. He's trying to be helpful, and I can appreciate the care.

I nod mindlessly, checking in with myself and inhaling before slowly rising to my feet.

"I'm okay now, I think."

He stands, too, towering over me as he peers down. "You're staying for dinner for sure?"

"Yes."

I'm not leaving this house without answers. Answers and a plan.

"Okay. You need some ginger ale to calm your stomach. We have all night to talk. Let's just get you feeling better first, deal?"

I came here fired up, ready to demand answers. I wasn't expecting to soften so quickly in his presence. But he's right—we have all night. Knowing he didn't have his phone on him and that he's still very much invested in this situation eases the sense of hostility that had been brewing inside me all day.

We have time. Time to talk. Time to figure each other out. I'm here now. He knows I'm pregnant. Maybe he's stalling when it comes to discussing the videos he knows I've seen, but we'll get to them, and I'm okay with taking things slow.

"Deal," I agree, taking the hand he's offering and letting him lead me out of the bathroom toward the back patio.

"I would honestly question your age if we didn't share a birthday, ya old man," Fielding jibes at his brother.

"Remember—when he—made us—go—last time?" Maddie gasps between fits of laughter. "You even wore suspenders!" she mocks, lifting a toned, perfect leg to nudge Fielding in the thigh. He catches her by the calf and yanks her so hard her whole body shifts in the pool chair.

"Those suspenders were perfect for a night at the orchestra!" Fielding defends. "And how else was I supposed to sneak in pot and roll you a joint?" Instead of releasing her, he locks his hand around her ankle and tickles the arch of her foot.

"No, no, no!" she squeals. "I'll pee! You know I'll pee!"

"You know how to end it, Little Wheeler."

Fielding keeps up the torture, and Dempsey just shakes his head at their antics. It's odd to watch them be so physical and affectionate with each other. But Dempsey doesn't seem bothered, and I'm just getting to know them both...

"Fine! Uncle Tony!" Maddie declares. All tickling and play-fighting stops in an instant. I gulp down a scoff at the mention of my ex-fiancé's nickname.

I'm both fascinated and curious about their dynamic. Maddie is younger than all of us—she mentioned she's about to start her last year of undergrad, whereas I'm twenty-six, and I think the twins are closer to thirty. Another thing I'll need to ask Fielding about eventually.

They're all extremely affectionate and comfortable with each other, which I like. Fielding and Maddie have a sitcom sibling vibe going on. And she's obviously head over heels for Dempsey.

She shoots Fielding a death glare before she retreats into her boyfriend's lap, wrapped in his big arms immediately. He engulfs her in a tender embrace like it's the most natural thing in the world. Then she runs a hand along the stubble of his jaw while he draws little circles near the hem of her shorts.

Their PDA borders on too intimate, and I give in to the urge to look away. But then the only other place to look is at Fielding, and that's definitely not the safest place for me to focus while I'm trying to keep my wits about me.

I can't stop staring at him—studying him—now that we're sitting side by side in broad daylight. He's somehow even better looking than I remember. As if his dazzling smile and lagoon-blue eyes weren't enough, his arms and hands are like works of art. Not following the tracks of veins in his forearms down to the strong flex of his fingers is all but impossible when I'm this close.

It doesn't help that I remember exactly how those hands felt on my body. The things they can do. The ways he can make me come undone.

"All right, boys," Maddie declares, smacking a kiss on her boyfriend's cheek before rising to her feet. "To the kitchen with you. Daphne and I will handle the steaks."

My stomach churns at the mention of steak—I'm not sure I can handle even looking at raw meat right now. She must notice because she offers me a sympathetic smile before whispering, "I've got you."

The boys haul themselves out of their seats but grumble about her bossiness. She just smirks and plants her hands on her hips. She looks between them with raised eyebrows before turning back to me. "Field can't be trusted—he gets distracted by his phone and overcooks everything. Dempsey makes the best potato salad. Ergo, I'm in charge of the grill. And now that you're here, you're sticking with me."

Fielding closes the space between us but doesn't touch me. I still shiver from the near-contact.

"You don't have to be stuck with her," he murmurs. "Will you be okay out here? Or do you want to come inside?"

I've already gotten the impression that Maddie's a force to be reckoned with. But I'm confident I can handle her. Besides, if we're really doing this, I want to get to know his family. I want them to like me, too.

"I'm good," I insist, mustering a smile I hope convinces him of the words I don't fully believe myself.

"I'll grab my phone from the car before we get started on the rest of dinner. Text me if you need anything." He brushes his fingers against the bare skin of my arm, leaving me shivering as he walks away.

Maddie follows them into the house, then comes back out with a foil-covered platter and a handful of seasonings. We're both quiet as she fires up the grill and gets things situated. After a few minutes, I break the silence.

"Can I ask you something? Did he already tell you..." I trail off, because if she knows, it'll be obvious what I'm asking. And if not, I'm not sure what to say next.

She meets my gaze over the top of the open grill lid and nods slowly. She must notice the grimace on my face because she's quick to defend him in the next breath.

"He told us, but he honestly thought he wouldn't see you again. He was... really upset. Upset enough to text Dem last night and ask us to come home."

"Home?"

"We live in California," she reveals.

I blink multiple times, working out what she just said. "You flew across the country to be here today?"

That's... extreme.

Maddie smirks as she closes the lid of the grill. "Being in a relationship with a twin is a *whole* vibe. You'll see—"

She looks away as soon as she realizes her potential overstep. Just because I'm here... and I'm carrying his child... doesn't mean Fielding and I are in any sort of relationship.

"Fielding and Dempsey are exceptionally close," she continues. "Dem moved out to Cali to be with me last year, but I don't see them living apart for much longer. I'm looking at law schools on the east coast and already plotting ways to get them back in the same time zone. They're best friends. They've been through hell and back. Their mom died last year—"

Emotion catches in my throat.

"—And their dad's a dick."

I snort at her shrewd assessment. Nice to know I'm not the only one with less-than-stellar parents.

"Their lives were sort of on hold for a while because their mom was sick. After she died, they both had to find their footing and figure out what was next."

She pauses then, looking toward the house. When she speaks again, her voice is softer, just above a whisper.

"Fielding's been working really hard to get his shit together. He starts med school next week. His reasons are absolutely not financial,"—she raises her hand with a flourish, indicating the over-the-top backyard and the literal mansion before us, "—but he's determined to make something of himself."

"So they're rich?" I confirm.

Maddie's eyes go wide, and she smirks. "Stupid rich."

We're making progress, she and I. She obviously loves her boyfriend and his brother, but she's not one to sugarcoat or bullshit. I press my luck and decide to see just how much she'll tell me.

"You said Fielding's working hard to get his shit together... so that implies it wasn't together at some point?"

I study her as she purses her lips, flips up the grill lid, and busies herself flipping the steaks. When she's done, she walks over and sits beside me on a pool lounger.

"It was not. He wasn't well for a while," she admits.

"And now?" I try.

She exhales, glances at the house, then looks back at me. "He's been working really hard."

I play with the ends of my hair, accepting that's probably all I'll get out of her. Her answers seem honest—but they do nothing to settle the uneasiness in my gut that kicks up when I think about the videos and the way Andy carried on last night.

"Before I met Fielding, I was engaged," I offer. I figure if she's being candid with me, I can do the same. "We met the night of my bachelorette party, even though I was calling off the wedding."

Maddie doesn't react—so she already knows this part of the story.

"My ex-fiancé's little brother showed me all these videos last night. Of Fielding at a party, drunk or high... or both... trying to make people fight him."

She pales at my words, but it's almost imperceptible behind her golden tan.

I stay quiet, waiting her out for a reaction.

Finally, she sighs. "I was there when those videos were taken."

I suspected as much. In a few of the videos, a petite blonde runs into the crowd and screams at everyone to stop. Most of the videos Andy showed me cut out around that point, so I don't know what happened after that. Now that I'm sitting here beside her, it all makes more sense.

"So you know what happened that night?"

She side-eyes me as she stands up, whether to check on the steaks or get away from me, I'm not sure. She smooths down the front of her shorts and blows out a long breath before looking at me with sincerity in her eyes.

"I do. But that's Fielding's story to tell."

Chapter 28

Fielding

"This is *so* good," Daphne practically moans as she cuts into her steak. She must feel my eyes on her, because she looks up and gives me a sheepish smile. "I haven't had an appetite all week."

I reach under the table and squeeze her thigh. I'm thrilled that she's eating. Hopefully, she'll be able to keep this down. And she's not wrong—Maddie did an excellent job with the steaks, Dem's potato salad is on point, and the rice pilaf and fresh sweet corn from the little farm stand we like down in the valley put the meal over the top.

We make small talk as we eat, which I'm grateful for. Daphne and I need to really talk—and soon—but it's nice to sit around the table and enjoy a meal together. I won't see my brother and Little Wheeler again until the holidays. Despite the melodramatic reason they rushed home, I'm grateful they're here.

When we were alone in the kitchen, Dem drilled into me how unnecessary their trip home now seems. He's not wrong, but never in a million years did I expect to be sitting around the dinner table with the woman who walked away from me last night.

Maddie starts classes on Monday, which I did not know when I asked them to come back to Hampton. After dinner they'll get their travel plans arranged, and thankfully, she won't miss anything because of me.

Dem stands up first to clear his plate, and I side-eye Daphne beside me. "Did you get enough to eat?" She nods, but I push back. "You're sure? You're growing a human. You need nutrients."

She smiles at me but rolls her eyes, declaring that she's stuffed before thanking Maddie and Dempsey for cooking.

I watch the easy way she interacts with my family. I watch her settle back in her seat and let out a little satisfied sigh. I could watch her do anything, really. She's so pretty. Her hair is down, curled in soft waves. I can't stop staring at the blush on her cheeks.

I know I should keep my defenses up after all the drama of last night... but something in me believes her. I *want* to believe she left with Anthony to prevent things from escalating. And I want her to believe in me.

Dem grips my shoulder as he reaches in front of me and picks up my plate. "We'll take care of cleanup and give you two some privacy."

He knows Daphne has seen the videos. He knows what's on the line.

I smile appreciatively as I turn to Daphne, take her hand, and help her to her feet.

"We'll be outside. If you're gonna go upstairs and bone, don't do it on the balcony where we can hear."

Maddie rolls her eyes and gives me a pointed look. Dem's cheeks turn red with rage. Daphne probably thinks I'm teasing them, but in reality, I know *a lot* of sordid details about their sex life courtesy of one or both of them getting drunk and oversharing. The balcony off Dem's wing of the house is one of their favorite places to get it on.

We head out to the patio, and I inhale the moment we step into the fresh air. It's August, but the nights are finally getting cooler, and there's a crisp, clean scent in the evening. Summer is holding on to its final days, but fall is definitely coming.

"Do you want to sit and talk? Or go on a walk?"

"Where would we walk? Up and down your long-ass driveway?"

I smirk at her sass. It really is an obnoxiously long driveway.

"There's a trail through the woods this way," I explain, nodding toward the path just barely visible from our backyard. "Our property backs up to the Cuyahoga Valley National Park. It's an even path, and we don't have to go far. It's a really nice, secluded trail. But only if you're up for it."

"I'm up for it."

We walk quietly for several minutes, finding our footing and maintaining a comfortable pace as we make our way along the trail, side by side. I focus on the song of the birds and the distant sound of traffic from the two-lane highway that runs parallel to this section of the park.

The peace doesn't keep as my anxiety nags at me to break the silence. We have a lot of ground to cover. I clear my throat and start with the basics.

"When did you find out you're pregnant?"

"Just a few days after my period was late. My back was burning at work—I'm an esthetician at a salon, so I'm on my feet all day. But everything just hurt worse than usual, and typically when my period's late, I don't have any PMS symptoms at all."

"And what you said last night... about the timing, with me?"

She peers over at me, rolls her lips, and nods.

"You make the most sense. I've had abnormal periods in the past, but even extending the window of when I could have ovulated, I'm almost positive the baby is yours. I looked up paternity testing—we can get it done as early as seven weeks. It's a blood draw for me and a cheek swab for you."

Shit. Why didn't I think of that?

"It's accurate that early?" I marvel, not because I don't believe her. I just wasn't aware that option even existed. I make a mental note to look up the details about the procedure on the school research database.

"Supposedly it'll either show zero percent chance of paternity or ninety-nine percent-plus. I feel like ninety-nine percent is probably good enough, don't you think?"

The quiver in her voice makes me trip over my next step. *Shit*. I wasn't doubting her or questioning her integrity. I'm not looking for an out. If the test says it's mine, then it's mine.

I really fucking want it to be mine.

"Absolutely. Everything I said to you last night... that's all still true, Daphne. I want to help. I want to be there for you. I want to be in this baby's life. You can count on me, I swear."

She slows her steps, and I shorten my stride to match her pace.

"That's nice to hear, but those are just words. I don't know you, Fielding. I appreciate everything you said last night, but your actions spoke louder. You didn't respond to any of my texts. I sent five. That's, like, stalker-level texting. Then, when I showed up this afternoon, you seemed..."

"Hungover and pissed off?" I supply.

She gawks at me, wide-eyed. I know how I acted when she showed up today, and I won't pretend that I wasn't being a dick. I was in defense mode.

"When you walked out of that alley last night, when you left with *him* and walked away from *me*, I texted my brother in a panic. Then I came home and got drunk off my ass."

I don't give her time to respond. There's nothing she could criticize about my behavior that I haven't already said to myself.

"I know my reaction was immature and stupid. But I felt so fucking helpless. In my defense, I thought I wasn't going to see you again. I thought... I thought that even though you were pregnant with my baby, you picked him."

We're both silent for a few breaths, the natural hum of the forest and the tiny bits of gravel crunching beneath our feet the only sounds rising above our even breathing.

"So it's fair to say you don't handle rejection well?"

Her tone is teasing. But the sting that results from her jab is hard to hide.

"I don't," I admit, my tone low and earnest. "That's my shit, though. And I'll figure it out. You don't need anything else to worry about. I'm sorry I didn't respond to your texts. And I hate that I was a defensive dick when you showed up here today. Forgive me. I promise it won't happen again."

"It's okay," she murmurs, linking her arm through mine in a gesture that tugs at my heartstrings. I resist the urge to stop in my tracks and pull her into a legitimate hug.

"Can you tell me about the videos?"

I blow out a breath and mentally negotiate with myself about how to approach this. I'll tell her anything—I want to be open and honest, and it's important we establish a rapport now if we're going to be in each other's lives in such a significant way.

But fuck. That night was awful.

"That was a really bad night for me," I start. "I regret how it went down, but I won't lie and try to sugarcoat it. The videos kind of speak for themselves…"

I was drunk. And high. I showed up at a party, and more than anything, I wanted to feel something that hurt more than the pain eating at me from the inside.

I would never hurt someone intentionally for my own comfort. I'm not a sadist. But I needed to feel *something*. I decided fists on flesh was what I wanted that night.

"It happened last summer?" "Yes."

"Is that—I mean, did that…" She doesn't finish.

"What do you need to know, angel? I'll tell you anything you want to know about that night."

She inhales and quickens her pace, looking straight ahead before she articulates her next question. "Did that used to happen a lot?"

"Not a lot," I assure her, before adding, "But I wouldn't be surprised if there is other random footage floating around out there of me acting like a fool or making questionable choices. It's okay if you judge me for what you saw in those videos, but I haven't been that guy for a long time. Which I'm sure sounds crazy, since I just admitted to getting drunk off my ass last night, but there's a difference."

She cocks one eyebrow in question but lets me continue.

"In those videos Andrew showed you—on a night like that—I was desperate to forget. I would go out looking for a fight. I used to do shit like that to numb the pain."

"And last night?" she pushes.

"Last night, I was desperate not to be forgotten. Or left behind. I called my brother before I did anything else. I made sure I got home and couldn't hurt anyone else."

I glance over out of the corner of my eye, anxious to get a read on her reaction. She's looking forward, focused on the path ahead and the trees that surround it. She's looking everywhere but at me.

"I told you the first night we met that I'm not a good man, Daphne. I've never been the hero in anyone's story. But I've been putting in the work, trying to be a better person. And you just gave me the ultimate reason to get my shit together and keep it together once and for all. I don't have the track record to back up my claims. I'm going to have to prove to you that I can do this. But I will. You'll see. I promise you—I'm in, and you can count on me."

Silence stretches between us. I regret suggesting a walk. If we were seated and stationary, I would at least feel like less of a creeper staring at her and willing her to respond.

"I can accept that."

I sigh out all the anxiety I've been bottling up since last night.

"I don't love what I saw in those videos, but with the way Andy was going on about it, I got the sense that there was more to the story. I can accept that it was something you did, but that it's not who you are."

Fuck. Yes. Okay. I can deal with neutral acceptance. Deeper trust will come with time.

I grasp for a subject change now that I know she's not running away in terror or basing her impression of me on those videos alone.

"That was the night Maddie and my brother first hooked up, you know."

She looks up at me in mock-horror when I wag my eyebrows in amusement.

"That's probably too much information considering I just met them a few hours ago…"

"Get used to it, angel. You're gonna hear plenty more about them if we're doing this for real."

A reluctant smile graces her lips, and I'm once again disarmed by just how pretty she is. How the hell did I land this angel? I hate that she's sick and that she was going through more than enough even before grappling with the life-changing reality of an unplanned pregnancy. But I'm sure as hell not mad at the Universe for bringing us back together. It's like I'm cheating the system somehow now that I know she's carrying my child. I passed Go and collected two hundred dollars, and it still feels like the best is yet to come.

"So where do we stand?" I ask cautiously.

"We?" "You and me." I move my hand down her arm and interlace our fingers, squeezing once for emphasis. "Us."

Her grip goes slack before she responds.

"I honestly don't know how to answer that…"

I wait for her to continue, but she doesn't.

Nope. That's not gonna work for me. She's here. She knows I'm in. We're both single, and the pull between us is just as strong as it was that first night. She's carrying my child, for fuck's sake. We know we're fire when we're together—something I'm fiending to experience again. If she's letting me in, I want *all* the way in.

"I meant what I said last night. I'm in. I want to be with you. Let's do this together."

She says nothing still. I tug on her hand with enough force to halt us both.

"Tell me what you're thinking, Daphne. What's holding you back?"

"You're not going to like my answer," she warns.

I wait patiently for her explanation as I start working up a counterargument in my head.

"I believe you want to be in the baby's life. And I want you to be involved where it makes sense. But I can't just hop into a relationship, if that's what you're asking me to do. I don't have the energy to deal with... with everything. I'm exhausted. Calling off the wedding... my entire life going off track... and now this?" She puts a hand to her lower abdomen.

"But you feel it." I argue. "I know you do. The connection between us—" I lean closer, pushing my luck and hovering in her space. "You feel it, and it's stronger than ever. We were *so* good together, Daphne. So. Fucking. Good," I remind her, putting emphasis on each word and resisting the urge to kiss her.

She closes her eyes and inhales, so I do the same, savoring the floral notes of her hair mixed with the fresh, woodsy smell all around us. God, I want her. Not just because she's carrying my child. But because she's *her*. That night—that amazing, mind-blowing night—was nowhere near enough. I need another fix. I want to cash in on that monthly pass. I'd gladly sign up for a lifetime of this feeling.

"We can't just act on attraction, Fielding."

"Why not?" I challenge, inching closer until I can feel her breath mingle with mine.

"I don't want to make this more complicated. We can't guarantee things will work out between us, so it's best if we don't even try. Now that there's another life involved, he or she comes first." She nods once before meeting my gaze, her resolve firmly locked in place.

"You're honestly telling me there's no chance for us?" I push, the back of my hand brushing a featherlight touch down the side of her neck. "You think we'll co-parent, spend all kinds of time together, and not want more? I already want more with you, Daphne."

She looks up at me then, a hint of sorrow in her gaze. "I wouldn't be a good girlfriend. Just getting through each day this week has been a struggle. I can barely keep my head above water as it is. If I keep feeling this sick, I won't have anything else to give..."

The actual fuck? I can accept no if she doesn't want me. But she's standing here admitting she's holding back because she's afraid she's not enough?

I refuse to accept that.

"I don't know what kind of assholes you've dated in the past, but I don't need anything from you except permission to be by your side whenever you need me," I declare. I fucking mean it. There aren't any rules or expectations for how we do this. I just want to try. We can figure this out—figure out what *us* means—together. If only she'd give us a chance.

Silence builds between us, but I let the awkwardness fester. Silence is better than rejection.

Unlacing our fingers, I skim my fingertips up her arm, then gently cup both sides of her face in my hands before tilting her head back so she's forced to meet my gaze.

"You're trembling," I realize, pulling her closer in case she's cold.

"You unnerve me," she admits as she nuzzles her cheek against the fabric of my shirt.

It's the closest we've been since that night. Wave after wave of intimate memories come flooding back to me. There's something so simple and beautiful about the way she leans into me. I never want to let her go.

I glide my arms down her back, and she shudders again under my touch.

"I like the way your body responds to mine," I whisper, emboldened by her reaction. "It's like it remembers—"

My words are cut off abruptly when she spins out of my hold, grabs as much of her hair as possible, and projectile vomits off the side of the trail.

For fuck's sake.

Is it wrong of me to think that our kid is already proving to be a cock block? I gather her hair in one hand and use the other to run soothing circles up and down her back.

"You're okay," I murmur over and over again as she loses what appears to be every bite of her dinner. When she finally stops throwing up, she looks back at me and cocks one eyebrow in challenge.

Joke's on her, though. I'm not scared of a little puke, or anything about pregnancy, really. It's going to take a lot more than morning sickness to convince me we shouldn't be together.

"I'm not sure I can survive eight more months of my body remembering yours," she finally jokes, panting and trying to catch her breath. When she straightens and gives me a quick nod, I assume the nausea has passed, and I interlace our fingers again and turn back to the house.

"Come on. Let's get you back."

She's right—the baby and her health are my top priorities right now. But the issue of *us* is up there alongside them, and I don't give up that easily.

Chapter 29

Daphne

If I felt foolish parking on the street and trekking down his driveway when I arrived, I'm mortified to have to retrace my steps now—with Fielding by my side.

He hasn't said a word, but I can tell by the way he's fighting back a smirk that he has plenty of thoughts about my selected parking spot.

"You obviously know the code for the gate. Next time, pull all the way up on the left side of the driveway. I don't want you walking back and forth like this."

I let him hold my hand—again—because even though I told him there won't be an *us*, I can't help but hope I'm wrong. So much of what I said is true: I can't imagine trying to navigate this new normal while also trying to do cutesy, new relationship things with him. But it's not because I don't want him. I just don't know how to reconcile the plans I had for my life with reality.

"You sure you're okay?" he asks again, grazing his thumb over my knuckles. By the time we made it back to his house, my stomach had settled. The fresh air and a full glass of ginger ale from his ridiculous Freestyle machine had me feeling good as new.

He insisted I take home all the leftovers—and that I try to eat a little something before I go to bed. I would have rolled my eyes at his concerned partner act if I didn't find it so endearing.

"I'm sure. I've gotten used to it this week, honestly. And I promise to eat something before I go to bed," I insist before he can remind me—again.

He opens the door for me when we finally get to my car and holds it open longer than necessary as I fiddle with the seatbelt and get situated. Then he has the audacity to roll down the window before he closes the door, leans into my space, and grips the doorframe for dear life.

He's stalling.

And for some reason, I'm not annoyed by it.

"I'm going to see you again, right?"

His words disarm me. There's no version of my future that he isn't part of. But given how we parted last night, and how noncommittal I was in the woods, it's fair that he's worried about what's next.

"You will. I promise. I'll even text you when I get home if it makes you feel better."

He smirks and shakes his head—looking up the road before gazing back at me. When he smiles, my insides flip-flip, and not in a nauseating way. He's got the best damn smile.

"I would tell you not to patronize me, but I really do want you to text me later."

He reaches into the car then, gently peeling my left hand off the steering wheel and kissing my palm before placing my hand low on my stomach and releasing it.

"Good night, Daphne."

He takes three strides back, watching me the entire time. His expression is a mix of apprehension and hope. There, at the top of the driveway, he stands, with the wrought-iron gates closed behind him, peering at me as I put the car in drive.

He lifts his arm in one last wave, but he doesn't turn back to the house.

I don't know what comes over me, but I can barely bring myself to pull away. Just as I find the courage to *go*, I remember something and slam on the brakes.

I had completely forgotten about this. In my defense, I showed up today ready to ream him out and put him in his place. This whole night has gone so unexpectedly off the rails; but now I feel bad that I didn't think to ask earlier.

I roll down the passenger window as he takes a tentative step forward.

"Um, so—I have a prenatal appointment and ultrasound on Wednesday morning. I know we don't have confirmation about paternity yet… but do you want to go with me?"

"I'm so fucking there."

I didn't think he could possibly smile any bigger—but there it is.

I shut the door as quietly as possible, hearing their murmurs stop when it clicks into place. I don't know why I bother attempting to sneak in or out of my parents' house—for one, I'm a twenty-six-year-old financially independent woman, minus my living situation. And for another? It's pointless. They could sense my approach even in pitch black silence.

"Daphne? Is that you?"

"Yes, just me." I stick my phone back in my pocket—I sent Fielding a text as soon as I arrived, so that's handled. Leftovers in hand, I move toward the fridge, lifting the plastic lid off the container and giving the food a whiff before popping a little purple potato in my mouth. It tastes just as good as it did earlier—thankfully. As awful as it is to toss my cookies on the regular nowadays, at least morning sickness hasn't turned me off to the foods I just threw up.

"What are you eating?"

I jump on instinct and lift the back of my hand to my mouth before closing the fridge and turning to face her.

"Nothing, Mom. You scared me."

She tuts her tongue as she looks me up and down.

"It's after nine."

I check the clock on the stove—and so it is. It's 9:07 p.m., to be exact. Heaven forbid the pregnant woman who's kept nothing but oatmeal down today sneaks a bite of potato. But she doesn't know I'm pregnant. And I don't have the energy to fight. I quietly slip on the impassive mask I wear in her presence and straighten my shoulders.

"Is Tahlia home?" I ask, moving to fill up my water bottle.

"Of course she's home. She's a twelve-year-old girl. Where else would she be?"

Seconds roll by as I wait for the impossibly slow stream from the tap to fill my bottle. I can feel her eyes on me—a strike is coming. My shoulders tense involuntarily when she speaks again.

"Have you talked to Anthony today?"

And there it is.

The delusion that perhaps if I just talk to him—give him a chance to explain himself—everything will be okay. That's getting old. It's been over a month. Things in my life are shifting and changing in significant ways. None of what I'm dealing with right now has to do with Anthony. I'm more than ready to close the door on that chapter of my life once and for all.

"I have not. And I won't be," I assert, turning to face her again as she narrows her eyes.

She doesn't need to know that I was with him last night when he drove me home. Or that I couldn't wait to get away from him.

"We raised you better than this, Daphne," she whispers, her words dripping in judgment.

Once again, we're at an impasse. The same impasse we've battled over for weeks. Her insistence that I fall in line and marry a man who intentionally set out to cheat on me is something I will never be okay with. But explaining that to her *again* will only bring us back to the same conclusion it always does: It's more embarrassing to our family that I ended my relationship than it would have been had I just sucked it up, gotten over his infidelity, and gone forward with our plans.

"I know you're disappointed. But your disappointment doesn't change who I am or how I feel. Good night, Mom," I murmur, effectively ending the conversation. It's not really over.

It'll continue to be a point—*the point*—of discussion for as long as I live under this roof. But at least we're done for tonight.

My hand instinctively rests on my stomach as I take the stairs two at a time. I will not bring a child into the world and force him or her to be subjected to this level of dysfunction. I was fully prepared to reach out to Serena's landlord about my old apartment, but that was before I found out I was pregnant. I want to be smart about this because I'll need help when the baby arrives. So for now, I'll stay put, save my money, and bide my time.

I sigh as I reach the top step, noticing the sliver of light shining from Tahlia's room. Either she heard me or sensed me coming, because her door swings open a second later. "You're here!"

Exhausted, I still return her smile. "I'm here. I told you I'd be home before bedtime."

Now that she's twelve, Tahlia has her own cell phone. I know my parents monitor it, but it's still nice to touch base with her and make plans like this.

"Are you too tired tonight?"

Her question twists in my gut. Twice this week, I couldn't follow through with our plans because I didn't want her to see me running to the bathroom or getting sick.

"I'm good. I just need to change. I'll meet you in your room in five."

I make quick work of throwing my hair into a messy bun and pulling on PJs. By the time I get to her room across the hall, Tahlia has everything set up for us. I grab my favorite blanket and climb on top of the covers, then arrange a pillow behind my head as she adjusts her reading light.

She finds our place and begins, and I do my best to not drift off to sleep as she dives into Percy Jackson's latest peril. I used to read to her when she was little—but nowadays she reads to me. Our nighttime routine is one of the few traditions I cherish about being back in this house.

I'm grateful my parents don't look at her the way they look at me. She's significantly younger—she was an oops baby, arriving fourteen years after I was born, but she still slotted into the role of the favorite naturally.

I don't mind. She's my favorite, too. She was my first baby—she always will be. I know she'll be thrilled when she finds out she's going to be an aunt. Tahlia's the singular bright spot for me while I'm stuck in this house.

I yawn when she turns the page. "I hope you get to go on a big adventure like this someday, TT."

"I don't want adventure. I just want to find my own Prince Charming like you," she retorts.

Ugh.

I've tried to shield her from the reality of what happened between Anthony and me. She knows we canceled the wedding, but I refuse to speak poorly about him in front of her. Which means she only knows partial truths and half the story. She has the luxury of still believing in fairy tales.

"Maybe you'll get both," I suggest. "I think living a life you love is more important than finding a Prince Charming. Especially at age twelve," I add as I tickle her side.

"Is that the real reason you aren't getting married?"

It's not. But maybe it should have been.

The saddest part of it all isn't canceling the wedding or ending a decade-long relationship. It's the harsh reality of how close I came to settling for so much less than what I deserved. I see that now. But I'm ashamed that it took me so long. If I'm honest with myself, I may have never seen it if Anthony hadn't taken his "free pass," and I hadn't shared that night with Fielding.

"I'm not getting married because it didn't feel right. I decided I needed a different kind of adventure." My answer is vague, but someday I'll tell it to her straight. And someday I hope she'll understand. My hand drifts to my low belly again, my body already keenly aware of the precious gift it protects. I can't help but yawn and snuggle into the pillow.

"Don't fall asleep," she whines, nudging my knee as I shake my head and try to keep my eyes open.

"I'm not," I insist through the yawn. "Keep going. I'm listening, I swear."

I wake up in her bed around two with the urge to pee but smile when I have to peel her lanky limbs off me before making my way to the bathroom and back to my own bed.

Chapter 30

Fielding

"Fuck, bro. I can't believe this is happening."

I let his words settle into my bones as I reach for my acoustic guitar and plop back down on the couch.

Not believing it wasn't an option for me. Time to exist in a state of disbelief was a luxury I wasn't afforded. I went from desperately trying to find Daphne, to being hit with life-altering news, to then being abandoned (or so I thought) in the alley.

I hate asking for help, but I did it anyway, and Dem and Maddie were here in record time. Then, before I could even talk things through with my brother, Daphne magically appeared at the house, and all was right with my world.

I'm suffering from emotional whiplash. But I'm also on cloud nine. I strum the chords to one of my favorite John Mayer songs as I consider everything that's happened over the last twenty-four hours.

"I can't, either. But not in a bad way. I sort of feel like I won the lottery," I admit.

"Are you kidding me?" Dempsey challenges, rubbing the top of his head against mine. I grunt, then use my legs to push against the arm of the sofa and dislodge him. We wrestle for dominance before finally settling back down, our legs hanging off opposite armrests as our heads meet in the middle of the couch.

"I've been thinking about her nonstop since the night I met her, Dumpy. At first, I thought it was because I had a responsibility to tell her about the condom... but honestly, I just wanted to be near her again. I feel... different when she's around. Calm. Settled. Whole."

He lets out a long, exasperated sigh. A sigh I know all too well.

"I'm not gonna fuck this up," I vow, strumming on my guitar quietly. Maddie already went to bed. They have to get up before dawn to catch their flight back to California.

"I didn't say you were," he retorts.

I scoff. He didn't *say* it. But I know how his mind works.

"Sort of crazy that I've made it more than ten years without some sort of pregnancy drama," I muse. "Nothing about this feels wrong, though, Dem. I wasn't trying to knock her up, obviously, but I'm really fucking happy with how things turned out."

"You really like her, don't you?"

"Yeah," I admit with a sigh, remembering how she looked up at me in the woods today, and the sizzle I felt before we almost kissed. "I really do."

"I don't think you would have been so excited about the prospect of being a dad if this had happened last year."

Last August, our mom had just passed away, and Maddie had left to go back to California. I had already decided I couldn't sit around this house pissing my life away anymore—I needed a change. I needed to *live*, and I was the only one who could make it happen. This time last year, I was encouraging Dem to go after what he wanted and trying to convince him I'd be okay without him.

He's right. A lot has changed over the last year. I'm different now. The way I view myself is different. My self-doubt and loathing aren't all-consuming. I'm fucking ecstatic that I get a shot at being a dad, maybe even at having a family of my own.

But Dem loves to scold me for getting ahead of myself. So I won't voice those thoughts just yet.

"Did you ever have a scare?" I ask, effectively changing the subject.

"Never."

"You're such a dick. You say it with such conviction. How do you know for sure?" I press.

"Think about it, bro. We're fucking loaded, and *I've* always had my shit together."

I swat my hand toward his head at the dig.

"If a girl thought she was carrying my kid, she would have made herself known. Plus, I *always* used condoms. Always. Until Maddie..."

I consider teasing him about raw-dogging his woman, but there's no point. They're the real deal, and they're both in it for the long haul. Plus, I'm certain Little Wheeler's got all her bases covered in the birth control department. She's recited her five-year plan to us so many times even I know that shit by heart. A baby doesn't fall into that plan.

"That was probably the only worthwhile thing Dad ever taught us, huh?"

"Don't be a fool," Dempsey starts before we finish the ridiculous motto in unison: "Wrap your tool."

We laugh at our asshole father's expense. And then we both go quiet.

Long ago, we decided we didn't want any sort of relationship with the man, but the stark reminder that it's just the two of us against the world never ceases to make me feel small.

"How do you plan to inform George Haas that he's going to be a grandpa?"

I smirk as I consider my options. "I'll probably just send his secretary a press release."

Dem chuckles, no doubt thinking about the time our dad told us he was moving to China for two years via press release. Like I said: he never was and never will be father of the year. That doesn't mean I can't vie for the title.

"I know you're just days away from starting med school, so maybe this is a stupid question..."

I suck in a lungful of air and hold it while I wait for him to continue.

"But you're doing a paternity test for sure, right?"

"Yes, Dumpy." I sigh, annoyed. The baby is mine; I know it. But I'll go through the motions to appease everyone around me.

"Okay, good. Did you and Daphne discuss how twins run in our family?"

Fuck. Nope. We did not. In my defense, I've only known about the baby for twenty-four hours. But shit—should I text her about it?

I blow out a long breath and try not to dwell on the possibility. Or let myself get too excited. That's probably not something she wants to learn via text, and I can't imagine it would do much to ease her stress to inform her she very well might be carrying twins.

"She has a prenatal appointment and an ultrasound this week," I remember. "I'm going with her. We should know then whether there's one heartbeat or two."

"You're gonna go all in with this, aren't you?" Dempsey groans. "Our lives are about to become all baby, all the time."

I don't bother arguing. My brother knows me better than anyone—he knows I only have one mode. If I am the father of this child, then all our lives are about to get turned upside down. It's going to be so fucking fun.

"Pace yourself with her, brother. I think she's great—Maddie really liked her, too. But sharing a kid means whatever happens between you two is going to affect your lives forever. It's going to affect another life, too."

His warning is warranted, but also in vain.

I'm already head over heels for Daphne: totally smitten, utterly mesmerized, and completely gone for this girl.

Chapter 31

Daphne

Having a full clientele with a steady waitlist has always been my dream—until now, when I have to shuffle clients and reschedule people to make it to the only doctor's appointment slot available that's long enough for an ultrasound and prenatal visit.

I worked for two hours this morning, and after my appointment, I'll go back and work until eight tonight. It's less than ideal, but without more notice, my schedule has little flexibility. It was hard enough explaining to our receptionist Bobbi why I needed to move clients today without flat-out telling her what was going on. It's going to be near-impossible to keep this pregnancy secret from the girls at work much longer.

I blow out a long breath as I pull in next to a huge silver SUV. Fielding hops out of the driver's side as soon as I park.

Of course he's grinning from ear to ear like he's thrilled to be here, and I can't help but smile, too—his enthusiasm is contagious. He's been nothing but wildly supportive, albeit a little overbearing, over the last few days. We've been texting nonstop. I've forgotten what it's like to not feel my phone buzzing over and over again in the middle of doing a bikini wax.

He's around my car and opening my door before I've unbuckled, then he's offering his hand to me.

"Hi," I greet him while I let him help me out. "Are you excited?"

"You have no idea." I don't doubt it. He's grinning so wide there's no way his face doesn't hurt.

Once I get checked in, I'm asked to "leave a sample" in the bathroom, then we sit among the other women and couples in the waiting room. I've barely had more than two sips of coffee today—my stomach just can't handle the acidity right now—but my knees are bouncing like crazy.

"This is going to be awesome," Fielding murmurs under his breath, brushing one of his large, tan hands down my trembling thigh. "I'm so grateful you asked me to be here."

His words calm me enough to stop fidgeting. That, or the sight of his hand and all those arm veins brushing up and down my thigh has done the trick. Without overthinking it, I smooth my hand over my pant leg, eventually letting it rest next to his. He doesn't hesitate to clasp it, interlace our fingers, and bring our hands to his lips.

"Wait," he whispers suddenly. "You washed your hands after leaving that sample, right?"

I snort—not my most lady-like move, I know, but he's ridiculous. He somehow always knows what to say to lighten the mood. I bump his rock-solid shoulder with mine, and I'm still laughing when a nurse calls us back.

After confirming my name and birthday, she asks me to get on the scale.

I cringe and look at Fielding. "Please don't look," I beg.

"I won't if you don't want me to," he murmurs, turning around to give me and the scale the privacy I asked for. Good thing, too. This doctor's office scale is rude as hell—it claims I weigh four pounds more than the one I have at home. Nothing about my body has visibly changed yet, but that hasn't stopped me from stepping on the scale each morning out of curiosity.

"Great. Have a seat. I'll take your blood pressure before we head back to imaging."

I cross my ankles and offer my arm, then try to calm my bouncing leg as the cuff tightens.

"Hmm... oh dear," the nurse mutters. "It's 142/85. Perhaps we'll try again..."

Next thing I know, Fielding is dropping into a crouch in front of me and resting his elbows on his knees with his hands clasped in front of him. "Give us one minute, please," he tells the nurse.

Surprisingly, she nods without hesitation.

"Hi," he murmurs, now singularly focused on me.

"What?" I demand. "What's wrong?"

Rather than answering, he uses one hand to pry my legs apart, making my eyes bug out of my head in the process.

"You're nervous."

"No shit," I spit back.

He tries to hold it in, but he still has the audacity to laugh, just a little. "I don't know if I've ever heard you swear before, angel. Not in everyday conversation, at least. You usually save the colorful language for when I'm—"

"Fielding," I scold through gritted teeth.

He bites down on his bottom lip and gives me a look that's highly inappropriate for a doctor's office.

"Okay. Let's try and get this blood pressure under control. Keep your feet flat. Take in a deep breath, hold it in, blow it out, then do it again. Don't talk."

Once I've followed his instructions for several rounds, he peers back up at the nurse. "Let's try again."

Fielding stays crouched in front of me, his eyes never leaving mine as we both breathe in, hold it, and blow out in unison.

"Ah, 122/78. *Much* better," the nurse declares.

Of course the praise goes right to his head. "We got this," Fielding whispers smugly before he winks, rises up, and helps me to my feet. "We're already the perfect team."

We're led back to a large room with a flatscreen TV mounted on the wall. The nurse records a few more vitals, the date of my last menstrual cycle, and current medications, then instructs me to undress from the waist down before she leaves the room.

"Do you want me to step out?" Fielding asks before I can even process her directions.

"No, you're fine. Just turn around so I can get situated."

He doesn't crack any jokes this time—thankfully—and a few minutes after I'm settled, the ultrasound tech knocks and enters the room.

I refuse to meet Fielding's gaze as the tech rolls a condom onto the internal ultrasound wand—I can practically feel the dirty comment on the tip of his tongue.

I close my eyes and lie back, feeling a bit of pressure as we start the tour of my internal organs. After making notes about the length of my cervix and each ovary, she finally homes in on what I've been so damn anxious to see.

Not only does she zoom in, but she turns on a speaker, and the room is immediately filled with a rapid whooshing sound.

"And right there is your baby."

She's going on about a yolk sac and the gestational age when Fielding grips my hand.

I look away from the screen, teary-eyed, and turn to meet his gaze.

He's not even trying to hold back. His lagoon-blue eyes pool with moisture as a single tear rolls down his cheek.

He grips my hand tighter before hovering close and tilting his face back toward the screen. "That's *our* baby, angel. We made that."

If his enthusiasm in the parking lot was contagious, this unbridled emotion is my damn undoing. Waterworks erupt as I nod up at him. I'm so overwhelmed—and so damn relieved. There's no question this man is in this with me, fully and completely.

We're doing this. And I'm so damn lucky to be doing it with him.

"Why are you being such a picky pickle?" Serena asks, nudging my knee with hers. Leave it to her to notice that I'm just pushing my salad around the takeout container. An enormous cheese-topped salad sounded great when she asked for my lunch order. But by the time it arrived, my appetite had betrayed me yet again.

"Do you really want to know?" I flip the lid closed on my container. Hopefully, this wave of nausea will pass and I can eat after my next client.

"Of course. It's my duty as your BFF to know all the things."

"Well, your job responsibilities as BFF are about to expand. How do you feel about being an aunt? I'm pregnant."

She jumps to her feet and spins to face me. "With a baby?" she demands.

I cock one eyebrow and laugh. "I mean, yes? What else would I be pregnant with, Re?"

Next thing I know, she's engulfing me in a hug and squealing.

"Okay, *okay*. Settle down. And *quiet down*. It's obviously not public knowledge yet, so you can't go carrying on—"

"When are you due? Who else knows? Holy shit, babe—who's the father?"

I tackle the most unexpected answer first.

"Um, remember when you had to pick me up in the middle of the night after my bachelorette party?"

"What? *Him*? No. *No!*"

She's saying no, but she's jumping up and down and clapping her hands, brimming with excitement.

"Holy shit. What was his name? Fleeting? Flint?"

"It's Fielding," I correct with a pointed look.

"Yes. Field-ing." She wags her eyebrows at me suggestively. She knows all the sordid details about that night. I told her everything because at the time, he really was just a one-night stand. I sort of regret the way I objectified him now that I know he's going to be in my life for, well, ever. We got the paternity test results back yesterday. Fielding is the father for sure.

"Holy shit—does he know?"

I inhale deeply and check my phone—eight minutes until my next appointment. "Re, I love you, but your enthusiasm is at a nine, and I need you to be at a three or four for this conversation."

"Okay, okay, okay," she insists, settling in beside me. "I know we don't have a ton of time—girls' night tonight so you can tell me everything?"

I wince at the idea of doing anything but going home and crashing after I finish out this day. "How about Friday? I work until eight tonight, and in addition to being super nauseous, I'm also bone-crushingly exhausted by the end of the night."

"Shit. Yes. Of course. My sister went through that when she was pregnant, too. Okay, Friday night, I'm taking you out. And you can sleep over if you want. Unless you have better plans..."

She eyes me suggestively, so I take the opportunity to set the record straight.

"Fielding knows about the baby. He went with me to the doctor last week, actually. But we're not together-together or in a relationship. I told him I needed to focus on myself right now. He—he wants more, I think, but I just don't have anything to give right now. Here..." I unlock my phone and show her the ultrasound images from our appointment. "Check these out."

Serena swipes through the images, her mouth forming into a perfect *O*. When she looks up to meet my gaze, she looks as if she's about to burst into tears.

"You're going to have a baby," she whispers. "You're excited, right? Happy?"

"I am," I admit. "Obviously this was so not the plan—but I've always wanted to be a mom, and Fielding has been nothing but supportive."

"I'm so excited. And proud. You're handling this so well." She gives me a side hug before resting her head on my shoulder. "You deserve to be happy, Daphne."

I scoff at her optimism but squeeze her back. "I had my shot at happy."

"No, babe. You had your shot at mediocre," she wisecracks. She wasn't Anthony's biggest fan, but sheesh. I side-eye her as she continues. "If you had married Anthony, things would have been fine. You would have been happy enough. But what if this version of your life is better than anything you ever imagined? You deserve true happiness. I hope this is the start of something great."

Chapter 32

Daphne

I worry my bottom lip between my teeth as I read his text again.

Fielding: Weird question. Can you send me Serena's address?

How do I respond to that? Fielding doesn't seem like the overbearing type—at least not in a way that requires him to know my plans or whereabouts. He's a lot, but he's not domineering or high-handed. I can't imagine him keeping tabs on me, even if I'm carrying his child. So why does he need—

My phone vibrates again and interrupts my overthinking.

Fielding: I'm not trying to crash your sleepover. I just wanted to drop something off for you.

I glance up to find Serena completely engrossed in the episode of *Gilmore Girls* we're watching.

"Um, so Fielding just asked if he could stop by," I offer, snapping her out of her Jess-obsessed reverie.

"Here?" she demands. "Like, now?"

I wince. I don't think he has any intention of staying, but if she doesn't want him here...

"He says he has something to drop off. But if you don't want him to stop by—"

"Daphne," she deadpans. "I know you haven't been in a new relationship for more than a decade, but if your gorgeous baby daddy wants to bring you something, the answer is yes. The answer is *always* yes."

I give her a pointed look and mutter under my breath about how we are *not* in a relationship. But I can't fight the smile when I reply to him with Serena's address.

Two episodes later, the intercom buzzes.

Serena squeals and rushes to the door. I follow behind, just as excited but not willing to show all my cards or get my hopes up.

My standoffishness is in vain. As soon as Serena buzzes him in, we're greeted by a grinning, gorgeous Fielding hauling multiple bags in each hand.

"Sleepover provisions," he declares with a wag of his eyebrows. "May I come in?"

He ducks his head and makes his way into Serena's studio apartment, smiling kindly at her before moving on to me.

"Hi, angel," he greets, bending to kiss me on the cheek. "I hope this is okay. I know you had a long week at work, so I wanted to surprise you."

"Let me guess. You brought pickles and ice cream?"

Fielding's gone all in with the baby books and mommy blogs. Not an hour goes by that he isn't sending me an article to read or a morning sickness remedy to try. It's not a stretch to think he'd bring something related to pregnancy cravings. Trouble is, I haven't had many of those.

"Something like that." He smirks as he takes me in from head to toe, amping up that electric connection that's always raring to go between us. I admittedly feel anything but sexy right now with my sweats rolled low and my end-of-the-day messy bun securely in place, but when this man looks at me... *sheesh*.

"Wait until you see this spread." He sets the brown paper bags on the counter and whips out an actual cloth tablecloth. He drapes it along the two-person kitchen table before setting a few candles in the middle.

Serena snaps her head in my direction, but I refuse to meet her gaze. If I do, I'll laugh. Not at Fielding, per se. Just at the absurdity of the situation.

"I wasn't sure what you were in the mood for," Fielding offers in my direction, "so I brought a little of everything."

He pulls things out of bags, one after another, and lines them up on the table. "Green juice. Kale chips. Protein bars..."

Serena catches my eye with an apprehensive grimace. Annoyance and something akin to concern passes over her expression. We've both been subjected to this game before: being offered health foods and green juice by my pushy mother—this move is a little too familiar.

But I don't think that's his intention here. He probably just wants what's best for the baby. Hopefully Serena can see Fielding's delivery for what it is: a thoughtful gesture, even if it does scratch at old wounds.

I step forward and place one hand on her elbow just as she defensively crosses her arms over her chest. Before she can say anything or I can intervene, Fielding continues.

"Oreos. Chinese food. M&Ms. Gummy bears *and* gummy worms, since I didn't know your preference. Fresh bagels for the morning. And, of course, the traditional pickles and ice cream."

He arranges the last of the items proudly before turning back to us, beaming.

A moment of silence passes—then Serena giggles, I burst into a grin, and Fielding glances between us like a little kid waiting for approval.

"Worms," Serena declares. "The answer is always worms." She practically skips over to the table to dig into the spread.

"You didn't have to do all this," I insist, stepping in front of Fielding. I reach out tentatively, prepared to give him a one-armed hug. Unsurprisingly, he pulls me in and holds me close, enveloping me in both arms and running one big hand up and down my spine.

"I wanted to," he muses, his words whispered softly just for me. "I want to do everything I can to support you and make you feel good."

I return his hug but extricate myself from his arms after a few seconds. The line between boyfriend and baby daddy is ill-defined and getting blurrier each day. Part of me is growing more and more tired of fighting our connection. But I don't want to give my wavering heart too much credence in the midst of such a swoon-worthy gesture.

Fielding is working hard to prove he's not going anywhere. But then I remember how little I know about him and how new all this really is. Slow and steady. I need to keep my head on straight and let things unfold over time.

"Holy shit—this is *so* good," Serena declares, pulling something out of one of the takeout cartons and popping it in her mouth.

"You like that, huh?" Fielding grins as he shifts over to the table and grabs a bite of whatever she's raving about. I shift from hip to hip and watch them interact. A surge of gratitude consumes me.

I never dreamed I'd see the day when my best friend and my—well, the man in my life would get along like this. Having them both so close feels like all I could possibly ever need.

Loved. Seen. Cared for. Supported. It's all new. But it's wonderful.

Fielding peeks over his shoulder and gives me a secret smile. A few seconds later, Serena turns around, wide eyed, and gives me a pointed look.

It's not just the effort he put into this. It's the gesture itself and the lack of expectations associated with it. He did this because he wanted to do it for me. He sincerely cares about me, and he's determined to proactively prove himself. I couldn't ask for a better partner—I'm overwhelmed by the way he's gone all in. This moment is so much more poignant and emotional than I expected.

Maybe slow and steady isn't necessary after all. I was with Anthony for more than a decade—it doesn't get more slow and steady than that—and yet I can't think of a single time he made me feel like this. Everything Fielding does feels right and real. Maybe right and real is what's been missing all along.

Chapter 33

Fielding

"Are you nervous?"

Daphne looks gorgeous, per usual. I picked her up from Serena's apartment this afternoon, and we're on our way to Sunday dinner with her family.

I'm meeting her parents tonight, and I feel absurdly underprepared. It's like not doing the reading for class and hoping the professor doesn't call on you, then finding out there's a pop quiz worth half your semester grade.

Existing in undefined relationship limbo isn't making things any easier. It's been almost a month since that first doctor's appointment—three weeks since we received confirmation that I am the father of the child in Daphne's womb. All I do all damn day is study and think about Daphne and the baby. Read baby books and send Daphne *thinking of you* texts. Lie in bed and fantasize about that night.

I know what I want. But I'm trying my best to play this right and give her space. So while I'm not nervous about meeting her parents, I have no idea what to expect, and I'm still unclear about my role in Daphne's life.

"Not nervous," I finally answer, reaching across the center console and squeezing her leg affectionately. "Anxious to meet your parents—yes. Excited to meet Tahlia? Double yes."

Desperate to know where things stand between us? Abso-fuck-ing-lutely.

I keep that one to myself.

"I want them to like me and understand how seriously I'm taking all this." My attention instinctively falls to Daphne's lap before I turn back to the road in front of us again. She doesn't have a defined baby bump yet, but she swears none of her pants fit, hence the pretty, flowy skirt she's wearing tonight.

What I wouldn't give to see exactly how her body is changing, up close and personal. I shake my head before my thoughts wander too far down that path. I can be a total horndog for my baby mama later. When I'm alone. Just like I've done pretty much every night since we met.

Right now, I need to focus.

"Are *you* nervous?" I ask, turning the question back on her.

She scrunches up her noses and side-eyes me.

"Honestly? I just want to get this over with. Now that they know about the baby and have sort of accepted what's happening"—Daphne told them she was pregnant once we received the paternity results—"I'm anxious for them to meet you and for things to move forward. Just please don't be offended if they come off as rude or unwelcoming. They loved Anthony, and our breakup has been really hard on them."

I shake my head in frustration but say nothing. She's given me the same warning multiple times over the last few weeks. No matter how she phrases it, it still pisses me off. Her parents are very much Team Anthony, which is just wrong on principle. Add in that fact that she's already making excuses for their behavior before they've even met me...

"Parents love me," I declare confidently. "It's like a universal rule or something. They can try to resist my charms, but eventually, they'll come around."

"Yeah, well, you haven't met my parents..."

I follow the GPS directions and turn onto Haymarket Street before easing into a driveway on the right. An inkling of recognition sparks in my mind as I coast to a stop. It's not that anything looks familiar; I just recognize the neighborhood from all those damn videos. The houses on this end of town are spread out, but I can still see the Adley residence next door from here. It's a historic home with an expansive yard and a two-story barn out back. I scowl at the house as if it's personally offended me. I hate that Daphne is stuck next door to her ex's family, even if Anthony doesn't actually live there.

"Park on the right side," Daphne murmurs, unbuckling her seatbelt and collecting her things as she anxiously plays with the hem of her skirt.

I park the car as instructed, then catch her hand in mine.

I smooth my thumb over her knuckles, tempted to kiss them or soothe her in some way. "There's nothing they can say or do to change things between us, angel."

She offers me a weak smile in return, like she doesn't actually believe me, before opening the door and exiting the car.

"Everything is delicious, Mrs. Knowles."

Daphne's mom lifts her gaze and offers a poor excuse for a smile in response to my compliment.

"This is okay. But it's not my favorite. What would your death row meal be, Fielding?"

"Tahlia!" Daphne scolds from across the table.

I fight back a chuckle. "Uh, I'm not sure what you're asking, kiddo. What's a death row meal?"

"You know—like if you got one last meal, what would you want to eat right before you died?" Her eyes are wide behind her glasses, and the two braids in her hair do nothing to calm the frizzy strands that have fallen out around her face.

This kid's hilarious. I love her already.

"Okay, assuming I get an appetizer, an entrée, and dessert—"

"It's not an Applebee's three-course meal deal," Tahlia snarks.

Seriously. Coolest twelve-year-old I've ever met.

"Hear me out," I counter, channeling my brother and giving her a stern look. I wait for her to nod before continuing. "I'm going for three courses, but with a distinct theme. My ideal last meal would be three versions of my favorite food: waffles. I'll start with a savory mushroom-truffle waffle covered in gravy, then go with a traditional hot chicken and waffles for my main, before ending the meal—*and my life*," I add ominously, "with Belgian waffles smothered in hot fudge and whipped cream."

Tahlia blinks twice from across the table. "Excellent answer," she admits, nodding to herself like I just passed some imaginary test.

"If you two are done," Mr. Knowles interjects, "maybe Fielding would like to answer some questions that actually matter."

"Martin," Mrs. Knowles murmurs under her breath, but the warning holds no heat. It does nothing to deter her husband from glaring at me, as if I wasn't just knocking it out of the park with his younger daughter.

I clear my throat and sit up straighter. "Absolutely. I'm an open book. I'm happy to answer anything you'd like to know."

"When did you and my daughter first meet?"

I freeze. Anything but that.

I have no shame about how we met and what happened that night. So many perfect, distinct memories from that night live rent free in my mind. But how exactly do I answer him without mentioning that we did, in fact, meet the night of her bachelorette party?

The question feels like a trap. It's got to be a trap. He's only asking it because he already knows the answer and he wants to watch me squirm.

"We met earlier this summer," I offer, "but admittedly, didn't keep in touch. Thankfully, we reconnected a month ago; once Daphne told me about our baby."

The table goes silent. I have no idea if I overstepped or under-delivered. I glance to my right, side-eyeing Daphne, but she just offers me a meek smile that does little to calm my nerves.

"Can you pass the potatoes please, Mom?" she asks, breaking the tension around the table.

Her mother clucks her tongue, making a show of lifting up the serving bowl in slow motion and holding it out of arm's reach.

"Be mindful, dear."

The actual fuck?

I reach past Daphne, anger coiling in my veins, and grab for the bowl that's being not quite offered.

"You're growing a human," I mutter, spooning a sizable portion of mashed potatoes onto Daphne's plate. And not only that. She's still getting sick multiple times a week, even though she's almost into her second trimester.

"I read an article online that said women in their first trimester only need about one hundred extra calories a day—the equivalent of a medium-sized apple. One hundred calories. Can you believe that? I wish I would have known that before I packed on the pounds when I was pregnant."

For fuck's sake.

"Do you want extra butter for your potatoes?" I ask, louder than necessary. I'm not going to sit here and listen to passive aggressive comments about how much Daphne should or shouldn't be eating. Is her mom a nutritionist? A doctor? I don't fucking think so. And she's saying shit like that in front of a preteen girl, too. Total and utter bullshit.

"It's fine, Fielding. Ignore her," Daphne pleads under her breath.

Ignore her? Is she serious? I think I'll do the opposite.

"According to the pregnancy books *I've* been reading, a pregnant woman should always eat when she's hungry, especially if her appetite is inconsistent because of morning sickness."

I look around to find everyone avoiding each other's gazes. Everyone except Mr. Knowles, of course, whose beady eyes are trying to burn a hole through my head.

"You'd do well to not disrespect my wife in this house, son."

Now it's my turn to glare. Is this guy for real? Did he not just hear his wife implying that his daughter—the mother of my unborn child—didn't really need a second helping of potatoes?

Does he have any fucking idea how sick Daphne's been, how stressed out she is about work and the wedding and the baby in general?

If they want to play games and pick sides, I can do that. But I only play to win.

"With all due respect, sir, I refuse to sit here and listen to anyone dribble on about the daily caloric intake of an expectant mother."

"Hmph," he scoffs. "Since you're in medical school, you must know everything, then?"

Some people have a fight-or-flight instinct. I'm only wired to fight.

"I would like to think I know the basics, yes. I've also been reading baby books non-stop, and I know for a fact that Daphne couldn't keep down her lunch today, so if anything, her body's operating at a calorie deficit."

He huffs again, but gives up, peering past me and directing his next comments at his daughter. "Looks like you've locked in a real smart guy here, Daphne. A smart guy with a big mouth."

The rage that sweeps through me is indescribable. It's one thing to pick a fight and not like it when I push back—it's another entirely to drag Daphne into this. She's literally only said four sentences all night, and one of those was to ask for more goddamn potatoes.

"We don't have to sit here and take this," I declare, shifting my chair back a few inches for emphasis. "We came here tonight with nothing but goodwill, but we don't need to stay if the feelings aren't mutual."

"Are you threatening me in my own house?" he sneers.

"I don't have any control over whether you feel threatened by me, sir."

His eyes double in size.

"I understand Daphne's your daughter and that you might be upset and disappointed by the situation we're in. But you have no right to make things harder than they need to be right now. She's handling everything with so much grace. We're figuring this out, the two of us, together. If you can't be supportive, you can at least be quiet."

He has nothing to say in response to my monologue. That doesn't mean he keeps his mouth shut.

"Smart-ass with a big mouth. Anthony would never—"

We're officially done.

I rise to my feet, desperately hoping Daphne follows or at the very least doesn't get upset with me for making a scene. Everything about tonight has been off—she's a different person inside these four walls, and I hate it. I've never once viewed her as anything but fierce and independent—but seeing her wilt at this dinner table, surrounded by people who supposedly love her, has opened my eyes to an entirely different part of her world.

"You can keep your assumptions and judgments about me. Hold on to those real tight. But don't you dare bring up her dirtbag ex-fiancé in front of me again. If that's your standard for an ideal partner for your daughter, then you and I are two very different kinds of men."

Daphne grips my hand, but I don't dare break eye contact with her dad. This is complete and utter bullshit. I refuse to back down.

As expected, Martin doesn't respond well. Rising to his feet at the head of the table, he wags a finger at me as he raises his voice.

"You think you can impregnate my daughter, then just show up here saying whatever the hell you want? You think you can come into my house and disrespect me? Who the hell do you think you are?"

"I'm Fielding Haas. And I'll be happy to show myself out." I turn to Daphne's mom then. "Thank you for inviting me tonight. I'm sorry it didn't go well."

I take a step back from the table, but Daphne doesn't drop my hand. Relief floods my body when she actually rises up to join me. I turn back to Mr. Knowles, who continues to mutter under his breath, a vein throbbing in his neck all the while. I don't bother asking him to speak up—I won't be able to hold it together if he articulates any of those sentences about disrespectful pieces of shit and whoring around. As it is, I can't help throwing down the gauntlet in response to his mumbles.

"I don't know if you have any aspirations about being in this child's life, or if you've dreamed about the day when someone calls you grandpa. But you'll have absolutely no contact with my child if you don't learn to hold your tongue and check your temper."

Mrs. Knowles gasps as Daphne squeezes my hand, but whether it's in warning or solidarity, I'm not sure. I'm probably out of line. I didn't set out to cause a scene. But I sure as hell will end this.

"Oh yeah?" Martin sneers. "And how are you going to prevent that, smart guy? Daphne lives in this house."

A wiser man would walk away. But I never claimed to be wise.

"Not anymore, she doesn't," I boldly declare.

Daphne pulls on my arm as she rises from her seat. I turn and peer down at her, meeting her frantic gaze. She opens her mouth as if she's about to argue, so I rush to make my case in a whisper.

"I can't stand the thought of you living here and dealing with this every day, angel. You can't stay here. You don't have to stay with me. I'll get you your own place if you want. But I can't leave you here like this."

Tears fill her eyes, and she quickly moves to swipe them away with her free hand. I'm literally holding my breath, waiting for her to respond. I glance down at our joined hands, desperately hoping that who I am and all I'm offering will be enough to sway her. Throughout this entire ordeal, she's held on to me—that has to be a good sign, right? *Please let this be enough*.

After what feels like eons of waiting for her response, silently imploring her to come with me, she bites down on her bottom lip and nods.

"I'm so sorry, TT," she whispers to her little sister across the table before turning to her mom. "I wish it wasn't like this. I hate that I've disappointed you. But I think it's probably for the best that I go." Her grip tightens around my hand as she steels herself for their response.

"Daphne Leigh Knowles..."

I don't hear what her dad says next because Daphne's already pulling me through the kitchen and heading for the front door.

"Wait. Do you want to grab anything before we go?" She'll have to come back eventually. I'm sure she has a ton of stuff to pack up, but grabbing a toothbrush and an overnight bag would probably be a good idea.

"I have a few changes of clothes at Serena's place. And all my work stuff is in my car. I'm afraid if I stop moving all the courage I feel right now will vanish."

"Then let's fucking go."

Chapter 34

Daphne

I'm physically shaking as Fielding and I walk out the front door of my parents' house, hand in hand. Despite the full-body tremors, there's a levity that washes over me with each step I take away from the house.

A crack of lightning parts the sky in the distance, jolting me back to the reality of what I'm doing. Things escalated *so* quickly between my mother's judgmental comment and the moment Fielding declared that I don't live in their house anymore—so quickly I still haven't processed it all. Then it was like someone hit pause, and from there, everything unfolded in slow motion.

I should have expected their digs and abhorrent behavior. Nothing about how things played out tonight was a surprise. My dad made snide remarks and not-so-subtly expressed his unwavering love for Anthony. My mom made passive aggressive comments about my weight and food intake. Tonight was nothing out of the norm where my family is concerned.

But seeing them through Fielding's eyes was jarring. I sat at that table feeling voiceless and transparent among the people who are supposed to love me unconditionally. It's so different from how he makes me feel. And although we hadn't discussed it up until now, he's right: I can't raise my child in that type of environment.

I hate that Tahlia had to witness that. It kills me that she'll be under their roof for several more years. I'll make tonight up to her—I have to. I'll prioritize coming over to visit and taking her out, just like I did before I moved home.

Hopefully watching someone stand up for me opened her eyes to how she should expect to be treated in a relationship. It certainly opened mine.

Thunder rumbles in the distance, but it's a removed sort of sound. Rain is coming. I can smell it in the air. The storm just hasn't arrived yet.

I'm lost in thought, still in a daze, as Fielding guides me toward his car. It was extreme, him pushing back and defending my honor or whatever it is he thinks he was doing in there.

But as much as the feminist in me wants to hate it, it felt really nice to have someone on my side for once.

When we reach the passenger side of his Infiniti, I blow out a long breath and squeeze his hand appreciatively. But before I can open my mouth to thank him, someone else is screaming my name.

"Daphne! Wait!"

My gut twists with dread as I spot Anthony tearing across his parents' front yard in our direction.

What the hell is he doing here?

Fielding crowds my space, trying to usher me into the car before Anthony reaches the driveway. I press my hand to his chest in protest. His eyes flare, and he opens his mouth, ready to object—but this isn't his battle to fight.

"It's okay, but please let me handle this. Just follow my lead..."

The conflict etched in every line of his handsome face is unmistakable as he studies me. Finally, he takes a step back and raises both hands, giving me enough room to slip around him and come face to face with my ex-fiancé.

I tentatively shuffle forward two steps. Fielding shifts beside me in a silent show of support. I have to stop myself from smirking at him in my periphery—there's no way he could sit this one out completely. He's too protective. Even though I told him I wanted to handle this, I'm grateful for his support.

"So it's true?" Anthony demands, glaring from me to Fielding, then to me again before he gawks at my stomach in disgust.

I gulp past the lump in my throat and pray my words don't waver.

"I don't owe you any explanations or have anything to say to you, Anthony. Fielding and I were just on our way out."

"Daphne, stop," he demands, taking a step closer as Fielding tenses beside me. I reach back and stroke a hand down his arm—reassuring him that I've got this.

Anthony continues. "It doesn't have to be like this. Even if you wanted to keep his bastard child, I'm willing to make it work. Don't throw us away because of your mistake. We can figure this out..."

"Throw us away?" I challenge, eyebrows raised.

He says it like he believes it—like I initiated our demise.

I plant my feet wide and cross my arms under my chest. "I didn't throw anything away, Anthony. You ruined us. I tolerated a lot over the years, and maybe that was my mistake—putting up with too much for too long. But the second you had Andy text me from that plane, you sealed our fate."

"I didn't think—"

I hold up a hand to stop him. I'm not interested in his excuses. My life has changed more dramatically over the last few months than I ever thought possible. The idea of him and me, of us together... it doesn't even make sense anymore. I haven't healed from the ordeal. But I'm over it.

"That's right. You didn't think. You decided a free shot in Vegas was more important than my feelings or the sanctity of our relationship."

"Come on, Daph. We weren't even married yet. You didn't really expect—"

I cut him off again. His face morphs from annoyance to disdain as I refuse to let him speak. He's not used to me interrupting him—or standing my ground.

"You're absolutely right. My expectations were wildly low to begin with. If I'm honest, part of me never expected you to be faithful. I was settling, because I spent the last ten years believing you were the best I could do. Thank God I realized my potential before it was too late," I quip, cocking one eyebrow for emphasis.

Fielding huffs a barely audible laugh beside me, catching Anthony's attention and reminding us both of his presence.

I'm shocked that he's stayed out of it until now—just like I asked. After the scene around the dining room table, I highly doubted his ability to hold his tongue.

Anthony takes two steps toward us—and Fielding immediately moves closer, placing one hand on the small of my back in a silent show of support.

Anthony sneers for several seconds before finally coming up with something to say. "People are gonna talk, Daph... the girls at the salon... all our friends. What's your grandma supposed to tell everyone at church?"

Fielding's hand flexes against my back at the change in tactics. What he doesn't know is that I'm more than used to the guilt and shame he's using to try and get me to go along with things. Anthony can be wicked with his words, but no one can top my mother.

When I don't react like he wants, he pushes harder.

"Everybody we know is going to be talking about the girl who cheated on her fiancé, got knocked up by this douche and threw away her life to have his baby."

Oof. Too far. I'm not even a little surprised when Fielding shifts forward and starts in.

"Shove off, asshole. Do you even hear yourself right now? You're not going to shame or manipulate her into getting back together with you. You're wasting your goddamn breath."

"He speaks," Anthony mocks.

What he doesn't know is that I asked Fielding to leave this to me. And he did. Until things escalated, at least.

"You don't know her like I do," Anthony pushes. "You won't take care of her."

Fielding doesn't have time to respond before Anthony's turning the verbal assault back on me.

"You think this guy's still going to be interested in you when your hips are even wider and you're nine months pregnant, Daph?"

Fielding springs into action before I have the wherewithal to hold him back. He gets so close, Anthony trips backward on instinct.

"You're done," he hisses through clenched teeth. I swear I can see the veins bulging in his forearms as he makes fists, then flexes his hands back open. "You know *nothing*. That's the mother of my child you're talking about—"

"She's my fiancée!"

"*Ex*-fiancée," I remind him.

Thunder cracks overhead, punctuating the air as both men stare at each other, trembling with pent-up rage.

Someone's going to snap. I don't want to let things go any further, but knowing Anthony the way I do, it's inevitable. I can feel his swelling eagerness as he goads us—he's desperate for Fielding to hit him, if only so he can say *I told you so* and double-down on his claim that the father of my child is a loose cannon. I'm not willing to play his game.

I take a few tentative steps forward, threading my arm through Fielding's in a clear show of solidarity before pulling back gently. "Let's go home," I urge, disregarding Anthony completely.

Just because I don't want things to escalate doesn't mean Fielding's on the same page.

He reaches for my hand and grasps it in his, so I know he heard me. But then he turns back to Anthony. Because of course he does.

"You hear that, asshole? *Home*. She wants me to take her *home*. You made your choice when you decided a Vegas hookup was more enticing than honoring the promises you made to this woman. You're a goddamn fool."

I tug on Fielding's arm. But apparently, he's not done.

"You think you know me? You know nothing about me. So let me spell it out for you."

Oh God. This isn't going to go well. I can feel it. Another boom of thunder rings out—louder this time—amping up the adrenaline in my veins and leaving me lightheaded with chaotic energy. I'm torn between getting out of here as quickly as possible and wanting to know what Fielding has to say.

"This woman here? This woman you couldn't keep? I see her. I see how gorgeous she is on the outside, how beautiful she is on the inside. All I want to do is get to know her better. Take care of her. Love her if she'll let me."

I gulp down a rush of emotion as his words crackle through the tension between the three of us.

"And all that has nothing to do with the baby growing inside her. That's just a bonus."

I don't need to look over at Fielding to know he's got his chin jutted out in that obnoxious cocksure way. I would be tempted to roll my eyes if he hadn't just practically declared his love for me.

Anthony is clenching his jaw so hard he looks like he's about to crack a tooth. I'm a mess as I battle with myself over what to do. Should I pull Fielding away? Do I let him continue? Is it wrong that I desperately want to hear more?

"I know Daphne's worth. While you were taking advantage of your self-granted "free pass" in Vegas, I was here showing her just how valuable she is. With my hands. With my mouth. With my—"

Good. Grief.

He was about to say cock. The man was literally about to brag to my ex-fiancé about how well-acquainted I am with his dick. For better or for worse, the word never makes it out of Fielding's mouth because Anthony is charging toward us and throwing a punch before he can finish.

"Enough!" I scream as Fielding careens back, his hand instantly going to his jaw.

"It's over, Anthony," I declare. "Don't contact me again. Don't try to start shit with my family. We're done. We're so done you should forget we even existed."

I reach for Fielding's arm and pull him toward the car. As expected, Anthony has to have the last damn word.

"This isn't over!" he growls. "I'm not giving up! You're making a huge mistake, Daph. You'll see."

Chapter 35

Fielding

The silence is thick as I back out of the driveway and navigate out of her parents' neighborhood. Leave it to me to take things to the extreme. As if it wasn't enough to get into a verbal spat with Daphne's father and consequently demand she move out of his house, I had to antagonize her asshole ex into throwing a pretty decent punch.

I gently probe at my jaw again—it smarts, but I've had worse. And just like I repeated over and over again tonight—it was absolutely worth it.

Except now we're driving away, and I have no idea how to play this.

Things between Daphne and me have been going well. We talk every day, and she's included me in every detail and decision where the baby's concerned. I hope to God I didn't just throw that all away with my back-to-back tantrums.

When we pass through downtown Hampton, she finally speaks.

"Did you mean what you said back there?"

Panic rises in my chest as I sift through all the things she might be referencing. I feel horrible that I fucking went off on her family, especially in front of her little sister. Tahlia didn't deserve to sit through that. But neither did Daphne.

Fuck it. I'm not sorry for standing up for her and calling them on their bullshit. I wish it had gone down differently, but they were horrible first.

There wasn't a single thing I said about her or in defense of her that wasn't true.

"Every word," I confirm, reaching across the center console without taking my eyes off the road. I let out a silent sigh of relief when she lets me interlace our fingers.

"Have they always been like that?" I hedge.

She hums under her breath and sighs. "You're going to have to be more specific about who you're talking about…"

"Your parents."

"I guess? It was all I knew when I was a kid. Then, as I got older, it didn't affect me as much, because I didn't live at home. I moved back in with them this summer since I was supposed to move into Anthony's place after the wedding," she explains. "I got so good at ignoring it that I stopped keeping track of when it happened. But seeing it through your eyes tonight…"

"That was bullshit. I meant what I said to your dad, angel." I squeeze her hand in what I hope is a comforting gesture so she knows I'm on her side. But I won't budge on this. "I know I can't fight all your battles for you, but I'll go to war to protect our child from that sort of gaslighting and vitriol. They'll control their tempers and their words, or they won't be around our baby."

Daphne says nothing for a beat, then another.

"I don't want to fight you on this, angel, but—"

She cuts me off before I make it any further. "I don't disagree. At all. I just don't know how to navigate this..."

"Leave it to me," I assure her. "I'll help you get your stuff moved out. I don't mind being the bad guy as long as I'm not the villain in your eyes."

"Never." She squeezes my hand reassuringly where it rests on the exposed skin of her thigh. I spread my fingers wide, craving more contact. I meant what I said to her parents. Every damn word I said to her asshole ex was true, too. I want this woman so much it hurts.

"If you're really moving out of their house... do you want me to take you back to Serena's?"

I hate the idea of driving up 480 to her best friend's studio apartment. Sure, it's closer to work for her, and it's infinitely better than being stuck at her parents' house... but it's farther away from me. I hold back my pout as I wait for her answer.

"Did you mean what you said?" she asks again.

I peek over at her quickly, our eyes connecting for a single second as we navigate what's next and what this means for, well, *us*.

"I've meant every word since I met you, angel. But you're going to have to be more specific about what you're asking—"

"Do you really want me to move in with you?"

I hold back a grin and breathe a sigh of relief.

"I've literally never wanted anything more in my whole damn life."

She pauses for a beat, then another.

We're dancing in the in between, figuring this out on the fly, relying on nothing but instinct and this undeniable connection between us to validate that what we're doing is good and real and true.

If she turns me down, I have to keep my cool. There's no good reason for us to live together—but I want it so bad it hurts. I just want to be near her. To take care of her. And yeah, maybe I want more time with her and more opportunities to woo her. If I can show her how good we could be together—remind her how good we already *are*—then maybe there's hope for more.

Fuck it. I don't want her to overthink this. I want her to move in. I need this chance to prove to her that I'm all in. Mentally rehearsing my first argument, I inhale deeply, preparing to sell her on the idea. But before I can get a word in, she puts me out of my misery.

"Then that's what I'll do. Take me home, Fielding."

Chapter 36

Daphne

I creep into the kitchen, using the flashlight on my phone to guide my way. I could flick on an overhead light—but I've only lived here for a few weeks, and I honestly don't know which switch goes with which light. Plus, I really don't want Fielding to find me out here.

I open the first few drawers of the kitchen island and close them just as quickly once I scan the contents. I skip the silverware and knife drawers because I'm already familiar with those. That just leaves the last two drawers at the end.

Bingo.

The contents of the junk drawer rattle loudly, leaving me even more frazzled. I aim the flashlight from one end of the drawer to the other, desperation itching up my spine as my efforts don't produce my intended result.

This is my literal last resort. I already switched the batteries around once. I also opened up the back of the remote controls in the living room. I just need two stupid AAs to magically appear in this drawer…

"Angel?"

I groan and slam the drawer shut.

"What?" I snap, harsher than intended, before blowing out a frustrated sigh.

"Uh, are you okay? What are you doing out here in the dark?"

His voice is laced with concern, which certainly isn't unwarranted. I'm sure I look like a hot mess.

I glance down at my bare feet and uncovered legs—I'm wearing an oversized T-shirt and nothing else. There is definitely a light sheen of sweat on my forehead, whether from exertion or frustration at this point, I don't know. I've literally never been *that close* and had my vibrator just die.

"I'm fine," I huff out, glancing over and groaning when I realize he's standing before me without a shirt. Because of course he is.

I blow out a long breath and try my hardest not to stare at the indents that create the peaks and valleys of his torso. He's rocking a literal eight-pack, and the way his pants are slung so damn low shows off the distinct outline of the veins on his hips.

Those aren't the only veins I love in that general area. I may or may not have been thinking specifically about a hard, veiny, ramrod straight part of his body before I lost my orgasm just now. I clench my thighs together on instinct, then squirm at the slickness still coating my core.

Why the hell didn't I put on panties before leaving my room?

"Daphne."

I snap up to meet his gaze. He's got that stupid cocksure smirk on his face—like he knows exactly what I'm thinking. The frustration in my glare is enough to put him in his place. He schools his expression, then speaks softer as he steps into the kitchen and flicks on a dim light.

"Can I help? What are you looking for?"

I side-eye him, then quickly avert my gaze before responding. "Batteries. Two AAs, which I can't seem to find anywhere in this damn house…"

When I peer up again, he's got his tongue in his cheek and his arms crossed over his bare chest.

"What do you need batteries for in the middle of the night, angel?"

It's that stupid grin that tells me he knows *exactly* what I need batteries for. Instead of answering or even shrinking in on myself, I explode.

"You did this to me, you know. This is all *your* fault!"

"Oh yeah?" he counters, leaning against the island and crossing one leg in front of the other while he assesses me up and down. He thinks we're flirting. He has no idea how close I am to biting his head off, praying-mantis style. "What exactly did I do?"

"This! All of this! You got me pregnant! You did this! And now I'm hornier than I've ever been in my whole life! All I can think about is that night… the way you… the way…"

"The way I what?"

I freeze where I stand. I just came way too close to admitting the truth to a man I can just barely resist.

"Forget it!" I growl in frustration, turning on my heel to storm out of the kitchen.

This place is a literal mansion. I'm sure I can find two stupid batteries somewhere if I look hard enough.

But before I can leave the room, he grips my arm and gently but firmly pulls me toward him. His hands slide down my sides.

His fingertips dig into my hips. He moves me where he wants me—right between his spread legs—then looks down at me in earnest.

"If I did this to you, let me fix it."

"Fielding," I warn, my hands rising to his chest on instinct. I'd like to believe I'm trying to push him away and put a bit of space between us. But a supercharged zing of arousal hits me the second my palms brush the taut muscle of his pecs.

Based on the way he sucks in a breath and goes still under my touch, I know damn well he feels it, too. I never stood a chance.

"What do you need, angel?"

He skims his hands down my hips again, then grips the hem of my T-shirt.

The way he's looking at me is familiar and so unbelievably hot. My breasts feel heavy and my lungs ache as I stare up at him, panting and silently pleading for him to put me out of my misery.

I know he knows what I need. I also know he's not going to make a move without explicit consent.

"Use your words," he murmurs as he dips his head low and brushes his lips down the side of my neck. It's a tease. An invitation. An offer of what could be if I'd just get out of my own head...

But we shouldn't complicate things. I'm still so unsure about so much.

His mouth rests right against the pulse point below my ear, each exhalation sending a fresh shiver of arousal through my body. I want him. I also really want to get off. I'm tired of overthinking where this man is concerned. That, or I'm too horny to worry about the consequences.

He's going to make me say it. To ask for what I want and what I know he could give me.

Decidedly, I wrap my arms around his neck and push up on my toes. His muscles lock up under my touch for just a second, then he relaxes and pulls me closer.

It's just us. But my words still come out barely above a whisper.

"I'm horny and my vibrator died. I'm desperate."

His devilish smile is the only answer I get before his fingers tease under the fabric of my T-shirt.

"This doesn't mean—" I start, suddenly panicked that he's unclear about what I'm asking.

He doesn't let me finish. One second, I'm standing between his legs. A second later, my feet lift off the floor. He spins us, strides forward, and sets my bare ass on the cool quartz of the kitchen island before bracing his arms on either side of my body and leaning in close.

"This doesn't mean anything you don't want it to mean," he confirms. "But I did this to you. And you have needs. So let me take care of you." His fingertips tease up both my legs, tickling the tops of my thighs as he caresses the delicate skin of my bikini line. "I told you I was all in, angel. It's time you trust that I know exactly what you need and how you want it."

Fuck.

I spread my legs wider, and he wastes no time flexing his fingers and spreading my lips apart.

"You're so fucking pretty," he praises as he zeros in on my pussy.

I take advantage of his distracted state and whip the T-shirt off over my head.

His eyes immediately rise to my chest.

"Goddamn," he groans in earnest. "You're fucking perfect."

I squirm under his heated stare until he lifts his chin and regards me.

"Just so we're clear; this is about you. You, and what I did to you." He smirks at his own joke. "I'm getting you off, then tucking you into bed. Got it?"

I'm simultaneously turned on and grateful that he's giving me a pass for tonight. It's not that I don't want him. Fuck, if I'm honest with myself, I really do want him—but I'm already so hot and bothered I can't think straight. I couldn't make a lucid decision about what to do or how far to go if my life depended on it.

I am, however, worried that his confidence is about to be shattered.

"Got it. But I should warn you—I don't know if this is going to work," I caution. "I had my vibrator on the highest setting right before it died. I doubt I could even get myself off right now without—"

He leans in and pinches both my nipples until I arch into his touch. "Don't you dare doubt me," he whispers haughtily before biting my earlobe and trailing more nibbles down my neck.

His hands graze down my front, caressing gently over my bump before he grips each of my thighs and forces my legs wider.

"Your orgasm starts in your brain, angel." He's back in my ear, his breath hot on my tingling skin as one single finger slicks through my folds.

"Do you ever think about that night?"

I whimper, already unable to form coherent responses to his questions. My brain can barely make sense of all the places he's touching me. His mouth on my neck, one hand woven into the hair at my nape. His other hand is trailing featherlight touches along my pussy, touching all my intimate parts while cruelly avoiding my clit.

"I think about it all the time. When I had you pressed up against my bedroom wall. When I sank *all* the way inside you for the first time?"

One finger enters me. Then another. I wrap my arms around his neck and rest my forehead on his shoulder. When he crooks those perfect fingers forward, I whimper on command. I'm so relieved I might cry.

"Fuck. You were *so* wet for me that night. You loved the way I touched you. The way my tongue felt on your skin."

He crooks his fingers forward again, then finally—mercifully—his thumb lands on my clit. He doesn't move, though. He just holds me. Holds me and presses hard on my G-spot and my aching, swollen nub at the same time.

"Do you remember sitting on my face, angel? Do you remember holding on to the headboard and riding me until you saw stars? I can't even look at my goddamn bed without thinking of you and remembering the force of you grinding down on me. The way you danced back and forth, begging me for more..."

The intensity of my moan surprises me. But the heat's already ebbing out from my core, and a familiar tingle starts in my toes. His hand is just barely moving now—his thumb rubbing hard, rhythmic circles over my clit as his fingers flex and dig into that perfect target inside me.

"I love it when you beg, Daphne. I love it when my name comes out of your mouth right before I make you gush."

"Fuck... I'm close... Fielding. Please..."

I grind my forehead into his shoulder, so fucking desperate for release.

"Please," I whimper one last time, right before the intensity of the buildup peaks.

"I'll give you anything, angel. Starting with this orgasm and ending with forever. Now come for me."

I shatter around him, against him, because of him. I shatter, and every little piece of me is made whole in that moment. I buck against his hand, and he works me through the orgasm, neither of us stilling until I'm completely wrung out and limp in his arms.

Appreciatively, I lean into his body and press my lips into the skin between his neck and his collarbone. He makes no move to pull away or put space between us. I ride out the gentle pulses of aftershock with his hand buried deep inside me until my body is lax, my mind is at ease, and all that registers is his arms cradling me against his chest as he carries me back to my bedroom.

Chapter 37

Fielding

Maybe it wasn't wise to plug in the waffle maker right where I made her come last night.

Yet here I am, leaning against the counter in the exact spot I was standing a few hours ago, stirring batter with the hand I had buried in her pussy. I adjust my boner in my gray sweatpants—*again*—just as she makes her way into the kitchen.

"Good morning," I greet as Daphne squints her eyes closed with a yawn. "Waffles will be ready soon. I've already got bacon and eggs on the table for you."

Most of her morning sickness has passed, but she still feels better if she eats as soon as she wakes up. Too long, and her stomach gets queasy. Then nothing sounds good by the time she gets to lunch or dinner.

Instead of heading to the table, she surprises me and starts into the kitchen. In fact, she's walking directly toward me.

I watch, desperately trying to play it cool, as she makes her way across the room and stands much closer than usual. Unsure of what she wants, I freeze. I refuse to fail if this is some sort of test to gauge if things are awkward or different between us after last night.

My muscles stiffen when she wraps both arms around my bicep and nuzzles against the fabric of my T-shirt. "Thank you," she murmurs, smiling sweetly before kissing my shoulder and turning back toward the table.

I don't bother asking for what. I refuse to push her when things are maybe, finally moving in the right direction. I refuse to fuck this up out of selfishness or greed.

My dick pulses with desire. My brain urges me to act. But I push down all my instincts in favor of honoring the promise I made last night. I told her I would take care of her and that I didn't expect anything in return. I'm keeping my word. Even if the blue balls kill me.

"Do you want syrup or whipped cream, angel?" I call out when the timer goes off for the first batch.

"Can I have both?" she asks as she skirts past me toward the coffee maker.

I stifle a groan and school my expression. "You know you can have anything you want. Always."

Chapter 38

Daphne

Fielding brushes one hand across my bare shoulders as he moves through the kitchen, messenger bag slung over one arm with a to-go coffee in the other. A shiver runs up my spine at his touch, and I instantly crave more contact.

"I've gotta get going, but your lunch is in the fridge."

I've been living in his house, or *our house*, as he loves to correct me, for a month. We've fallen into a comfortable, easy routine: one where he goes to school, I go to work, and my every whim, craving, and need is both anticipated and enthusiastically met by this gorgeous man.

Even my most pathetic moments of need. Like last week, in this very kitchen, up on the counter. I shudder and shove down the memory—that hasn't happened again. I refuse to let it.

Was it one of the most intense orgasms of my life? Yes. Yes, it was. But I had practically edged myself to tears before he finally made me come. These pregnancy hormones are unreal. Still, we're better off keeping our boundaries clear. Even if I do think about that stupid kitchen counter incident every single night.

That encounter aside, cohabitating with Fielding is effortless—it's honestly a joy to live here with him. He makes breakfast and packs a lunch for me each day. He keeps track of both our schedules on a dry-erase calendar on the fridge, jotting down my doctor's appointments and weekly development milestones for the baby. Every afternoon, he texts just to say hi. At night, he rubs my shoulders, then puts his wireless headphones in so we can be in the same room while he studies and I watch TV.

I miss him when we're apart. I'm calmer in his presence. I'm not worried about saying the wrong thing or doing something that will piss him off. Fielding makes it easy to co-exist beside him.

It's a gift to not have to mold myself into a certain shape or play a specific part in his presence. By that same logic, I'm mortified that I did those things to please others for so long.

Being here with him in "our house" makes me realize that I've never really felt a sense of home. I've never been in a place physically, mentally, or emotionally where I could just be. Until now.

"Hey."

I snap out of my reverie as Fielding sets his things on the counter and slips on a leather jacket.

"You look really pretty today," he tells me, smiling, his eyes lingering on my face before trailing down my body.

How does the saying go? *Feed me and tell me I'm pretty?* That shit's not a joke when you're pregnant, horny, and living with a six-foot-two Adonis who has made it very clear he wants you.

I'm so flustered I barely manage to squeak out "thanks" before he scoops up his things and heads toward the door.

"I'll text you when I'm leaving campus. I have Teddy's thing tonight, but I'll come home and we can have dinner together before I have to be there."

Right. Teddy's thing. Fielding's going out tonight, back to The Oak, and although he invited me along, something about going out and being surrounded by his friends doesn't appeal to me.

How would he introduce me? What would I do at a bar while everyone else drinks? And how would I handle being back in the dark space where his eyes first locked with mine and I decided to take a chance on myself by choosing him?

It would be like heading back to the scene of the crime. It feels like asking for trouble.

"See you tonight," I call out after him two seconds too late as the door closes and I'm left alone, missing him already.

I listlessly push a gnocchi around my plate as I look everywhere but at him. I'm seated at the bar, and he's standing across from me on the other side, the way we eat dinner most nights. Fielding insists that after a long day of lectures and commuting back and forth to Cleveland, he can't stand to sit down.

He was sweet enough to pick up my favorite meal from Little Italy—but I can barely taste the food as I torture myself with made-up scenarios about how tonight will play out for him.

This whole thing is stupid—I've got myself completely twisted up about the idea of Fielding even talking to other women tonight, yet I refuse to define our relationship or have a real conversation about what we're doing.

I have no right to think these things. And yet I can't stop my mind from spiraling.

"Are you listening?"

Nope. I most certainly am not. I give him a sheepish smile. "Sorry. I'm tired. I'll probably just go to bed early tonight since I have to work in the morning."

He considers me through narrowed eyes, shifting his weight from foot to foot before resolve settles in his expression. "I won't stay out late. I'll pop in to tell you good night when I get home."

His reassurance is anything but. I already know he'll peek into my room and tell me he's home when he gets back. He does it any time he has to stay late on campus, and he did it the one time he went to a John Hughes double feature at the drive-in with a few of his buddies.

The idea of him coming home to check on me when he could be hooking up with someone else instead leaves an acrid taste on my tongue.

I hop off the barstool and clear my plate without replying. He hasn't said or done a damn thing to make me feel this way, and yet I'm literally on the verge of tears.

I'm rinsing the red sauce off my plate when he sidles up behind me.

"Are you okay, angel?" he whispers, brushing my hair to one side so he can speak directly into my ear. His hands reach past my hips, resting on each side of the sink, effectively caging me in.

I shiver at his proximity while simultaneously craving more contact. A few inches forward for him—or a slight lean back for me...

I'm desperate for our bodies to connect. To be held. To melt into his frame and let him have his way with me.

But that desperation is no match for the galvanized armor encasing my still-raw, tender heart.

So instead of leaning into him, I shift forward, pressing my belly into the edge of the quartz countertop because there's nowhere else for it to go.

"I can stay at Serena's for the night," I offer. Thankfully, my voice comes out soft but callous—I refuse to let him hear how affected I am right now.

Fielding staggers back as if I've burned him. He gently grasps my shoulder, turning me in place, then stares down at me with an assessing glare that's borderline angry.

"I just—I didn't want to make things awkward if you wanted to bring someone home," I stammer, crossing my arms under my chest in hopes of conjuring up a confidence I don't feel.

He glowers at me, then shakes his head. "I'm not interested in bringing anyone home. I would *never* do that to you while you're staying here."

"What's that supposed to mean? We're not together, Fielding."

I thought he was glaring before, but his lagoon-blue eyes harden in a way I've never seen in response to my question. He's silent for several seconds, standing still as stone, before he finally spits out a reply.

"Well, I'm not available."

It's what I want to hear. It's everything I secretly wish for when I let myself dream beyond the limitations I've placed on our situation. Yet it seems too good to be true, and I refuse to be made into a fool. Again.

"Because of me?" I demand. "Because of *this*?" I wave one hand up and down my body for emphasis. "I don't want your loyalty," I assert, my tone intentionally harsh to mask the vulnerability coursing through my veins.

His glower turns into a full-out scowl, and that little wrinkle between his eyebrows appears, signaling that he's working overtime to figure out how to play this.

"Too bad," he finally declares, shrugging. "You already have it. While you're living here—while you're carrying *my* child—you have me. Completely. Exclusively."

It's everything I want. Why can't I just let myself trust this moment?

Motivated by self-defense and fear, I can't stop the words that tumble out of my mouth.

"And let me guess. I'm expected to not hook up with anyone else either?"

If looks could kill.

I've never once felt threatened by or scared of Fielding. Until this moment, when his eyes darken and his nostrils flare, I hadn't fully appreciated the intensity of this man.

His chest rises and falls at a rapid pace, and he runs his hands through his hair over and over again as he lets out long, controlled exhales. Finally, when it seems like he's settled back into himself, he speaks.

"I would never tell you what to do or ask that of you, considering we're not in a relationship. It's your body."

"That's carrying your child," I retort, but my words don't hold any heat.

"Still your body." He shrugs as he turns on his heel, grabs the rest of the dishes, and gets to work cleaning the kitchen. He's clearly done fighting me.

Tense silence settles around us as we work together to load the dishwasher and wipe down the countertop. We move in perfect synchroneity, falling into a rhythm we've perfected over the last few weeks.

I'm barely holding back tears by the time we're done. Frustration that he won't duke this out with me wars with anger and disappointment reserved exclusively for myself.

I'm attracted to him. I love spending time with him. I might even be falling for him. But as eye-opening and life changing as life with Fielding has been over the last few months, one thing is indisputable: I am a horrible judge of character.

What if I'm getting this all wrong? What if he doesn't really want me, but just loves the chase? Or what if everything he claims to be feeling is situational because of the baby? My heart won't survive another round of breaking.

The reward would be so damn good. But the risk is still right there.

I push in my barstool and take a deep breath, intent on heading to my room and putting myself to bed. He catches my wrist before I can leave the kitchen, so I let him pull me into his orbit. As much as the undefined hurts, I can't deny that the little pieces of him I let myself indulge in are incredible.

He wraps his arms around me, slowly, tentatively, like I'm something to be both cherished and feared.

Returning his embrace, I nuzzle into the soft cotton of his T-shirt, savoring the way he smells and feels and relishing in this moment, because right now, he's mine.

His hand blazes a trail of tingles up my arm until his fingers find my chin. He tilts my head up and leans down so close I fear he might kiss me.

My deep inhalation stops him in his tracks. His mouth hovers a few inches above mine, his eyes searching, then sad.

He holds the position, just like I knew in my heart he would. He doesn't push. He doesn't take. But his expression speaks volumes: he doesn't like holding back. He looks as desperate as I feel.

"You're the boss here, angel. I haven't pushed my luck or tried to force a conversation out of respect. You just got out of a years-long relationship. You called off your wedding. You already warned me you weren't going to hop into anything new... so I'm biding my time until you *are* ready to make that leap.

"It's your call. When, where, how, on what terms. I'll do whatever you say. I'll be whatever you need. Just know—I'm already yours."

He steps back and walks out of the room, leaving me light-headed and more confused than ever as my heart and my mind wage war against each other in a savage battle of lust and survival.

Chapter 39

Fielding

I push into the house and exhale. It's the biggest breath I've let myself take all day. I spent the night only half-invested in the goings-on around me at The Oak. The urge to be here—with her—is all-consuming. Never before has this house felt so much like home. It's the only place I want to be.

Especially on a Friday night. After a long week of classes, all I want to do is sprawl out on the couch and watch her watch the ridiculous reality shows she loves. Once she gets home tomorrow, whether she likes it or not, we're not going anywhere until Monday morning. She needs rest. And I need—*fuck*. I just need her.

I creep through my own house as quietly as possible. She really does need to sleep—she has back-to-back clients in the morning. I hate that she works every Saturday. Maybe tomorrow I'll swing by Jersey Bagels and surprise her. I haven't felt bold enough to just show up at the salon yet, but I think that would be okay now.

We're settling into ourselves. Finding our rhythm. Or at least I thought we were. Things were clearly off tonight. But she's tired and probably feeling the heft of the end of the week. I'll try and get all my studying done while she's at work so she can be my sole focus for the rest of the weekend.

I automatically glance at the space below her closed bedroom door as I make my way down the hall toward my room. There's no hint of light—not even the barely there glow from her phone or Kindle. I assume she's asleep. But I still feel compelled to check on her like I promised.

I silently push her door open partway and squint through the dark to where she lies in the middle of the bed. Instead of being fast asleep as I expected, she sits upright the second I turn to close the door.

Shit.

"Sorry—I didn't mean to wake you. I just wanted to say good night."

She's silent as I hover at the threshold. Maybe she's not really awake. I take a tentative step back into the hallway and reach for the knob.

But then she speaks.

"Fielding."

I push the door open again so quickly it creaks on its hinges.

Smooth.

I take two steps into the room, scanning her bedside table. Maybe she needs water. Or antacids. I'm no stranger to the *can you bring me more Tums?* texts these days.

She shifts in the dark, sitting up a bit straighter and arranging the covers around her.

Her voice comes out a whisper—raw and emotive in a way I wasn't expecting.

"When you left... you said this—us—that it's my call... that it's up to me..."

She strings the words together in a barely coherent thought. But the way she's sitting there, the way she sounds so soft and open and—*fuck*—hopeful? This moment is so much more than recapping our earlier conversation. It has to be.

I stay quiet. I don't trust myself to not jump to conclusions or put words in her mouth. If there's even a glimmer of hope that she wants what I want...

I hear her inhalation. I sense her vulnerability. I clench my fists at my sides, willing her to go on.

She audibly swallows before she finally speaks again. "I don't want us to be undefined anymore. I'm tired of tiptoeing around how I feel. I know this is complicated and rushed and it's not just us we have to worry about... but if you meant what you said earlier..."

"Every fucking word," I swear, taking two more steps toward her like a man possessed.

"Then I'm yours. I want to be yours."

All the nerves in my body light up like fireworks on the Fourth of July. Every emotion, all the longing, every ounce of attraction I've shoved down and buried over the last few months fire off in rapid succession.

I rush to the bed, then force myself to halt at the edge—too eager and excited to even make sense of what to do next. I bend low and brush the hair off her face. Even in the dark—even when I can't see her clearly—I know. I just fucking know. She's never looked more beautiful.

"I'm going to kiss you now," I murmur, cupping her jaw with one hand and tilting her chin up.

She presses her fingers to my lips before I can make good on my promise.

"I want you to do so much more than kiss me," she whispers, both her arms circling my neck and pulling me down until our lips collide.

Chapter 40

Daphne

He lifts me effortlessly, holding me to his body as he strides across the hall. When he kicks the door open, he grips me tighter, the muscles of his forearms flexing beneath me.

All that holding back. All that restraint. Now we're here.

"You're sure?" he asks on an exhale, placing me on the edge of his mattress before standing up to pull off his shirt.

I nod and eagerly drink him in. I've seen him shirtless plenty of times over the last month. But not like this—not when I could look and touch and appreciate every ripple and contour of his body.

"Just to clarify..."

The doubt in his voice breaks me out of my trance, and I study his face, taking in how his lips are pressed together.

He runs a hand through his hair like he's nervous, looking over at the huge windows against the far wall before scrutinizing me, shameless vulnerability radiating from him.

"This is for real? Not just for tonight?"

My heart hammers in my chest as my insides melt to goo. This man routinely disarms me. But never more so than in this moment—when he's confirming for his own peace of mind that I want him, that this is real, and that it's not just a moment of weakness or a fleeting desire.

"For tonight. For tomorrow. For as long as you'll have me—I want to be yours."

"*Fuck.*"

I barely have time to process the reverent curse before he's closing the space between us and crushing his lips to mine. "Do you know how badly I've wanted to hear those words from your mouth, angel?"

I pull him closer and open myself to him. Our kisses turn frantic, the heat between us so far beyond boiling that I don't know how we'll stop kissing long enough to take things further.

Not that we even need to. He's dominating me, skimming his hands over my body and caressing his tongue against mine. These touches alone could send me over the edge toward an orgasm.

"Take your clothes off," he demands, sinking his teeth into my bottom lip until I moan. I'm so desperate and greedy I can't even manage to sass back. "I need to see you now that you're mine."

The way he says it makes my bones go soft. It's not a request—it's a *need*.

I shimmy out of my sleep shorts, then press a hand against his chest, encouraging him to step back. When I pull my tank top over my head, his breath hitches.

"Mine."

His hands are back on me before my shirt even flutters to the floor.

"Look at you," he praises as he strokes and explores, his eyes shining with reverence. His gaze drops to my midsection, his expression dancing between lust and wonder. "Look at what we made."

In any other circumstance, with any other person, I would cower under this type of assessment.

Although a blush creeps onto my cheeks, it's motivated by desire, not insecurity. I blossom under his adoration. I want him to see me. Fielding has never once made me wonder if he's attracted to me. It didn't even cross my mind to be self-conscious about my fuller breasts, darker nipples, or the fresh, angry stretch lines creeping their way across my lower stomach and hips.

"If anything hurts or doesn't feel as good as it should—"

"I'll tell you," I insist before he even has a chance to finish. "But I'm still me. And I'm horny as hell. Don't you dare go easy on me or treat me differently. You know exactly how I like it. You know what I want."

He considers me for a beat, then another.

"This is what you want?" he teases, pulling his belt out of the loops with a salacious smile that tells me we are on the *exact* same page.

"*You're* what I want," I clarify, biting my lower lip as he unbuttons his jeans and shoves his pants and boxers to the ground.

Enough moonlight illuminates the room to create a luminescent halo around his form. From the cut of his jaw to the curve of his shoulders—from the planes of his chest to the veins of his forearms—he is all man. And now he's all mine.

He lets me drink him in as he stands before me, his erection solid and heavy between his thighs. I swear I can hear myself panting. My cheeks hurt from grinning so hard.

After several seconds, he smirks, cocking one eyebrow in question.

"Are you done?" he teases, taking one tentative step forward, then another.

He comes to stand between my open legs at the edge of the bed, the tension between us tighter than an over-tuned guitar string.

I place my fingertips on his lower abs, smoothing down the hard, indented valleys of his hips. Biting my lip, I peer up at him through my lashes.

"Honestly? I'm just getting started."

Anticipation crackles between us. We both know what comes next. For as much as I've hated the last month of not allowing myself to touch, to taste, to give in to the pull we both felt so many damn times, I'm in no rush now.

I use my tongue to trace a line over the prominent veins on his hip. He groans on contact, spurring me on. I can't help it. I want more.

Nipping and tasting and teasing, I kiss his thighs and cup his balls with one hand while intentionally ignoring his cock.

"Angel…" he murmurs, breathless, weaving a hand into my hair.

I slide off the bed and lower to my knees.

"All those orgasms that first night together," I muse, finally gripping the base of his dick. "And I never once got to taste you."

I wrap my lips around the head of his cock, loving the way he hisses and nearly loses his balance. He catches himself on the bed, then braces his arms on the mattress.

I hollow my cheeks and suck, lavishing him with the same intensity he has bestowed on me each and every time we've been together.

He tastes delicious—salty and clean, with a hint of crisp apple I identify with him without thinking. I take my time savoring his length, running my tongue under the head of his dick and sucking him so deep he moans.

"Enough," he eventually declares, stepping back so I can't continue my rhythm. "I need you."

He's helping me up the next second, crowding my space until I'm clambering back toward the headboard.

Once he joins me on the bed, he traps me with a searing kiss and looms over my body. My legs wrap around his strong, taut frame. He's deliberately holding back and trying not to crush me as I cling to him and desperately pull him closer.

There's something beautiful about the way we ebb and flow in the bedroom. This is what we are. Push and pull. Desire and restraint. The tension between us is stronger than ever.

There's something sacred about these final moments of resisting each other. Now that we're here—now that we're really doing this—I have an even deeper appreciation for all the restraint, space, and respect he's shown me over the last few months.

Because this? The way I feel right now, with his body hovering over mine, his eyes roaming my frame, and goose bumps erupting all over my skin? It's almost unbearable.

I'm propane. He's the flame. How we've gone this long without combusting is unfathomable. I want him more than anything. To burn with him—to be engulfed in his personal brand of fire. To bask in the way he touches me, teases me, uses me. To savor how he makes my body ignite the way no one else ever has.

When his erection grazes my center, we moan in unison.

"Hold on," he grits out, reaching for the bedside table in the next breath.

Catching his arm, I stammer over my next words. "We don't—I mean, I don't think—"

He freezes, then searches my face.

I take a deep breath to steady myself. I have no doubt about what I'm going to say—I need him to know I've already thought about this and that I'm sure.

"Part of my prenatal bloodwork was a full STI panel. I'm clean. You said you got tested once you found out the condom broke…" I trail off, realizing my potential miscalculation too late. There was a solid month between our first time and Fielding finding me again. Now we're nearly four months past that moment. It's silly to think—

"I'm clean. I haven't been with anyone since you. It's just been me and my fist, jacking it every night to memories of *this*." He cups my pussy when he says "this," his fingertips dipping into my folds.

My heart leaps into my throat at his confession.

His eyes light up with amusement.

"What?" he teases. "You really think anyone could top this perfect cunt? You ruined me, Daphne. That night—wrapped up in you, drowning in the way you made me feel—it was everything. You're all I've dreamed about since we were together this summer."

He shifts backward then and repositions his head between my thighs, hovering so close his breath tickles my clit.

"I'm going to devour you. Then I'm going to fuck you raw."

When he does finally bring his mouth to my center, it's with so much force I jerk my hips in response.

"Shh. I've got you," he soothes, placing his hands on each thigh to hold me open and pin me down.

He really does.

There's no hesitation as he nips and sucks, laps and licks. He's starving, and I'm the only thing that can quell his hunger.

He holds nothing back as he eats me out: his tongue and teeth working together to devour me, as promised. His big hands caress my thighs, then part my pussy lips. He fucks me with his tongue hard enough that I almost come.

Just when I think it can't get any better, he flicks the tip of his tongue over my clit in rapid succession. Building me higher. Pushing me further.

"You taste so fucking good... like you're all fucking mine."

The first tingles of release dance up my spine. Before I can make a sound, he's right there, engulfing my clit. He sucks hard and holds on tight as I buck and writhe in his grasp. It's the push and pull that I crave with him—it's his intensity and determination that throw me over the edge.

My orgasm washes over me while simultaneously taking me even higher. The walls of my pussy clench around nothing, desperate and needy but so damn satisfied at the same time.

Fielding is relentless, his vacuum seal on my clit driving me higher and higher even as I unravel. My body spasms again and again until he finally nips at my clit and comes up for air.

He's got that cocksure grin on his face that I secretly love. I can't be bothered to do anything but pant and catch my breath as he smirks at my satisfied state. I'm literally still riding the waves of my climax when he sits back on his knees, hauls my body into his, and lines himself up. He pushes just the tip in—and my greedy pussy pulsates on contact, trying to pull him deeper.

"You're sure?" he asks solemnly.

Beyond sure. I want to feel his heat and solidness without anything between us. I bite down on my lip and nod. But instead of plunging in, he jumps off the bed and drags me with him.

Rising to his feet, he captures my calves in his huge hands, placing each leg on a shoulder before repositioning his cock. He thrusts into me with one fast, hard motion, then grinds the heel of his hand into my clit as he bottoms out.

My shock and thrill come out in a soundless scream, inspiring another smirk on his smug, gorgeous face.

Yes.

Fuck.

This is what I love. This is what I need.

He knows exactly how I like it. There's something so damn sexy about him not only remembering but straight-up manhandling me. He pounds into me less than a dozen times before I'm coming again, this time clenching around his cock like my life depends on it.

I'm lost to the orgasm, back arching and limbs tingling, so much so that I don't even feel him slow down until I've settled back into the mattress. We're still connected, but he's not moving anymore.

"I need a minute," he admits, leaning forward to pepper kisses on my breasts and neck. "You feel way too fucking good with nothing between us." I feel the slickness of his sweat drip down my body. He bends and kisses the mound of my stomach, brushing both hands gently over my hips.

I don't mind the breather—I'm still coming back to earth, content to fully savor all the soft kisses and gentle caresses he'll give me.

When he finally rises back up, his eyes are on my pussy—right where we're joined.

"You're so fucking pretty. I could finish just from looking at my dick buried inside you. We're a perfect fit, angel."

I thrust up at his praise, spurring him on.

He growls in response, shoving into my soaking core and wrapping my thighs in his arms, holding me open to him. He's hitting the perfect spot, all the while continuing with his flattery and worship.

"It's not just this gorgeous cunt that does it for me"—he reaches down to caress the place where we're joined—"it's all of you. The way we fit together. The way you take me so well. It's like you were made for me, angel. Made for me to please. Made for me to care for. Made for me to ruin."

I'm a panting mess from his words. From the way he's toying with my clit while he fucks me deep. From the way the head of his cock nudges against my G-spot, over and over again, locking me in a trance of pleasure.

I can't think of anything else. I can't focus on anything but him.

When he presses harder into my clit, I gush around him. Gripping the sheets, I'm sure I look like a writhing, sweaty mess—but right now, I don't fucking care.

I'm so close, and I don't even have to ask. He knows just what I like and how I like it. But I know what he likes, too.

"Fielding... please."

He groans as he surges harder into my pussy. "I fucking love it when you beg. If I go any harder, I'm not going to last. Is that really what you want?" "Give it to me," I plead.

He smirks before thrusting so hard it takes my breath away. He's a machine—hammering into me at a breakneck pace, fucking me so intensely my body jolts against the mattress with every movement.

Another orgasm builds deep inside my belly as he slams against my G-spot over and over again. The strain on his face is evidence that he's ready to let go as soon as I'm there—but I know he won't finish until I do.

I tumble over the edge, the very first tremor of my core taking him right along with me. He chants my name as I swear my soul lifts out of my body and transforms into something new. Something beautiful. Something whole.

I'm different with this man. I'm more myself, and yet someone unfamiliar. I don't have to worry. I don't have to hold back. There's just us in this moment, reveling in mutual pleasure, both of us opening and giving and being more authentic than we've ever been before.

He rests his forehead against mine for a few minutes before finally lifting up. He pulls out slowly and kisses me with such reverence, I have half a mind to pull him back into my body and never let him go. His release drips out as I shift on the bed, and by the way he's staring at the apex of my thighs, I know he sees it, too.

What I don't know is how to react when he bends low, swipes two fingers through his cum, and massages it against my over-stimulated clit before pushing it back into my pussy.

"So fucking perfect," he repeats, his eyes hungry as he eases in and out of my aching cunt. "And finally all mine," he adds, plugging me up with his fingers before climbing onto the bed and kissing me senseless.

I'm just as giddy as I was hours ago when I climb back into Fielding's bed after my third trip to the bathroom. I don't know what I was expecting to feel after finally giving in to what we both want, but there's nothing but glee inside me as I reposition the pillow and snuggle up beside him.

The excuses I've been clinging to are quieter now. They're not gone completely—there's still a nagging curiosity about his past, along with a whisper of doubt about any sort of long-term commitment. But I'm starting to recognize that the voice that loves to doubt Fielding sounds a lot like the voice that often has me doubting myself.

It doesn't matter what he's done or who he was. The man I see, the man he is now, is admirable—desirable—and I'm willing to bet on this version of him. Just like I'm willing to put my faith in a new and improved version of myself.

If the last few months have taught me anything, it's that I'm so much more resilient than I ever thought possible. I don't feel strong, necessarily, and I still worry about how the hell I'm going to do any of this well: motherhood, a new relationship. These aren't exactly things I thought I'd be facing anytime soon. But I've been through enough this year to know that I can endure.

Maybe that's what strength really is at its core. It's not about being unbreakable. It's about being flexible enough to shift and change without shattering.

Instinctively, I inch back until my ass is resting against Fielding's side. He wordlessly shifts his hips toward me before one arm snakes around my front and pulls me closer.

Our bodies align perfectly under the covers. Our souls settle with contentedness, too.

I take a deep, cleansing breath and let it out, knowing I need to give myself more credit: to trust myself, and to listen to that little voice of knowing that echoes loudest when he's near. How could anything bad or dangerous feel this good? It's not just the sex. Or the money and security. Or his incessant need to dote on me and take care of me in ways I've never been taken care of in my life.

It's this. This feeling of calm. This sense of peace. It's the way my thoughts go still when I'm in his arms.

My brain isn't working overtime. My body isn't tingling with discomfort. For the first time in my life, I can just *be*.

I interlace my fingers with the ones he has splayed over my midsection. I lift our joined hands to kiss his knuckles before resting our hands against my chest.

He squeezes my hand in return, flexing his fingers with enough strength that I know he's awake, too. I take a chance and roll my hips into his crotch. I'm met with a drowsy moan.

His palm flattens against my chest, smoothing between my breasts and over my baby bump before coming to rest against my core.

I swivel my hips with more force before pushing forward into his hand. He cups me firmly with intention before bringing his lips to my ear.

"Yeah?"

I turn in his arms, capturing his mouth in a kiss that's tantric and deep. I'm more than satisfied after our reunion tonight, so this isn't rushed or frantic like before. Now I want to make love to him; to make sure he knows what he does to me and how utterly grateful I am to have found him.

"Yeah," I whisper against his lips, pushing his shoulder hard enough that he gets the idea. As soon as he rolls to his back, I climb on top, determined to show him exactly what he means to me.

Chapter 41

Fielding

I've always been a hard sleeper. Except when it comes to middle-of-the-night romps. Apparently, I have no problem rising to the occasion when drowsy, intimate sex is on the table.

So I'm not surprised when I wake up in the early morning light to find Daphne sitting on the edge of the mattress, fully dressed and ready for work.

"What time do you have to leave?" I ask groggily. I'll gladly get up and make her breakfast if she's not rushing to get out the door.

She doesn't respond right away. She doesn't even turn to look at me.

"Daphne?"

Her voice is eerily calm when she finally speaks. "Is this from last night?"

She passes me her phone, and I have to blink several times before the pixels on the screen organize into something that makes sense. Squinting, I realize I'm looking at a grainy picture captured in the dark in the parking lot behind The Oak.

"It is," I hedge, handing back her phone as I shove up to sit. "Do you want me to explain it, or—""I don't want anything from you, Fielding."

Fuck.

Dread swirls in my gut at the prospect of this—of us—being over before we even had a chance to start because of one stupid picture without context. I've done plenty of shitty, incriminating things in my life. But this isn't one of them. Whether she wants it or not, I have to explain.

"That's Tiff. She works at Clinton's. I've known her for a few years."

Silence lags between us, so I continue my explanation.

"She had a shit night. She and Teddy hooked up a few years ago, and she's had a thing for him ever since. When she showed up to celebrate his birthday with us, he was already wasted and had his sights set on someone else. He barely acknowledged her."

I don't bother delving into the details of their messy relationship. They've always been hot and cold—fire and ice—each one making strategic moves against the other in a twisted game of situationship chess.

"She just wanted to go home, so I offered to walk her to her car on my way out. She was really upset, and I didn't want her crying while she was driving. That picture is me holding her door open and trying to make her laugh and lighten the mood before she left. Any questions?"

Her back is still to me. She's recoiling—shutting me out before I've even had a chance to dig my way back in and get reacquainted. There's no version of this situation where I'm in the wrong, yet guilt and shame are my default settings. I push them both down and clear my throat.

"Well, I have a question. Who sent you that picture, Daphne?"

It's an awful shot. Grainy and dark. I'm leaning against Tiff's open driver's side doorframe, which I probably only did for a few seconds. Without context, the photo looks incriminating. There's an endgame here.

She answers with more silence, which just pisses me the hell off.

I sit up straighter, staring at the back of her perfectly styled hair, willing her to at least turn the fuck around so we can discuss this like adults.

"Did you ask someone to follow me last night?" I press.

Her head whips around so fast I would have missed it if I blinked.

"Of course not!" she defends. "This was sent to me unsolicited."

Her hair might be perfectly styled, but her eyes are red and puffy, like she didn't get enough sleep and she's been crying for a while. The lack of rest I'll cop to, but the tears aren't my fault.

I level her with as much sincerity as possible, clenching my jaw until it aches. I don't dare move a muscle—but fuck, I wish I could hug her right now.

"Who do you think sent that picture, angel?" I ask softly. She's not the villain here. I have to keep my cool. If anything, she's more of a victim in this than me.

"If I had to guess, I'd bet it's from Anthony or Andy."

The answer doesn't surprise me. But it still pisses me off.

Fucking Adley assholes. When will they get a clue? They have no case to make—no business interjecting themselves into our lives. I'll be damned if I let them have any power over me.

"You think? Or you know?" I run a hand through my disheveled hair and blow out a long breath.

Daphne sighs but finally meets my gaze. I don't know if it's relief or disappointment on her face, but I'll be damned if I'm ever responsible for making her feel whatever she's feeling right now.

"I honestly don't know. I blocked both their numbers a while ago, but they keep finding ways to get through..."

She trails off as my fury rises. They have absolutely no right to be contacting her. I don't give a shit if they want to follow me around, trying to "catch me in the act." They can find me on campus, hunt me down in the library, or follow me around downtown Hampton any damn day of the week. I have literally nothing to hide. The truth is that no matter where I am, it's not where I actually want to be.

The only place I ever want to be is wherever she is. In this house. Lounging on the couch. Snuggling in my bed.

Fuck.

She asked me to take her to bed last night.

It was perfect in every way. *She* was perfect in every way. Ethereal, like a dream.

The Adley assholes are trying to morph this dream into a nightmare, but I refuse to let them.

"I don't have anything to hide. Like I've said before, I'm an open book, and I would never, under any circumstances, do something to make you question my loyalty. I wanted you to come with me last night," I remind her.

"I know." She sniffles, adjusting her position so she's a few feet closer.

"And he fucking knows exactly what buttons to push to get under your skin."

She scoffs as she dabs the sleeve of her shirt under her eyes. "Of course he knows which buttons to push. He's the one who put them there in the first place."

My blood pressure spikes. What's it going to take to shake this guy?

"Contacting you after you blocked him is harassment."

"I warned you," she counters. "Anthony has a temper. When he's determined to see something through—"

"That's not an excuse!" I fist both hands in my hair, livid that this is even a topic of discussion. "Did you reply to that picture and tell him to stop?"

"Of course not! I didn't tell him anything."

She looks down at her hands and sighs. By now I've freaking had it. I rise out of bed, find my boxers on the floor, and pull them up quickly before coming to sit by her side. She's not doubting me anymore—but that doesn't take away from the intensity of the drama hanging over our heads.

We can't live like this. Watching over our shoulders. Wondering if and when he's going to contact her again. This isn't love or pining. This is manipulation and control.

I wrap one arm around her, grateful when she melts into my side without hesitation. "This has to stop," I whisper, tilting her chin to look into her eyes. "He can't keep harassing you like this."

"Why? Are you afraid there's something he could do or find that would hurt us?"

I'm shocked silent by the question. She doesn't really mean *us* in this case... She means me. I hadn't even thought about it like that until now. My resolve is firm where Daphne's concerned: I want her. I want us to be a family.

I won't do anything to make Daphne question my integrity.

That doesn't mean my past can't come back to haunt me in very real, life-altering ways.

That my past indiscretions could be a sleeper cell and detonate everything I want in the present moment hadn't even crossed my mind.

She knows about the night at Adley's party. But there was another night in the not-so-distant past that was worse. My memories are as grainy as the picture on Daphne's phone. I can't defend or deny what could be said about one of the darkest nights of my life. Hell, I don't even have a firm enough grasp on what the hell happened to explain it.

I only recall how I felt during the days leading up to that night when the woman I thought wanted more blocked my number. Then there's the self-loathing that seeped from every pore when I woke up the next day. Everything between those moments is a blacked-out mystery.

"I'm sorry," Daphne whispers before I have a chance to gather myself. "It's not fair for me to question you because of my own insecurities."

Oh, but it is fair. Fair. Warranted. Maybe even necessary. I just don't know how to explain what I did. I have yet to reconcile who I was then with who I'm trying so damn hard to be.

"I don't know how to do any of this relationship stuff as an adult," she admits, nuzzling into my shoulder. "I haven't been in a new relationship in over ten years... all the old insecurities and worries I clung to as a teenager are bubbling up again. I shouldn't have even let myself react to that picture without talking to you first."

I sigh, accepting that nothing is going to get figured out or solved this morning.

"You don't have to apologize for your past, or for the things that bother you. I hate what he's doing to you—what he's trying to do to us. But I swear on the life of our child that I don't want anything more in this world than you. I'm not going anywhere. I won't do anything to make you question my feelings or loyalty. You have my word that I won't hurt you, angel. I will spend every day of the rest of forever making you feel safe and loved."

She sniffles quietly with what feels like weary acceptance as I grapple with the promises I've just made.

Every word of it is the truth: I won't fuck this up. I refuse to let my past actions or behaviors affect our future in any negative way.

Although I'm firm in my promise, that doesn't mean we're home free. That night—what I did; the role I played in someone else's misery—and the choices I made in the past could very well destroy our future.

Chapter 42

Daphne

Days turn into weeks. Life moves forward, both slowly and at a rapid pace. It's officially November, which, according to Fielding, means the holiday season has begun. It's cool and crisp in the mornings—perfect weather for sweaters and snuggling up in front of the fire.

We've fallen into the comfiest, coziest rhythm. Fielding goes to school, I go to work, then we come home every night and make the most of our time together.

Nights and weekends have become sacred. As exhausted as I am by the end of each day, our evenings together magically recharge me, and I'm more than ready to stay up late with my boyfriend by the time we go to bed. A few hours together each night just does it for me. It also helps that Fielding continues to rub my back, massage my feet, and dote on me every chance he gets.

I would feel spoiled if he made it seem indulgent in any way. But everything he does comes from a place of sincerity and obligation, as if it's expected of him.

We've had a heck of a time scheduling some of my prenatal appointments, mostly because Fielding has class every weekday and he has a forty-five-minute commute.

But this appointment is a priority. It's the twenty-week anatomy scan, a.k.a., the second ultrasound. This is when they'll check her growth and make sure everything is progressing. We already know we're having a girl, and we're both over-the-moon excited to see her on the screen this afternoon.

Fielding squeezes my hand repeatedly as the ultrasound tech rolls a barrier onto the internal probe. I once again avoid looking at him for this part—but for an entirely different reason. Whereas before it was just *awkward*, now I expect he'd purposely make a joke or tease me.

"All right, mama. Just lay back and relax. I have to take some measurements and update your chart before we get to the good stuff and see baby."

I blow out a long breath and focus on the flatscreen TV as Fielding rubs soothing circles around my knuckles.

"You good?" he whispers, concern lacing his words.

I smile my assurance. "So good."

He kisses our joined hands, then focuses back on the screen.

The internal probe doesn't hurt, but my bladder's full again, and every bit of pressure has me tensing.

"Hmm. Do you already know your placenta is low?"

The question catches me off guard. This is only the second ultrasound we've had—I don't know a single thing about my placenta. Am I supposed to?

"I—no, I didn't know that. What does that mean?"

"The official term for the condition is placenta previa. It means the placenta is covering your cervix along the bottom of your uterus. It's not uncommon, but it can cause issues if it doesn't move as the pregnancy progresses."

"What sort of issues?" Fielding demands.

"The doctor will answer all your questions after the appointment," the tech replies casually, clicking around the screen as she captures various angles of my insides.

His hand tightens around mine, but I don't dare look at him. The mood in the room just nose-dived. I'm on the verge of tears, and I don't even know what placenta previa means.

"Hey," he murmurs, calling my attention to him as the tech swaps out devices and lowers the paper cover to squirt cold gel onto my belly.

"They didn't stop the appointment or call a doctor in," he points out, scooting his chair closer so we're almost nose to nose. "She's okay. *We're* okay," he assures me and kisses me quickly before glancing back up at the screen.

"And there's baby!" the tech announces, pressing the transponder into my belly button as our daughter takes shape on the screen. "Do you already know what you're having?"

"A girl," I confirm, completely transfixed by the black and white images on the screen. The first thing I see is a nose. A perfect, pointed little nose. Then the inset of her eyes, the curve of her lips. A tiny fist raises up and covers her face a moment later.

"She's waving hi," the tech coos.

I can't help but side-eye Fielding, fully expecting to see him biting back a laugh about all the commentary.

But he's captivated by the screen.

"Look at her, angel. Just look." His tear-filled eyes are on me for an instant before he's focused on the screen again. "That's our girl."

The rest of the scan goes by in a blur, the tech babbling happily about how everything's measuring in range and printing off a dozen grainy pictures for us. It's not until we're sitting in the exam room afterward that my nerves ratchet up again.

The physician I'm seeing today is new to me. She enters the room in a rush, apologizing for keeping us waiting. Normally, I wouldn't mind. But today I'm unbelievably anxious to get some answers.

She glances at her notes, then looks back at me with a sympathetic smile. "Is this dad?" she asks, nodding toward Fielding.

"Yes. We're together," I confirm. Anything she has to say can be said in front of Fielding. I *need* him to hear it. He'll understand more about what this means than I will, and he'll know what sorts of questions to ask.

"Everything looks great with baby. Our only concern right now is the placement of your placenta. With the way it's positioned, there's a good chance it'll shift and move to the back of your uterus as your pregnancy progresses. But placenta previa does come with an increased chance of bleeding, and if the placenta doesn't move, vaginal delivery is out of the question."

"What am I supposed to do?" I ask, panicked. I haven't done a ton of research about birth options yet, but I hate that I might already be headed for a c-section.

"There's nothing to do besides wait, I'm afraid. We'll schedule another ultrasound for twenty-eight weeks to see if the placenta has moved. Until then, you're on pelvic rest. Nothing inside your vagina from now until the next ultrasound."

Tears spring to my eyes. I'm still processing the information when Fielding starts in with his questions.

"She's on her feet all day at work. Is that a concern?"

"Not unless you experience cramping or bleeding," the doctor answers, looking at me. "Any sign of bleeding whatsoever warrants an immediate call to our twenty-four-hour nurse line."

"Got it," Fielding confirms, typing furiously on his phone.

My chest goes tight with affection. *He's taking notes.* Good thing, too. Because I'm still fixated on one phrase.

"When you say nothing in..."

"No vaginal intercourse. No toys, hands, or any other contact. External orgasm is fine. We just want to minimize contact and potential irritation to the cervix since your placenta is *right there*."

Fielding asks more questions. The doctor goes into detail about uterine growth patterns and the lip of my cervix. I'm completely zoned out thirty seconds into the conversation.

I'm still fighting back tears. Which is silly, really. The baby looks great. Everything else is fine.

But things with Fielding are so fresh. And so good. Like, so, so good. We finally settled into this version of our relationship, and now sex is just off the table? *Shit.*

He's Fielding—he won't give me one ounce of grief about not getting any for the next two months. I doubt he's even thought about himself yet as he sits in that hard plastic chair, back ramrod straight, firing off more questions for the doctor. And that makes me feel even more guilty and even more sad about what this means.

We've come so far in such a short amount of time.

What comes next now that we have to pump the brakes?

Chapter 43

Daphne

I cried in the shower. I cried again trying to get through my skincare routine. I'm a fountain of feelings tonight, and nothing seems to ease the ache in my heart.

I've been texting Serena all afternoon. She demanded to see close-ups of every ultrasound picture, although I can't identify the subjects of half of them. She had the wisdom (or lack thereof) to do a quick Google search for placenta previa and has been sending me her findings ever since.

Like the ultrasound tech said, the condition is common. It really does resolve itself the majority of the time, and most women go on to have full-term, healthy deliveries.

But I doubt any of those women were in relationships that were just getting off the ground.

I change the bed sheets to distract myself—methodically pulling the tight elastic corners over each side of the mattress and tucking in the top sheet just how I like it. Halfway through the project, I'm out of breath, so I'm sitting on the edge of the mattress trying to steady my breathing when Fielding by passes the open door of my bedroom.

"Do you need help?" he asks, leaning against the jamb wearing nothing but basketball shorts with his shirt slung over his shoulder. He's either finishing up a workout or on his way to the shower.

"No, I'm fine. I can finish this, then I'll probably just go to bed." I shrug in what I hope is a casual way, turning my head to stare out the window before he gets a chance to really look at me.

"Daphne..."

I swallow past the threat of tears.

"What's wrong, angel?" The mattress shifts as he sits beside me.

I refuse to breathe life into my insecurities. I can't explain this to him. Instead, I press my lips together and shake my head, still watching the scenery outside the window.

"What are you doing in here anyway?" he pushes, his tone more serious now as he stares at the rumbled sheets on the floor in my bedroom.

I focus on them, too, rather than meeting his gaze.

Softly, but with as much determination as I can muster, I explain, "I figured it would be easier for both of us if I just slept in here again."

He doesn't say anything for a beat. But tension coils between us as realization sinks in.

Maybe this really is the first time he's put two and two together. He went into concerned dad/future doctor mode at the appointment today, which is admirable. But now that the truth I've been bitterly trying to process all afternoon is sinking in for him too...

His fingers find my jaw, startling me, and turn my head. He assesses me with a sharp, searing glare. I'm not sure I've ever seen him look this serious before.

"Are you fucking kidding me right now?"

"I'm sorry. I know it sucks, but you heard what the doctor said. We can't—"

He cuts me off before I can explain my thinking.

"You're right. I heard her, and I took notes, and then I came home and did some research. We have to avoid some things, but none of that matters to me. You. You and our daughter and your health. That's what matters. You have to know that—right?"

He's on his feet a moment later, pacing the room like an animal being taunted in a cage.

"There's no fucking way you're sleeping in this room. No one said there were rules against holding my girlfriend while she sleeps."

Oh.

Oh.

My cheeks heat with embarrassment. He's not upset about not getting any for the next few months. He's angry because he thinks I'm shutting him out.

I mentally backtrack. I assumed he wouldn't want to be intimate if he wasn't getting it in. But Fielding has always made me and my pleasure his highest priorities when it's come down to it. Why would this be different?

It's a rhetorical question. But that little voice of self-doubt in the back of my mind is more than happy to remind me that under different circumstances, with a different person, my assumptions would have been spot-on.

I lift my head and meet his gaze, waiting for him to still. "I don't *not* want to sleep with you, but you know us," I defend with a pointed look. "What if we get carried away?"

His answering smirk would be condescending if it wasn't so damn cute.

"Angel, I slept with my rock-hard dick in my hand for weeks before we defined things. And as much as I'm a hoe for your pretty pussy, not even that could make me put our child at risk. Please come sleep with me."

I don't know whether to laugh at him calling himself a hoe, or to cry because he's too damn perfect. So I let out a mix between a scoff and a defeated whimper. He drops to his knees in front of me and wraps me up in a hug.

"Please?" he whispers into my hair.

How could I fathom that things between us would change because of what we're facing?

"If you're sure," I hedge.

"Damn sure," he declares as he rises to his feet and gently pulls me up to stand. "Get your sexy off-limits ass across that hall and in my bed right now, woman."

Chapter 44

Fielding

I didn't bother closing the blinds. There's a full moon peeking out behind the clouds, and I love the way she looks in the moonlight.

She's been asleep for hours, aside from the every-other-hour trips to the bathroom she practically sleeps through. I haven't closed my eyes once.

I'm tired, and it's been a fucking day. But between seeing my daughter on the ultrasound screen and doing a deep-dive into placenta previa and all the possible outcomes, my brain's working overtime tonight. I don't stand a chance against my pharmacology exam in the morning.

But none of that matters now.

The only thing that does—the singular purpose of my existence these days, it seems—is her.

Taking care of her. Supporting her. Making sure she feels good, knows she's safe, and knows how much she's wanted. That's the endgame here.

I cuddle closer, curving my body around her soft form under the covers. Why sleep when I can spend the whole night holding her like this?

I was fucking livid when she assumed that I wouldn't want to sleep beside her because I can't get it in. Livid and a little insulted, if I'm honest.

But old habits die hard, and that's how trauma works. At some point, the idea that her worth is tied to what she can offer was instilled in her. That couldn't be further from the truth as far as I'm concerned.

I see what's beside me. I know what I'm holding.

She is so much more than I ever thought I deserved. I'm going to spend the rest of forever making sure she fucking knows it, too.

I want to be where she is. Always.

When I called Dem to give him the ultrasound updates, he started in again. Hassling me about falling for her. Warning me to curb my enthusiasm, to not get ahead of myself when it comes to this relationship.

Joke's on him, though. I'm not falling for this woman.

I've already tumbled over the edge and accepted my fate.

I am undoubtedly in love with Daphne.

Chapter 45

Daphne

I really need to wash my hair. Brush my teeth. Start on my makeup. I've got a million things to do before my baby shower today. And yet no matter how hard I try, I can't get out of this bed.

Okay. Fine. Maybe I'm not trying *that* hard. Between the way Fielding's holding me and his stupid-comfortable sheets, I have a lot of compelling reasons to stay under the covers.

"What time do you want me there today?" he asks, skimming a hand over my bare hip in a blatant tease. I really do have to get going. He knows this. He also knows that every touch, every graze, makes it harder for me to leave.

I roll to face him and prop up on one elbow. "Serena thinks we'll be ready to open presents around three. What are you going to do until then?"

Dempsey and Maddie are in town for the shower. And although I worried it would be awkward having them in the house with us all weekend, it's been anything but. It helps that the house is huge and that Dempsey has his own wing on the opposite end of the second floor. The four of us have had a great time together. So much so that I'll miss them when they head back to California tomorrow.

Fielding yawns before answering. "I talked Dem into going up to Holt for a pickup game of ice hockey. But that's at noon, so we'll have more than enough time to clean up and make our required appearance at the shower."

I flush at the thought of the two of them sauntering into my shower that's being held in the private room of The Grille. Most of my friends and family know so little about Fielding—my mom, in particular, is going to flip when she finds out he's a twin.

"What's that look for?" he teases, leaning forward to pepper my jaw with kisses. I place a firm hand on his chest to fend him off. If he gets started—again—I'll never be ready in time.

"Nothing. Just thinking about the two of you walking into the shower together. Hopefully, I'll be able to tell you apart."

His lips still against my neck, his mouth warm and damp on my skin.

"I'll wear something you'll recognize. I won't try to trick you," he assures me.

I scoff at his concern. "I was teasing. Do you really think I can't tell you two apart?"

Sure, they're identical twins. But Fielding and I have been living together for months. We sleep beside each other every night. I watch him move throughout his day and practically drool over his existence on an hourly basis. Whether he realizes it or not, I've completed a masterclass in Fielding Haas.

"Your eyes are one shade lighter than his," I start, kissing each of his closed eyelids in reverence. "Your hair is wavier, too. That, or Dempsey styles his more often so it's not quite as unruly," I tease, tousling his bedhead for emphasis. "You both get this little crease between your eyebrows when you're thinking too hard," I press into the wrinkle above his nose, "but Dempsey's is deeper."

"That's because I don't have to think as hard as he does," he retorts. "You did well, choosing the smarter twin."

I roll my eyes, but I'm not done.

"Your smile is wider. You slouch more than he does. You're much more animated when you talk. But even without the physical differences, I could tell you apart in an instant by the way I feel when you look at me," I conclude.

Fielding doesn't say anything right away, his gaze fixed on me as we lie quietly in each other's arms. A thickness starts to swirl between us—a blend of things unsaid and things we want to say.

"I—you are—"

With a fingertip to his lips, I silence him. I wasn't fishing for a response. He needs to know this.

"I see you, Fielding Haas. I know the shape of your heart. You may be a twin, but there's no one like you. You're inimitable, and I'm so lucky you're mine."

I peck his lips softly, and he immediately deepens the kiss. Right here beside him is literally my favorite place to be. So much passes between us in this space—lying in each other's arms, sharing the barest versions of our souls. But I meant every word. Despite all the craziness and the never-ending plot twist that is my life this year, I'm so damn lucky to have him by my side.

Before things can get too heated, I pull back—I would *not* put it past this man to cast a spell and keep me snuggled up in this bed all day. But we both have places to be.

"I thought of another name last night," he murmurs as he shifts back to give me space. He's still got a hand on my hip under the covers, albeit innocently. I exhale a shaky breath anyway. I always have a hard time focusing when in such close proximity to him.

"Dem reminded me of our mom's nickname when she was little."

I don't know much about their mother. She passed away last year, and she struggled with addiction, which worries him where our baby is concerned. When he talks about his mom, he always has this detached air about him, like it's too hard to remember just how much he loved her.

"Which was?"

"Her first name was Gloria, and her middle name was Winnifred."

I hold back a wince at the ostentatious tone of both options.

"But when she was little, she went by Winnie."

"Winnie," I repeat, testing it out on my tongue. It's sweet. But juvenile. Will our daughter resent us for naming her Winnie when she's in her thirties or job searching?

"It could be short for Elowyn. E-L-O-W-Y-N."

Elowyn.

"That's beautiful," I murmur softly. "Elowyn Serena Haas."

We've already agreed that the baby will have his last name, and that I get to pick the middle name. Her first name is supposed to be a decision we come to together.

"I love it," I confirm.

"We don't have to finalize anything right now—"

"Fielding." I interrupt. "I love it. It's the perfect name for our girl."

He captures my lips in another slow, searing kiss as his hand trails across my hip, over my stomach, and between my thighs. I'm too swept up in the feel of him to remind him we're short on time. The stubble on his jaw sandpapers over my neck as he works his mouth lower while his fingertips tickle over my core.

"Fuck... I love your body like this, angel."

I preen under his praise, then squirm when he dives down to kiss my belly.

"Don't get me wrong—it was amazing before—but now you've got me love drunk and possessed knowing you've got my baby in there."

He scatters kisses all over my stomach before peeking up through hooded eyes.

"How many kids do you want?"

I scoff in response, jolted out of the seemingly sexy moment by his new line of questioning. If he's love drunk, he just sobered me up real quick.

I prop up on my elbows and pull a face. "I honestly have no idea."

It's true. I always wanted to be a mom—but facing the logistics of how to blend that dream with our reality has been a wake-up call. Everything's expensive. The advice contradicting. There are a million ideas out there about parenting and what's best for baby. And I haven't even begun to think about childcare or school choices. It's all overwhelming.

But not for Fielding, apparently.

"I want to put at least two more babies in you. Maybe three." He licks down my stomach, obviously turned on by the idea.

My insides twist at the very thought.

"Slow down, Nick Cannon. Let's see how we handle one before we commit to creating our own soccer team. We haven't even figured out how to take care of this baby once she's born," I remind him.

I shimmy up the bed and pull the duvet up to my neck. I really do have to get ready. And suddenly sexy time doesn't feel quite so sexy.

"I have some ideas about that," he offers, undeterred by my sudden retreat. He joins me with his back to the headboard and turns to give me one of those megawatt smiles I'm a sucker for.

"Oh do you?" I challenge.

"I do." His expression falls as he takes my hand. "I know we haven't really talked about what'll happen once she's here, but I've given it a lot of thought."

This is news to me.

"I assume you still want to work?"

There's no inflection to his tone—no indication as to whether he has an opinion about my career or what I should give up when our daughter is born. Anthony was always adamant he wanted me to be a stay-at-home mom, like his mother. It was a point of contention between us, so we just kept tabling the issue.

"I do," I confirm, tentatively.

"I figured. What if I switched to a lighter course load and took night classes during the spring semester? Then I could be home to take care of her. Winnie"—he grins—"during the day while you're at work."

The way he says her name melts my heart.

"You would do that?"

He furrows his brow as he considers me. "Of course I would. I'm not giving up on med school, but I'm in no rush. We don't need the money. My grades are solid, and I've got more flexibility now while I'm only taking classes and labs. Let's try it. If the schedule works for us, I'll take classes in the summer, too, so I can keep up with my cohort."

This is the most disarming thing about Fielding. Big picture, life-changing decisions are just—easy. I don't have to overthink things. I don't have to make my case or steel myself for an argument. I hadn't brought up the issue of childcare because I honestly figured it was my problem to solve. That he's come up with a solution and that he views each of our careers so equitably—it's unexpected. And so deeply appreciated.

"Thank you," I murmur, leaning into his side as he wraps one arm around me. The ease he brings to every situation washes over me yet again. I can breathe deeper and trust harder than ever before.

"Having you home with her during the day will make everything so much easier. Maybe my mom could watch her one night a week so I could still take evening appointments," I consider out loud.

"At our house," he asserts, squeezing my shoulder and giving me a pointed look.

Things are better with my mom. Cordial and sometimes even pleasant. She's come over twice, and we text on a regular basis. I haven't had the courage to ask her, but I get the distinct impression that my father is *not* privy to our reconciliation.

It hurts my heart. But it gives me more context for our relationship. There are countless things my mom has done or said over the years that just—hurt. But Fielding's showdown dinner most definitely struck a nerve, because I can tell that she's making an effort to be in my life.

"Agreed."

Fielding pulls me closer and kisses my hair before adding, "I trust your judgment, angel. I want your family to be in her life as long as they respect both my girls."

His words wrap around me, filling the cracks chiseled out by years of gaslighting. It's hard to fathom that something as small as him talking about "both his girls" can feel so significant to my heart. I can't help but marvel at how whole, cared for, and loved I feel in his arms.

Chapter 46

Fielding

10 Weeks Later

The last thing I want to do is drag my ass out of this bed and go to The Oak tonight. It feels like I was just there. But it's been a few months according to all the nagging I've been dealing with the in the group text.

It's Anwar's birthday—the big three-oh—and the guys are threatening to show up at my house instead of the bar if I don't make an appearance.

It's not that I don't want to see my friends. But so much has changed. The guys I used to work and live with assume everything is status quo: different day, same shit. That I'm the same as I've always been.

That couldn't be further from the truth.

I'm different. I'm different in a million ways, all of which are major improvements. I've never felt so content or this wonderfully alive.

"Do I have to go?" I whine, as if Daphne has any say in the matter, rolling to my back but dragging her right along with me. I position half her body over my bare chest, careful not to jostle her too much or put pressure on her midsection.

"I just want to stay here. Cuddle you. Make you come again," I tease, licking up the side of her neck as she mewls in my arms.

Now that she's into the third trimester and we're sure her placenta isn't covering her cervix, we've gotten the all-clear to resume normal activity. We've spent the vast majority of our time together in bed over the last few weeks making up for lost time.

I'm always sure she'll be too tired after a long day on her feet, but the farther into the pregnancy she gets, the more insatiable my woman becomes.

She rolls her hips against my leg, but she's just teasing me at this point. We're both sated and slack in each other's arms: wholly satisfied after an entire afternoon of fucking.

"You promised your friends you'd be there," she reminds me, running her hands through my curls as we cuddle. "Plus, based on the little I know about said friends, I wouldn't put it past them to make good on their threat and show up here if you don't go to them."

She's not wrong.

"Are you sure I can't convince you to come out with me?"

She sighs against my shoulder, then kisses my bicep before answering. "The Oak isn't exactly my scene right now. I already picked up a stranger there and got knocked up with his child. I've officially peaked."

I kiss the ticklish spot between her neck and shoulder until she's writhing and begging me to stop.

"And I invited Serena over for a girls' night, remember? Go out and have fun with your friends. I doubt you'll get many more chances like tonight once Elowyn is here."

Blowing out a long breath, I sit up. I need to shower. And eat something. I might as well get this over with so I can come home as soon as possible. "You're right that I won't have many more nights like this—but I can't wait for Winnie to get here. Then I'll have a legitimate excuse to blow off everyone else and stay home with my best two girls."

I swivel on my bar stool, somehow both bored and overstimulated by all the chaos that is The Oak on a Saturday night. Jake's behind the bar working his tail off since half the staff is sitting beside me, celebrating Anwar. I'm surrounded by friends: guys I've known for years, people I used to live with on a part-time basis, and yet I feel lonely and out of place.

It's strange to experience a sense of detachment in this particular group. I honestly think I have my shit together more than every single one of my buddies—Dem excluded, of course—which is embarrassing for them, considering we're all edging toward thirty. Speaking of my brother... I'm surprised he didn't get wrangled into coming back to town for these shenanigans. I make a mental note to ask how the hell he got out of this when I talk to him next.

"All right, boys, let's throw one back for the man of the hour," Teddy declares, passing around shots like they're candy.

Begrudgingly, I stare at the little tumbler and consider my options. I've been nursing the same beer all night. Knowing this group, throwing back this shot and accepting that I'm stuck at the bar for another hour or so will likely be easier than trying to get out of it. Worst-case scenario: I can call a Lyft to take me home if I want to leave sooner.

I run my finger along the rim of the precariously full shot glass, waiting on everyone else to get situated. Sliding my phone out of my pocket with my other hand, I do a double-take when I realize I have a text from Daphne. In all the chaos, I didn't even feel it vibrate.

I dim the screen and open the Messages app to find a selfie of her and Serena, both with some freaky-looking face masks on their skin.

Yep. That. Right there on the screen. That's exactly where I want to be right now. Sitting on the couch, relaxing with my woman. I'd even let her put a damn face mask on me if it would make her smile.

Accepting my fate, I stash my phone and look at Teddy, waiting for him to stop rambling so I can throw back the shot. I didn't bother asking what it was, so the distinct singe of cinnamon in my nostrils is the only warning I get before Fireball slides down my throat.

I'm not even done grimacing from the burn of the whiskey when a meaty hand grips my shoulder, digging in hard enough to make me hiss.

I bat the hand away and spin around, wishing I had any shits left to give when I come face-to-face with Anthony Adley.

This fucker.

He's smirking already, which immediately puts me on edge. A quick glance tells me he's alone, which also doesn't work in my favor. If his asshole brother was with him, I'd just call Jake over, and they'd both be gone.

Looks like I'm on my own.

"Can I help you?" I deadpan, staring at him with a blank expression.

His smirk deepens before he replies. "How'd I know I'd find you here?"

I roll my eyes, but I don't bother arguing with him. This fool doesn't know a damn thing about me. I had to force myself out tonight, away from the woman he treated like garbage. There's only one place I really want to be right now. It sure as hell isn't in this bar.

Pushing off my stool, I give him a dismissive nod. "Good talk." I look behind the bar, hoping to make eye contact with Jake. Maybe I can duck into his office for a few minutes, call a ride, and sneak out the back.

I don't spot him right away, though, and Anwar's making his way over to me with another round of shots.

"Just wanted to warn you," Anthony threatens, stepping in front of me and blocking the only clear path out of the overly crowded bar. He leans in close enough that I can smell his stale, putrid beer breath.

"I know who you are," he taunts. "I know what you've done. Got the proof, too. I'm biding my time—but she'll know soon enough."

The actual fuck?

I pitch back and cock one eyebrow dismissively, which only agitates him more.

He clenches his jaw, along with his fists. "You think people in this town don't talk? That you could keep your dirty little secrets forever?"

Every reasonable part of my brain warns me not to engage. He's goading me. And he's doing a pretty piss-poor job of it, if I'm honest. I don't give two shits about what this guy thinks he knows about me. But I can't deny the prickle of frustration running through me at his vague accusations. I've done plenty of shitty things in my life. He'll have to get a whole lot more specific if he wants me to have any clue what he's threatening me with.

"I don't have any idea what you're talking about." I shrug, then shift to the side, fully prepared to step around him and head to the back.

"Just wait until Daphne finds out about *her*," he yells in an attempt to be heard over the crowd. "Just wait until she knows the real kind of man you are."

Her.

Her?

My mind flashes to a blond-haired girl with kind green eyes—to the way she'd look at me in a crowd and the way she'd lean on me when she was tired. I can't help but picture the woman I once thought I was in love with.

Fuck.

I made so many stupid, selfish, ridiculous mistakes where Tori was concerned. There's a lot I regret—but nothing that I can't explain.

Unless...

I turn back to search Anthony's face, only to find his gaze set on me with that knowing smirk still firmly in place. Either this guy's a helluva drama king, or he really thinks he has something on me.

There's no way he could know about that night. *I* don't even know much about that night.

I used to revel in not knowing. It was easier to play the victim and claim I didn't remember what went down. And although I'll get little bursts of retrospect from time to time, all I really recall are the emotions that consumed me leading up to the incident and how I felt the next day.

I hate who I was back then. I shudder to think about having to answer for the blanks in my memory from that night. But if someone else knows something... If this jackass could shine a light on the darkest version of the person I once was... I have no doubt he'll use it against me.

There isn't a single conscious action I couldn't explain to Daphne.

But parts of me I don't remember have the potential to destroy us.

I clench my fists but calm my breathing and turn on my heel before I can react to his implications. He may think he has something on me. He may even be right.

But I won't be blindsided by this asshole. I'm not as powerless in this situation as I once claimed to be. There's someone I need to talk to if I'm ever going to make sense of this and form some sort of defense. And that man's not anywhere near this bar tonight.

Chapter 47

Fielding

I should have gone to my own damn room.

But it's across the hall from where Daphne and Serena are sleeping tonight, and I didn't want our voices to carry.

There's no place but the floor to sit. The walls are painted, and the dresser, crib, and changing table are ready to go. We're still waiting on the rocking chair to arrive because Daphne wanted to special order it, and I want to give her everything she wants.

I let my head loll against the light lavender wall as I wait for the FaceTime call to connect.

It's dark enough in here that I won't be all that visible. He's going to be resistant to what I'm asking him to do, but I need him to understand how important this is. I want him to look me in the eye and tell me the truth.

"Hold on," he greets in a whisper, the quiet shuffling of his feet the only sound for several moments. He closes a door quietly before he steps into the light and I can really see him on the screen. He's shirtless, and his hair's a rumpled mess. He's three hours behind me in California, but he looks like he might have already been asleep.

I gulp past the tension clogging my throat and stare straight into the phone before I make my request. "I need you to do something for me."

"What's wrong?"

He knows I'm not okay. Probably knew it before I opened my mouth, but I don't want his concern or pity. I just need fucking answers.

"I need you to tell me what happened the night I went to Wheeler's house."

He glowers at me through the screen, the little wrinkle above his nose working overtime when his eyebrows knit together.

"Fielding..."

It's a warning. His attempt at talking me off the ledge. It's one thing to have my brother want to protect me from something. It's another when the thing I need to be protected from is myself.

"I have to know," I counter.

"Hold on..." he mutters, moving through another dark room and eventually stepping out onto the balcony.

"Isn't Maddie asleep?" I challenge once I realize what he's doing.

"She is. But I don't want her to overhear any part of this conversation."

For fuck's sake.

"Why not?"

"Because she loves you," he snaps, pulling at his hair with his free hand in clear frustration. He settles into a chair but doesn't continue for several moments. Finally, just as I'm about to open my mouth and demand he get on with it, he speaks again. "She loves you, but it was her brother's marriage you tried to shatter. Unless she specifically asks, I refuse to let her hear any of this. Ever. I refuse to let your lowest low change things between you two."

I close my eyes in anguish. It was bad. Really fucking bad. I knew that. But to think that I committed atrocities so severe it could change the way Maddie feels about me...

Fuck.

I can't let who I was ruin who I am to Daphne. I'll give anything to remain the good guy in her eyes... even if it takes finally making peace with the worst version of myself.

"Tell me everything," I plead.

He scowls into the phone. "I don't *know* everything. No one does."

We stare at each other, his words settling in to the broken, empty space around me. No one knows everything—but there are others who remember a hell of a lot more than I do.

"What happened that night was horrific. But so much is unclear. I couldn't get a hold of you for three days beforehand. We were splitting time between the Valet House and our house back then, but three days of darkness was a damn long time."

"Tori called Jake at the bar. She was scared, saying you were in the backyard, screaming for her to come outside and talk to you."

I wince at the audacity.

"Jake grabbed me on the way out without explanation until we were in the car and on our way. Tori called Jake again just as we pulled into the driveway. He put her on speakerphone. I'll never fucking forget how she sounded."

I close my eyes and sink into the dark, harrowing familiarity of shame. It's on the tip of my tongue to tell him to stop. But the only way past this is through it.

"You were drunkenly balanced on the diving board above their pool. It was already closed and covered for the season."

My eyes widen in horror.

"It was raining, so everything was wet. I didn't even notice it all at first..."

"Notice what?" I prod.

"You honestly don't remember?"

I rake through the depth of my memories, searching for a recollection or a spark of a memory that would make all this less embarrassing.

"No," I finally choke out.

"It was glass. There was glass everywhere. All over the ground, in Tori's hair..."

"What the fuck?" I gripe, completely dismayed.

"You had broken a tequila bottle before she came outside. Then Jake said you threw another bottle at her... or to her"—Bile shoots up my esophagus and threatens to spill out—"which shattered and cut her up pretty bad."

I throw the phone down in anguish. Who the fuck did I think I was? There's absolutely no way to justify any of that. I was a child. A selfish, indulgent child, throwing a fit because I didn't get my way.

But that's not an excuse. Despite my tantrum, I was a fully grown adult. I thought I was in love. I don't know shit about love—clearly, I never have—but I'm pretty sure it's not supposed to maim.

I peel myself off the wall and pick the phone back up to find my brother waiting on the line. He's always had the patience of a saint. He's always needed it with me.

"I'm good," I assure him, before urging, "Keep going. I need to know it all."

He continues. I listen. Listen to every word. I wince at the details but force myself to focus and take in every syllable. Absolutely nothing rings a bell. The story is much more foreign than familiar.

He eventually trails off, his voice low and gravelly.

I'm a dick for making him relive all this shit.

He sucks in a deep breath before another announcement. "That's not all."

I bark out a laugh. I'm so fucking pathetic. What else could there fucking be?

What he says next rocks me to my core.

Because this? The admission I spewed? One my fucked-up mind must have thought would convince her to leave her husband for me? This part isn't a shocking revelation. But I thought it was a secret I'd keep to myself forever.

When Dempsey tells me about the confession—about how I accidentally told him, Tori, and Jake that I handed Rhett Wheeler the keys the night he drunkenly crashed his car into the train bridge—I lose it.

Sobs rip through me, the tears falling faster than I can wipe them away. I'm not upset that the truth came out—serves me fucking right. But it's clear now that I caused incomprehensible heartache to a close friend—to someone I thought I *loved*. I got drunk one night and set out to do my worst. And fuck, did I go full out and deliver. I hurt Tori in ways I didn't even know I was capable of.

Who's to say history won't repeat itself? What if I do it again?

I groan in anguish as the tears keep falling. Dem is quiet, but I don't have to glance at the phone to know he's still on the line.

Fuck. I don't deserve his love. I don't deserve *anyone's* love.

I hurt someone I cared about—physically, emotionally—then I left the mess of destruction for someone else to clean up. For *years*. How the fuck did Jake even begin to forgive me? How can Dempsey stand the idea of sharing DNA with me?

What if I hurt Daphne like that? What if what I did back then is enough to ruin everything we have right now?

Now that I know the details, the severity of what Anthony Adley might have on me...

I can't fucking take it. It's too much. I would do anything to shed my own skin and never look back. I would do anything to change what I did.

But that's not an option now. Not after all this time.

Still.

I have to own up to it. Live with the knowledge of who I am. Completely.

This is what I'm capable of. And now that I know the full story, it's my job to make sure something like this never fucking happens again.

I hurriedly wrap up the call with my brother. There's someone else I still need to talk to tonight.

Chapter 48

Daphne

I'm only half awake as I pad into the kitchen for water. The baby only wants it cold these days, so I've resorted to coming out here in the middle of the night to fill my bottle with fresh ice.

Fielding offered to put a mini fridge in our room, but that's a bit extreme. It's not like I'm not up half a dozen times to pee anyway.

I halt in my tracks when a shadow moves in front of me. Within seconds, I realize it's just him.

"Hey, you," I whisper through the dark so I don't startle him.

Despite my effort, he jolts when he sees me.

"What are you doing up?" he demands, his voice scratchy and raw. Bizarrely, he doesn't wait for my response before he snatches his jacket off the back of a barstool, and—slides it on?

The clock on the microwave behind him confirms that it's almost one. If he's just getting in, then why is he putting a coat on?

"I just needed a refill," I explain through a yawn, lifting my empty water bottle for emphasis. I set the bottle on the counter, then make my way over to him and lean in for a hug.

His entire body stiffens on contact.

"Hey—what's wrong?"

"Go back to bed, Daphne. I can't do this right now."

Panic swirls in my chest as I realize his arms are slack at his sides. He manages to pull out of the hug and turn back to the bar to grab for his keys.

"Are you leaving?"

"There's something I have to do."

"What's going on? Are you—"

"Just leave it," he snaps. "You shouldn't be up. I didn't want you to see me like this."

"Like what?" I volley back defensively as I take a step away from him.

His eyes dart around in the dark, focusing everywhere but on me. He looks harried, almost desperate. He very clearly doesn't want to be here or answer me right now.

"Nothing's wrong," he huffs out unconvincingly. "There's just something I need to do."

I chew on my bottom lip as my insecurities churn in my gut. I reach for him again, only to have him recoil, all but stumbling over himself to avoid my touch.

"Fielding—" I implore.

He looks out the window, toward the garage door, then finally—*finally*—back at me. When our eyes meet, I barely recognize the man staring at me.

"Did I do something wrong?" I whisper. In all our time together, we've never had a fight. Sure, we've disagreed, but we always talked it out and worked through our issues by being open and honest.

But the way he's looking at me right now—like he desperately wants to be anywhere but here—makes me question every layer of trust I've allowed to build between us.

"No." He sighs before impatiently running a hand through his hair. "You didn't do anything wrong, angel. It's not you. It's me."

His words should be reassuring. They should comfort me in some way.

But my anxiety is clawing at me in a panic.

It's not you. It's me.

Those words strung together paired with his aloofness scream *breakup* in my head.

"I don't know how long I'll be gone. Don't wait up."

That's the last thing he says before he turns and walks out the door.

Maddie gave me her number, as well as Dempsey's, months ago, insisting I could text or call anytime. I doubt she expected me to reach out in the middle of the night like this. But I don't know what else to do.

I creep past my room where Serena's sound asleep and push into our bedroom—*his* bedroom—and crawl under the covers before sending off the text.

Daphne: I'm sorry it's so late, but I'm worried about Fielding, and I don't know what to do.

His response comes through immediately.

Dempsey: Can I call you?

The phone vibrates in my hand before I even have a chance to reply.

"Hi," I answer tentatively. We've never spoken on the phone. We've never interacted at all without Fielding around to act as a buffer.

"Hi." His greeting is weary, like he was almost expecting me to reach out. That alone is a comfort in some small, morbid way. If Dempsey's not panicking, that means Fielding's okay. It doesn't bode well for me or the state of my relationship—but at least he's okay.

There's no point dancing around the inevitable.

"Do you know what's going on?" I hiccup. "I do," he replies hesitantly, like he's trying to find the right words. "But it's his story to tell..."

"God," I breathe out, frustrated beyond reason that everyone always seems to know something I don't. "That's the least helpful thing you could say. I need you to give it to me straight, Dempsey. I'm weeks away from having a baby. If this is over, if I need to find another place to live, I need to know that *now*. I don't have time to wait for Fielding to confide in me. I caught him in the kitchen sneaking out just now! He just—he just left! In the middle of the night! I went into the kitchen to get a drink, and he was upset that I caught him. He walked out the door and told me not to wait up. He just left..."

I trail off as I run out of steam, painfully embarrassed by my outburst. My relationship with Fielding's brother is casual at best. If this is a situation in which sides have to be taken, there's no way he won't side with his twin. It's pointless for me to go on. It was probably pointless to even text Dempsey in the first place.

I consider just hanging up. But before I can, he breaks the silence. "He's okay. I think I know where he's going, and he's not in any danger," he promises.

"I just don't understand how he could freeze me out like that. How could he just leave?" I sniffle.

"You caught him off guard, Daphne. He's trying so damn hard to fix things that might not be fixable... but for the first time in his life, he cares enough to try. He cares because of *you*."

His words give me the courage to ask the question I almost don't want to know the answer to. "So you don't think he's about to break up with me?" My voice comes out trembling. Soft and pathetic. I sound like I'm twelve. I *feel* like I'm twelve.

"Fuck," Dempsey grunts. "Absolutely not. I'm sorry if he made you feel that way. I'm sure it was hard to see him like that, but try not to hold it against him. When my brother gets fixated on something, he's laser-focused. He'll come around. And he'll come back—I know it. I swear to you. Just give him a chance to explain. Don't give up on him."

I nod wordlessly, letting Dempsey's words sink in and wrap around me.

"He wasn't running away from you, Daphne. He was running away from himself. Now more than ever, he's motivated to change, to make amends for his mistakes, to be a better man. He wants to do it for you."

"Okay," is all I can manage before we hang up. I don't know what I was hoping to hear, but Dempsey's words did bring me a sliver of comfort—even if the details were vague.

I bury my face in his pillow and pull in a long breath. Notes of salt, musk, and apple consume me as I commit his scent to memory.

Dempsey says this isn't the end of us, but I refuse to be jilted again.

I want so badly to trust in this relationship—to count on Fielding, and to believe in the possibility of us. But he has to show up and meet me halfway. He has to stay.

I gather up my pride and look wistfully around the room before trudging back across the hall. Nothing will be resolved tonight. Especially without him here.

Chapter 49

Fielding

I don't even bother trying the front door. It's well past last call, but his car's still here, along with a few others. That means there's still hope.

The employee entrance swings open with ease. I stride through the dimly lit back hall, intent on finding one man and—*fuck*. I don't even know what I'm trying to accomplish. Too much time has passed. This probably won't make a difference. What am I even doing here? Is this just a desperate attempt to expunge my conscience of the crushing guilt consuming me?

I can't breathe. I can't think or formulate any sort of plan that makes sense.

Cole's eyes go wide when I stalk up to the side of the bar, confirming that I look as manic as I feel. "Looking for Jake?"

How the hell would he know—

"Your brother called. Told us to expect you."

I exhale and try to steady my breathing.

"Jake's next door helping Cory close up," he explains before he winds up and tosses me a ring of keys.

Without so much as a goodbye, I'm backtracking and swinging open the side door of Clinton's Family Restaurant.

I don't come here much anymore.

Actually, that's a gross understatement.

I avoid this place like the plague.

Sure, the tots are the best in town, and these four walls harbor dozens of bright moments and happy memories for me. But there's too much history. There's just so much of *her* in this place.

I'm halfway around the bar when I finally look up and spot him. Not just him—them.

Jake's here, as expected. So is his husband, Cory. They're plastered against the back bar. Cory's hands are in Jake's back pockets while Jake's got one hand gripping the back of his husband's head. I've clearly walked in on an intimate moment. And they have yet to realize they're not alone.

I clear my throat to get their attention, watching as Jake slowly turns his head and juts his chin in my direction.

"I—" I have no idea what to say or how to do this. "I need to talk to you," I try.

Jake holds my gaze for several seconds. I hate to imagine what exactly he sees when he searches my expression. Eventually, he sighs, leans into his husband, and gives him a slow, chaste kiss.

"Let me take care of this alone, baby. I'll meet you at home," he murmurs, cupping Cory's face in a way that makes my insides ache. The connection they share—the intimacy that flows between them—*fuck*. That's all I want in life. And maybe I've found it. I shudder at the thought of losing her and missing out on a lifetime of that, all because I made horrifically shitty choices in the name of love.

Cory looks over Jake's shoulder and eyes me warily. He and Tori had been friends for years before I came into her life. He has every reason to loathe me. Taking time with his coat, he darts a look at Jake, then back to me before he eventually walks out from behind the bar and heads out the side entrance.

As soon as the door clicks closed, I speak.

"I didn't know. I didn't fucking remember anything about that night. Everything leading up to it—everything that went down later—I knew. But that actual night—*fuck*. Dempsey told me everything just now. I didn't fucking know."

I grip the edge of the bar—a place where I used to sit and watch her work. Where Jake and I grew close, our friendship turning into a brotherhood. I hold tight to the bar where I spent as much of my free time as possible during a time when life really was good. Before I blew it to bits and fucked up everything.

"I'm not here looking for pity. I just—I just needed you to know that I didn't know, but now that I do, I'll never stop regretting what I did."

He walks over to where I'm standing, jutting his chin toward a barstool in clear invitation.

"Would it be funny if I offered you a shot of tequila?"

His delivery is flat, but he cocks an eyebrow when I lift my head to meet his gaze. I let out a breath I didn't know I was holding and hoist myself onto the stool, accepting his unspoken invitation. Head in my hands, I fight the urge to run out the door and never look back.

The irony is that even if I wanted to run, I have no place to go. Unless I actually do want to seek solace in the bottom of a bottle, there's no way to escape this situation because I can't escape myself.

Jake fills two cups with ice and pours us each a water. I take a long sip before sitting up straight. If he's giving me the time of day, I'm going to make the most of it.

"Was she okay?" I manage to choke out.

"No."

I close my eyes in anguish. I assumed as much but hearing it out loud hits different.

"It took your brother and me a long time to piece together what happened and how it all went down. In the end, there are still things we don't know because Tori refused to talk about what happened before we got there. Knowing her, she left out the worst of it as a way to protect you." He pauses and gives me a pointed look.

I nod, desperate for him to continue.

"Physically, she had a lot of surface scratches and scrapes. It took me almost an hour to get the glass out of her hair and clothes, and her hands and legs were all cut up."

I clench my fists in my lap.

I did that.

Then I ran away. I did that, ran away, and never looked back. Never gave any fucking indication that I was sorry or remorseful. I obliterated a friendship and physically maimed a woman I cared about to what end—to prove my devotion?

I'm sick.

I'm sick, and I infect anyone who gets too close to my particular brand of toxic.

"The damage wasn't just physical. You shattered her spirit. I didn't sleep for days after it happened, worried it would all be too much and that you might have actually broke her. But she didn't stay broken. She healed herself—figured out what she wanted and did what she had to do to fix her marriage and move forward."

"It helped that you never tried to contact her again, and that you finally loosened your grip. Eventually, I got over it and forgave you because I realized you were going to leave her alone. I never knew if that was intentional, or if you really didn't understand the severity of what you did and were just an arrogant asshole. I was just so fucking grateful it was done."

His confession does little to soothe me. The decision to let her go wasn't one I initially made for myself. I woke up the next day with him and Dem—my two closest friends—in my face. They laid into me about what happened, and I nodded along wordlessly as they made their demands. They insisted I leave her alone forever. The severity of their anger was strong enough to scare me into compliance.

I spent the next several months on a short as fuck leash. Dem moved us out of the Valet House. Jake made a point of forgetting my existence. My world turned upside down, and I just went with it, assuming it would be enough. Enough distance. Enough repentance. Tori moved away, and although I pined for her, I accepted that I lost. That she picked him. That I finished second.

Never once did it occur to me that I wasn't the victim in the whole damn situation.

"I fucked up."

Jake snorts, and I can't help but match his reaction. No words exist for the severity of what I did. That much is clear.

"There's no going back, Fielding. For any of us. I need you to recognize that and to promise me you won't contact her ever again. You almost destroyed the most hard-earned love I've ever witnessed between two people I consider family."

He continues. "I get that Maddie and Dem's relationship makes it inevitable that you'll see her at some point in the future... family gatherings, weddings, funerals... but the only way any of us moves past this is if you swear you won't attempt to contact her."

I hate being told what to do—or in this case, what not to do.

"The kindest thing you can do is leave her alone. Forever."

But as much as I hate it, the voice inside my head knows he's right.

There's no going back. There's no making up for what I did. It's time to accept it and let it shape who I become.

"I wouldn't dream of contacting her now," I vow. And I mean it. He's right—there will eventually come a day when I have to see her and accept that the pain she feels when she looks at me is all my own doing. But knowing my brother and Little Wheeler, it'll be a long-ass time before that day comes around.

Sighing, I bring my glass to my lips. I take a sip of water, letting the icy blast quench my thirst and calm my frazzled nerves.

"No apology will ever be enough," I lament, meeting Jake's gaze and doing my best to convey the veracity of my words.

"You're right," he agrees, before adding, "So stop punishing yourself and just do better."

As if it's that easy.

I search his face as he stares back in challenge. The takeaway is clear: I'm the only one who can change the narrative. I have to accept the past and make peace with who I am and what I've done. Forgiveness isn't an option. Acceptance may not be what I deserve, but it's the key to moving forward.

Chapter 50

Daphne

My eyes flutter open when light creeps into the room. I blink away sleep, yawning, and glance over to see Serena lying peacefully next to me.

A shadow overtakes the light, casting the room back into darkness as a figure approaches the bed.

He draws closer—slowly, tentatively. Something in my gut tells me he's warring with himself—trying to decide between taking another step or turning around and leaving. I sit up and meet his gaze through the dark to let him know I'm awake.

Suddenly he's moving quicker, closing the space between us, then swooping low until his lips are close enough to brush against mine.

"Can I take you to our room?" he whispers. His voice cracks when he adds, "I need you."

I nod sleepily, propping myself up when he hooks his arms under my knees and lifts me effortlessly. I automatically wrap my arms around his neck, nuzzling into the warmth of his T-shirt and jacket as he quietly carries me across the hall.

He places me gently—so gently—on my side of the bed, then perches on the end of the mattress. Brushing the hair out of my face, he studies me. When he speaks, his words come out whisper-quiet and laced with regret.

"I'm sorry I ran out like that earlier. I'm so sorry I left without any explanation. I had to go, and I was afraid if I didn't just get it over with—"

I rest my fingertips on his lips to silence him.

"I talked to your brother," I explain, hoping my touch and reassurance will soothe him. "He didn't tell me much, but I know whatever you're going through isn't about us."

He shifts back when I rest my head on his shoulder, but I scoot closer and force him to accept my comfort. After what feels like a drawn-out battle of wills, he finally relents, settling in and wrapping an arm around me.

"I'm so sorry, angel. I'm so fucking sorry."

"What are you apologizing for, exactly?" I nudge my head against his shoulder, desperate to transfer any semblance of peace I feel to him.

"Everything!" he exclaims before collecting himself and continuing. "All of it. Everything I've done. Everything I'm bound to do to fuck this up. I'm so damn scared I'm going to fuck this up…. That what I've already done will fuck this up…"

His words are urgent and incessant. But they seem misplaced—like they aren't even intended for me.

"Fielding—" I start, only to be interrupted by another stream of consciousness.

"I want to be better for you. But I don't know if I can be, angel. I'm so fucking worried I'm going to fuck this up. I don't know how to not hurt the people I love."

I'm at a major disadvantage here. He isn't just talking about what happened earlier. He can't be. The demons he's dealing with are so much bigger than a middle-of-the-night kitchen spat.

His demons are still a mystery to me. But I don't want to push him further into this spiral. I search for something—anything I can say to break the trance and help him focus on the here and now.

So much has been uncertain and unsteady over the last several months. But the thing that's made it all okay is him. He's been my anchor; my guiding light. Everything hard and scary feels less so with Fielding by my side.

Emboldened by how I would want to be treated if our roles were reversed, I climb into his lap, straddle his hips, and kiss him so hard he's forced to part his lips and kiss me back.

I nip at his bottom lip, then slide my tongue against his, setting a rhythm with my mouth and my hips that he quickly matches.

All the energy and anguish coiled tight inside him starts to unwind as we sink deeper into the moment. He grips my hips, then eases up until his hands are resting loosely against my sides. His jaw tics through several kisses before eventually relaxing.

When he's sated, calmer, and less frenzied, I pull back slowly and rest my forehead against his, forcing him to meet my gaze.

"Trust me," I whisper. "As someone who grew up being constantly hurt, just a little, by the people who were supposed to love me—I promise you're doing more than okay."

His eyes shutter closed, but I'm not in any rush. I wait as he treads through whatever's going on in his mind. I kiss his cheeks, his eyelids, and his forehead, until he finally opens back up for me.

"I know who you are. You show me every day. I don't know why you're upset, but I can accept that what you did in the past is in the past. I don't want to be defined by who I once was, either," I admit with a shaky exhale. "You won't mess this up. You can't. I know you too well, and I love you too much to let anything change that now."

He rears back like I've slapped him. I just wrap my arms around his neck and pull him right back, doubling down on my declaration.

"I love you, Fielding."

"Don't say that," he chokes out, throwing his head back and grimacing.

"First of all, don't tell me what to do."

He tries to hold back his smile, but he can't hide the way the corners of his mouth turn up slightly.

"Second—why can't I say it if it's true?"

He keeps his head tilted up, refusing to meet my gaze. "You don't know what I've done. You have no idea what kind of mistakes I've made or the shit I've fucked up."

He's not getting it. But he will.

"You are not your mistakes or your worst decisions. None of us are."

I take his hand in mine and kiss it before sliding it down between our bodies and placing it firmly on my bump. "Sometimes our lowest moments lead us to the most beautiful places," I remind him. "I love you, and you need to accept that. I love you for who you are today, for who I believe you'll be tomorrow. As you are right in this moment, I love you."

He doesn't respond right away. I don't push him to reciprocate. We sit in silence, leaning into one another, coming together as we are.

I don't need him to say it back to me. At least not yet. As long as he doesn't shut me out, we'll be okay. As long as there's hope he'll eventually come around, I know we can get through this.

He grazes his hands up my arms before gently cupping my face. "Fine. I'll work on accepting it. But don't think just because you said it first means the feeling isn't mutual. I think I've loved you from that very first night in the alley."

My heart stutters in my chest.

"It was more than attraction that brought us together. I've never felt like that in my life," he admits. "I just wanted to be near you. Even when I was balls deep inside you that night, it wasn't close enough."

"Thanks for the visual," I snort.

He grins and cocks one eyebrow, and I breathe a sigh of relief. *There he is.*

The man I know—the man I *love*—he's still in there. We're going to be okay.

"I'm not good at any of this, angel. I'm bound to fuck it up over and over again. But I want to be good for you. For a long time, I didn't know what love was. But now that I've found it, it's obvious. It's wanting to be better every damn day for the sake of someone else."

I catch his lips with mine, pouring all my gratitude and admiration into the kiss we share. He's exactly right: neither of us is perfect, nor do we need to be. But being better versions of ourselves is something we can both strive for.

"I love you, angel," he whispers when we finally come up for air. "You were made for me."

Chapter 51

Fielding

She stayed in our room without me having to ask, granting me the comfort of holding her all night long. Thank fuck. I need her tonight.

The darkness hasn't had a grip on me like this in years. Part of me still hates myself for what I did. But drowning in the shame and guilt over the past isn't an option for me anymore. I have something to live for: someone who makes me want to do better.

I nuzzle into her hair as she sleeps, feeling nothing but peace and resolve.

Dempsey says it's over. Jake said to leave it alone.

I can't change a damn thing about what I've done or who I once was. Dwelling on it accomplishes nothing. Acceptance is the only way. It's time to move on.

As I hold this sleeping angel in my arms, I decide to do just that. Grateful doesn't even begin to describe how I feel about being given another chance, the opportunity to somehow deserve her love.

I won't waste it. I'm going to take this fresh start and treat it like a gift. Work every moment of every day to be the best partner and parent I can be.

It doesn't matter what Anthony knows or what he tells Daphne. It doesn't matter what happened in the past or what atrocities I've committed.

She's in. She's not going anywhere. I have to trust that. What she and I have found—what we've created together—it's the kind of love and acceptance we both craved individually for years.

I refuse to fuck this up.

I'm the only one who can prove I've changed—that I'm reliable, dependable, capable of a selfless, unconditional kind of love. I'll spend every day of the rest of my life showing up and playing full out for her—playing full out for both of them.

She stirs and turns her head on the pillow, and I take the opportunity to gingerly pull her closer. I work my arm under her head so she can use it as a pillow just the way she likes. I rest my palm on her stomach, and Winnie gives me a hard, determined kick.

My girls.

I have something to prove, something to live for—someone, two of them actually, who makes this life worth living. It's more than I deserve, but I'm going to savor it, appreciate it, work hard to earn it. I drift off to sleep with a stillness in my soul that I haven't felt in years.

Chapter 52

Daphne

Now that my prenatal appointments are every other week, I've had to schedule them at odd times to fit around my clients. It might as well be the holidays all over again with how busy I've been—apparently, everyone needs a Brazilian before my maternity leave, even though I only plan to be off for eight weeks.

I really like the midwife I'm seeing today, which makes it easier since Fielding couldn't make it to this appointment. His course load is lighter this semester, but he's working on a huge group project that's due at the end of the week, so he's on campus all day trying to wrap that up.

The countdown is on. Just one month to go until we meet our baby girl.

"Hmm," the midwife hums as she measures from my pubic bone to the top of my uterus, which is practically bumping up against my lungs. "You're measuring a little behind, but that could be due to her positioning. Where are you feeling movement today?"

Elowyn gives a swift kick to my bladder, making me wince and clench my legs together. "All her kicks are low," I admit. "It feels like she's dancing on my bladder right now."

The midwife places her hands on my stomach and gently presses into different sections of my swollen belly.

"I'm almost certain she's breech, so that makes sense." "Is that bad?" I stress.

"No, not at this point. She technically has another week or so to get into position. You just have a little gymnast in there," she reassures me, smiling as she updates something on the computer.

"I'll place an order for an ultrasound so we can confirm position. If she is breech, and if you do want to attempt a vaginal delivery, we'll need to talk about the conducting an external cephalic version."

"What's that?" I rush to ask. I'm grateful they already took my blood pressure—my heart rate is surely increasing by the second. I wish Fielding were here to ask the right questions.

"It's an external procedure used to physically reposition baby. It's not without risk, and we don't even attempt it until thirty-seven weeks, so you have some time to consider your options."

"Is there a chance she'll turn on her own?"

"Oh, absolutely," she assures me. "We'll schedule the ultrasound this week so we know where things stand then."

I grimace at the prospect of having to carve out another chunk of time at work. There's literally no time left in my schedule this week—I'm already working late every day to squeeze everyone in.

"I—I don't have much time available this week. At least not during office hours." I feel like shit implying I can't make time for my baby's health. But maybe there's another location that offers earlier appointments.

"Tell ya what." The midwife purses her lips. "Why don't I see if the ultrasound tech has time to squeeze you in right now? You're already here, and we can at least confirm positioning now so we can start planning for a version."

"That's perfect," I exhale, relieved, as she gets up to leave the room.

I adjust my pants and waddle off the exam table, then fish my phone out of my bag to text Fielding the updates. Only a few minutes pass before they're whisking me away to imaging.

I'm treated to more cold goop all over my belly, but I don't mind. Fielding is upset he's not here for this impromptu ultrasound, so I ask the tech if she can please print out lots of pictures.

She spends a few minutes adjusting the transponder, pressing it into my stomach at various angles. "Definitely breech," she notes, pointing out Elowyn's head near my rib cage. One of her legs is also hooked overhead so it looks like she's doing the splits.

"Did the midwife mention you were measuring small?"

"She did," I confirm absentmindedly, totally transfixed by my daughter squirming on the screen. Her little fist is opening and closing near her face. It almost looks like she's sucking on her thumb.

"That's because you have almost no amniotic fluid left."

The words don't mean much. But her tone has me searching her face. "What do you mean?"

She squints at her computer, pressing the transponder harder into my stomach in a way that's almost painful.

"I can only find two pockets of fluid when there should be four, and those two pockets barely add up to three centimeters."

I'm once again at a loss—I feel like I need a translator. I should have FaceTimed Fielding before the ultrasound started.

"You're most likely having this baby today," the tech declares.

The computer spits out black and white ultrasound images, the hum of the machine impossibly loud as everything else around me goes still.

Today? Today.

I'm having a baby today.

Chapter 53

Daphne

They told me to go straight to the hospital. I convinced them to let me stop at work and home on the way.

Bobbi had a cow. She didn't even know I had a doctor's appointment today since I scheduled it before any of my clients. Now she's left with the task of rescheduling dozens of appointments on my behalf. There are two other estheticians at the salon, but knowing most of my clients, they'll cancel and wait for my return.

Which is now questionable because I'm about to have a c-section.

I know next to nothing about the procedure. The recovery. What to expect or how to prepare. This wasn't the plan.

Thank God for Fielding.

For a man who loves to make people laugh and flirts shamelessly with anyone who'll give him the time of day, he's been nothing but steady and stoic since he arrived. I've teased him more than once about having sent his twin in to handle this.

He pointed out that Dempsey couldn't have gotten back to Ohio on such short notice since I'm about to have an emergency c-section.

He's got me there. I was at my doctor's appointment less than three hours ago. Now we're about to meet our little girl.

Fielding's fully scrubbed in and dressed for surgery. He's trying his best to keep from bouncing off the walls—but I know him well enough now to know he's brimming with restless energy.

He doesn't channel any of that my way, though. He's all soft whispers and soothing words for me: the perfect balm as we prepare for an unexpected storm.

A nurse pops into the room to let us know it's almost time. I'm sitting at the edge of the bed, clinging to the thin sheets beneath me.

Cautiously, Fielding approaches me and crouches low, taking both of my hands and smiling.

It's that perfect Fielding smile—all white teeth and blinding charm. "It's almost time."

I can't bear to respond. I'm just barely holding back tears.

"Are you more scared or disappointment right now?"

He rubs his thumbs over my hands, the steady strokes reminding me that he's right here.

"Can I be both?" I manage. A single tear escapes, but he brushes it away before it's halfway down my cheek.

"You can be anything you need to be right now, angel. I've got you. I'll hold us up—all three of us. I swear you can count on me."

His words are honest and his promises are true. I have complete faith in his ability to support me through this.

I can't help but think back to the moment I saw the first set of double lines on the pregnancy test all those months ago. The thought that hit first, the one that filled me with dread, was *how am I going to do this alone?*

But I'm not alone. Not anymore. I'll never have to be alone again.

The greatest gift this man has given me is himself.

"I trust you," I tell him.

"And I love you," he replies.

It's the last private words we share before two nurses come in and usher him into the hall so they can prep me for surgery. It's the words that galvanize me as they wheel me down the hall into surgery.

Chapter 54

Fielding

She's here.

Elowyn Serena Haas.

My little Winnie. My perfect girl.

She's tiny. And feisty. She's been screaming nonstop since they took her off Daphne's chest and placed her in this incubator. My little girl is a fighter, and I fucking love it. I've never fallen in love this fast or this hard. And that's saying something, coming from me.

I knew life would change once she arrived. I just never expected it to happen so quickly.

Within minutes of her birth, she was whisked away to the NICU. Daphne asked me to go with her, but I waited until she was stitched up and on her way to recovery.

Now my heart's splitting in two—I'm desperate to be with both my girls. I watch with a keen eye as the NICU nurses chart and record her stats.

She weighs five pounds, nine ounces, which is pretty damn impressive for being four weeks early. She's eighteen inches long and makes these little gurgled grunts each time she breathes, which is an indication of fluid in her lungs. There's not much they can do for that while she's being observed, but, based on her oxygen saturation levels, I won't be surprised if she ends up needing CPAP.

The nurses keep asking me to move as they get things set up. I'm happy to oblige, but I refuse to go far. They should probably get used to the hovering—I'm about to redefine what it means to be a helicopter parent.

I snap a few more pictures, searching for a decent angle without the glare of the heated incubator distracting from the shot. I also strategically keep the IV on Winnie's hand out of the pictures. I understand the need from a medical perspective, but I don't want Daphne to worry about that right now.

I send off pictures to my brother and Maddie, then send a separate text to Daphne's phone so she'll have them to look at as soon as she's out of recovery.

I get another idea then.

"Say hi to Mommy, little angel," I whisper, recording our daughter as she fusses and carries on.

I shouldn't be surprised she's giving the nurses hell. I hold back a chuckle as her tiny fist displaces the pulse ox they're trying to secure around her wrist.

"She's perfect, Daphne. Our daughter's perfect. She's beautiful, like her mommy, and she's ornery, like her dad. Look at this little angel we made."

After I've ended the video, I stash my phone. I swear I can't even blink without feeling like I'm going to miss out on something crucial. I don't want to take my eyes off her. I don't ever want to leave her side.

Chapter 55

Daphne

We're finally settled in our room—without our little girl. I won't get to see her for another three hours because I have to wait for the catheter to come out before they'll let me go down to the NICU.

I haven't stopped crying since recovery. I honestly wish I would run out of tears—if only because my face physically hurts from being puffy and swollen.

Fielding won't stop peppering me with kisses and telling me how amazing I am.

I don't feel amazing. I feel like a failure.

"What can I do for you?" he implores, smoothing back my hair and staring at me, helpless, with those big lagoon-blue eyes.

I didn't even get a chance to see if her eyes were blue like his before they took her away.

Another sob ripples through me. And thanks to the spinal block wearing off, a singe of pain shoots through my lower half, making me hiss.

The anesthesia is fading, which is good, because they won't take the catheter out until I have feeling in my legs. But also—*ow*.

"Maybe you should just go back and be with her," I half-heartedly suggest.

"Absolutely not," Fielding counters, pulling his chair as close to the hospital bed as possible. He strokes my face, but I can barely stand to look at him.

"She's fine. She's more than fine. She's getting the best care possible, and they won't let me hold her while she's still in observation anyway," he explains. "*You* are where I need to be."

"I'm sorry," I whisper again. My lower half may be partially numb, but I feel so vastly empty. "I'm so sorry she came early."

He sighs and wraps me in a gentle hug, careful not to jostle me. "You're allowed to feel however you need to feel right now, angel. But you have nothing to be sorry about. Just wait until you see her. You'll be the first one to hold her," he promises. "I know this isn't the way it was supposed to go. But I promise we'll look back on this day and we won't remember the hard parts or the scary parts."

He shifts back in his seat and pulls out his phone. "Look at what you created." He beams, swiping through the fifty plus pictures he's already taken of our daughter. "Look at what we made together. Do you know how proud I am of you? Do you know how grateful I am?"

He tilts his head and smiles softly at an image on the screen.

"You're amazing. You're perfect. I know you feel like shit right now, but someday soon, this will just be a memory. One tiny moment in a lifetime of memories we get to make together with our daughter."

Chapter 56

Fielding

"Back to break another record?" Roberta asks as I make my way over to the sink to scrub in.

"You know it," I reply smugly with a wink. Daphne's back is to us, but I'd bet she's rolling her eyes. I've only been gone for a few hours—I ran home to get us both a few changes of clothes and to wrestle with the infant car seat in the privacy of my own damn driveway. But it feels like I've been gone for days.

I dry my hands quickly before striding over to the rocking chair and crouching low to peek at my girls.

"Why does she look bigger?" I pout, pulling down the edge of the swaddle blanket where my sweet little Winnie lies sound asleep on her mommy's chest. I can't help but inhale—she smells so fucking good. Like fresh soap and warm blankets and love.

I've very quickly become addicted to baby cuddles. And baby smells. Pretty much anything to do with this baby is my new favorite. I love it all. I simply can't get enough.

"Shh," Daphne urges. "You've only been gone a few hours. I promise she didn't grow in that time."

"Hmph. Easy for you to say. You've been here getting all the snuggles while I was cursing out a car seat base," I tease as I peck her on the lips. She also smells divine—like herself, but with this new layer of sweetness from the breastmilk.

"Did you get it figured out?"

"Of course," I assure her. I don't mention the three YouTube videos I watched—more than once—to get the install just right. But both bases are safely installed in our cars, and those suckers aren't going anywhere.

I smooth Daphne's hair and cup her face affectionately. "What do you need? Do you want to eat before her next feeding?"

She glances at the clock and grimaces—she's got less than twenty minutes before she has to nurse again.

This is one of the most insane parts about being in the NICU—intuition and baby-led anything are completely disregarded. Winnie has to nurse at a specific time, just like she has to be changed and weighed at a certain time. She takes nearly an hour to nurse on both sides. Then we weigh her again to calculate her intake.

If the weigh and feeds aren't enough according to the powers that be (a.k.a., the crabby nurse practitioner who's made Daphne cry no less than three times this week), they have to push the remaining feed through an NG tube. Since Daphne is determined to breastfeed, that means every nursing session ends with her having to pump, too. Then the whole shebang repeats three hours later.

It's brutal. And yet she keeps going.

"Please eat," I encourage her. I'm useless in a lot of ways right now, but making sure Daphne is fed, somewhat rested, and staying up on her pain meds are things I *can* do to contribute.

Plus, Winnie's had two great nursing sessions so far today. If she keeps this up, they plan to remove the NG tube tonight, and she can do her car seat test tomorrow, which puts us one step closer to going home. Hence why I rushed home to get the car seat bases installed this afternoon.

"I missed my little angel, and I haven't gotten to hold her since this morning," I push, shucking off my shirt before making gimme hands.

Daphne gives me a look, and I know better than to challenge her objection. She's overheard more than one nurse talk about the "hot dad" in room 207. But what does she expect me to do? Skin-to-skin is beneficial for bonding and for helping Winnie regulate her body temperature. It's practically required that I walk around shirtless.

She shifts forward and lets me scoop up our sweet girl. She's a warm, pliant ball of love in my arms. Bracing Winnie against my chest, I use my other arm to help Daphne up, letting her ease into it as she stands and finds her balance.

Daphne's had a few teary-eyed moments over the last nine days, but one thing's for damn sure—my woman is a fighter. I think she surprised even herself with the ferocity with which she's taken to motherhood.

Aside from being the hot dad (a moniker I fully intend to put on a T-shirt), I swear the nurses are grateful for the levity I bring to the room. Daphne is on top of everything: constantly asking questions, insisting we handle all the diaper changes, and Googling every damn thing they tell us to verify that it's the most up-to-date information and that she understands it. She's a badass, but she doesn't stop. Hence my need to lighten the moments, to make her rest, and to draw out those smiles.

"I'll be back before her next feeding," she tells me, grabbing her bag and looking over wistfully.

I settle into the vinyl-covered recliner and get comfy, rearranging Winnie's legs and making sure none of her EKG wires are tangled. When I look up to give Daphne a reassuring smile, our eyes lock, and it's like my whole world falls into perfect harmony.

"Love you," I mouth before placing my lips on the top of my daughter's forehead and breathing her in. Why do babies smell so damn good?

I fish out my phone and snap a selfie to send off to Maddie and Dem, asking if they want to FaceTime later. Then I close my eyes contentedly and rock my daughter in my arms.

Chapter 57

Daphne

"I don't know what to do. She doesn't want to nurse. She won't burp. Her diaper's clean. She's so—she's just—"

Fielding's moving across the room and lifting her from my arms before I finish my train of thought.

"She's just a baby. And you're a fucking rock star," he adds, giving me a sympathetic smile as he cuddles her tight to his chest.

She stops crying immediately. As soon as the wailing dies down, he repositions her tiny body to wrap around his forearm, and I'm almost pissed when she visibly relaxes and finally starts to settle. Thankfully, I can't muster the energy to actually be upset. All I really feel is relief.

There's something so painstakingly unfair about the newborn stage. At least in our dynamic. I'm on the brink of a breakdown, and he's somehow standing there cool, calm, collected, and looking like a freaking snack with a baby in his arms.

"How many times did you wake to feed her last night?" Fielding asks as he sways in place and shushes her in a calm, soothing tone.

I open the tracking app on my phone. "Eleven?" I exclaim in disbelief. And that's probably a low estimate. At some point around four a.m., I stopped counting. Getting up, getting her out of her bassinet, and trying not to nod off as she ravenously bopped around like a barracuda was almost more than I could handle.

"Fuck," he mutters under his breath. "She's cluster feeding. It's just a phase, but you need sleep. I have breakfast ready for you in the kitchen. Go eat, then you're going to take a shower and a nap. You *have* to sleep, angel. I'll keep her with me while I get things ready for today."

Ready? That's right. My parents and sister are coming over to meet Elowyn. I'm already a harried, stressed-out mess. I groan as I think about coming face to face with my father for the first time in months.

"We can cancel," Fielding reminds me. We've had some version of this conversation several times over the past few days. I'm not even upset at his constant reminders. He's just looking out for me and trying to protect my already feeble mental health. "We can tell them it's not a good day. Just say the word—"

"No," I insist. "I'll feel better once I've eaten and showered. I just want to get this over with."

"Text me if you need anything." He pads over to the bed, our baby still balanced on his forearm, and kisses me before threatening, "And don't you dare interrupt my baby time."

He's teasing. And trying to make me feel better about desperately wanting a little time to myself.

I tear up at his covert kindness. "If she—"

"She'll want for nothing," he insists with a pointed look, backing toward the door. "And if she gets sassy with me, she and I will negotiate. Are you okay with me giving her a bottle if you're napping?"

I work my lip between my teeth. Am I? Am I more desperate for sleep, or the assurance that I'm doing all I can to keep up my supply?

"If you sleep through a feeding, you can pump when you get up," he reminds me.

I sigh with relief. That's all the convincing I need.

I rise to my feet slowly—my low back and shoulders ache from being hunched over and trying to get her to nurse so many times throughout the night—and make my way over to where he stands in the doorframe.

"Thank you," I whisper, leaning into his side as he wraps me in a hug.

That meager sentiment doesn't begin to cover all the ways he's supported me and lifted me up over the last three weeks, but it's all my exhausted brain can muster. Fatherhood undoubtedly looks good on Fielding Haas. Unconditional love looks even better.

"Daphne."

I barely register my name through the fog of deep, delicious sleep.

"Daphne."

I squint my eyes open, then sit up too fast. My head spins and my incision aches—I'm probably going to need a few ibuprofen to feel human today. I reach for my phone out of habit, shocked to see that it's almost two.

"I'm so sorry to wake you, angel. But your family will be here soon, and I figured you wanted to feed her and pump before they arrive."

A slow, full-body yawn consumes me as I come to enough to make sense of what's happening. I fell asleep immediately after my shower. I've been asleep for more than five hours, and I haven't felt this rested in weeks.

"I can't believe I slept that long."

"You needed it," Fielding insists, grabbing my nursing pillow and helping me get situated before handing over our daughter.

He moves around the bed and pulls open the blinds, filling the room with sunlight. Elowyn closes her eyes against the sudden brightness, her blue irises disappearing for a few seconds before she reopens them, focuses on me, and smiles.

"Fielding! She smiled! She just smiled at me!"

My heart melts as I hold her close, breathing in her delicious fresh baby scent. Of course she roots around on contact and even tries to latch on to my neck. The little fiend.

"She did that for me earlier," he admits, coming over to brush her downy hair. "She took one bottle while you slept, then I held her off for as long as I could to give you some extra rest."

As if she knows we're talking about her, Winnie whips her little head back and forth rapidly, mouth gaping, desperate to latch. My boobs are fuller than they've ever been, and instant relief hits the second she starts nursing.

"I have to finish up a few things in the kitchen. Do you want me to come get her when she's done so you can pump?"

"I can manage," I assure him, and for the first time in the two weeks since we've been home, I feel like it's true. It's amazing what a shower and a five-hour nap can do. That, and having a supportive partner.

Almost an hour later, I make my way into the living room, cradling a sleeping Winnie in my arms. She conked out on me as soon as she finished nursing, so pumping and getting ready were a breeze. Plus, she smiled twice more when I held her. It's turning out to be a pretty fantastic day.

I pat her bum and step down into the sunken living room, overcome with glee at the sight of my little sister sitting on the couch, staring at her phone.

"TT!" I whisper, desperate not to wake the baby but so darn happy to see her in person.

Tahlia jumps off the couch and dashes toward me but freezes once she's within arm's reach.

"Oh my gosh. She's so little! Can I hug you? Can I hold her? I washed my hands when I got here. Fielding said you're still sore, and that I have to be careful..."

I roll my eyes and wrap my sister in a one-armed hug, holding on to her for much longer than normal.

Speaking of Fielding...

I don't have a chance to ask before I hear him somewhere in the house. His voice is muffled but grows stronger when my father's voice carries into the room.

I guide Tahlia back to the couch and raise one finger to my lips. She nods, probably thinking that I want her to be quiet while the baby sleeps. Really, I'm just desperate to know what they're saying.

"There should be no confusion: I have clear boundaries for today and all future visits."

I gulp down a sense of dread, bracing for my father's rebuttal. But I don't hear his reply. I only hear Fielding speak again.

"You're here because I'm allowing you to be. If I hear one passive aggressive comment, or if you make one remark that doesn't land well, you're out. Even if you say something that *accidentally* sets her off, you're out. Don't test me. There won't be second chances. Have I made myself clear?"

Months ago, I would have cowered at the idea of someone speaking like that to my parents. Now, I practically crave it. I can stick up for myself, but there's so much comfort in knowing I'm not in this alone.

I glance down at Winnie and find her bright eyes staring right back at me. As soon as I look at her, she gives me another smile.

Lifting her into the air, I bring her little body to rest on my shoulder. "You're so lucky," I croon. Your daddy will always stand up for you like that. You won't ever wonder if he loves you or if he wishes you were someone else. He's already so good at loving you."

Fielding walks into the room at that moment, followed by my parents. Our eyes lock as he gives me one of his megawatt smiles. I swoon from the sincerity—from the absolute adoration—in his gaze.

"He loves us so much," I whisper to my daughter again, knowing it's undoubtedly true.

Chapter 58

Fielding

Five Weeks Later

"I was *not* prepared for that," I lament, blowing out a long, dramatic breath as we make our way to the car. "I mean, seriously. You could have warned me."

Daphne giggles and rolls her eyes, but I'm pretty sure even she was surprised at the way her coworkers swooped in and went gaga for Winnie.

Daphne's best friend Serena has met her multiple times already, of course. She was at the house two nights ago for dinner and to do Daphne's hair. But the rest of those women circled us like vultures: cooing and clamoring to hold the baby. I'm lucky to be leaving with all my limbs.

I hit the remote start button on my key fob as we make our way across the parking lot. It's still chilly in the mornings, even though it's almost Memorial Day.

As we approach my SUV, someone steps out from the other side. My hackles instantly raise.

"Hold up," I murmur, placing one hand on Daphne's back as we slow our stride.

Fuck.

The audacity of this asshole. My rage rachets up tenfold as I realize someone at the salon must have told him we'd be here today. There's no way this isn't a setup.

Daphne wordlessly hands me the baby, the first indicator that she wants to handle him herself. As soon as she's perched in my arms, Winnie grabs at my face. I don't have a chance to speak before Daphne is stepping forward and calling out to him across the length of two parking spots.

"What do you want, Anthony?"

His eyes flick to my face. I snarl on instinct, then school my expression for Winnie.

Focused on Daphne again, he takes a step toward us. I match his stride and glare.

"Heard you might be stopping by here this morning. I thought you'd want to see this," he taunts, waving a manilla envelope in the empty space between us.

I stride forward and snatch it from his hands, then hand the thing to Daphne. I try to steady my breathing, swaying and humming to keep Winnie calm, but the motion does nothing to stop my own heart from racing with panic. This fucker looks way too fucking smug right now.

I have to assume the contents of that envelope are his hail Mary shot: the big reveal, the storm of leverage he thinks he has on me.

But what Anthony doesn't realize is that Daphne knows everything now. I told her about the woman I thought I loved, about the year I spent trying to convince Tori in subtle and not-so-subtle ways to be mine. Daphne knows everything I can remember—as well as the things I don't, thanks to Dem filling in the blanks.

I'm not a good guy. But I'm trying my hardest to be a better man.

I just hope I've done enough over the last ten months to prove to her that I've changed. That I won't spiral. That she can count on me, and that I won't be that person ever again.

Daphne holds the envelope away from her body and turns it over like it's rigged to detonate. She's not wrong to be wary—if he's waited this long to make his move, I'm sure the contents of that envelope are damning at best.

Searching my face, she silently places the decision in my hands.

I nod. I just want this over with. "It'll be okay," I whisper and do my best to crack a smile. I decided months ago that living in fear of the person I used to be isn't fair to her or Winnie. Or to me.

I can feel Anthony's beady eyes on me as Daphne pinches together the metal clasp. Winnie coos in my arms as my angel slides out what appears to be a stack of photos, all blown up to 8x10s, black, white, and grainy from where I'm standing.

I watch, desperate and tense, waiting for any clue as to how this will go.

But then Winnie wiggles in my arms and uses her pudgy little hand to grab my face again. The reminder of who I am now—a dad, a partner, a med student, and more—slams into me as my daughter draws my attention to her.

At the end of the day, when it comes down to it, this is all that matters. Daphne, Winnie, and me. My family. My future.

I don't give a shit about Anthony Adley, his brother, or what anyone thinks of who I used to be. The only people who matter on this whole damn planet are the little lady in my arms and her mama.

Daphne's eyes stay glued to the stack of photos as she leafs through them. After a few seconds, she glances up and catches my eye, both brows raised. Then she smirks.

It's that sly little grin—something I'm pretty sure she learned from me—that tells me, without knowing anything about the contents of the envelope, that we're going to be okay.

"You're right, Anthony. These *are* bad. Almost pornographic, honestly..."

The actual fuck?

I told myself I didn't need to see the pictures. But now I'm curious as hell.

"Did Andy ever mention to you that Fielding is a twin?" she asks, amusement lacing her tone.

The smug expression on Anthony's face disappears instantly as confusion blossoms on his stupid mug.

"He's an identical twin, actually. I thought for sure Andy would have mentioned it, since said twin beat the shit out of him in the downtown parking lot a few years ago."

Daphne doesn't give either of us a chance to speak as she steps forward, stands straighter, and continues.

"From what I know, they had a misunderstanding about a girl named Maddie. Andy thought she was available when she very clearly was not. She's the girl in the pictures here, actually. The girl sitting on her boyfriend's lap, topless, in the hot tub.

"Although calling her a girl is a bit of an understatement. Maddie's a force to be reckoned with. She's headed to law school soon, and I wouldn't be surprised if she and Dempsey get married one day. I don't think either of them will react well to these pictures."

Little Wheeler got my brother into mild exhibitionism? And that's what this fucker thought he had on me this whole time?

My face hurts from smiling. What goddamn luck. I'm half-tempted to pull out my phone and record the rest of this. I already know I'll want to relive this moment over and over again.

"You know what these look like to me?" Daphne muses, fanning through the pictures again in mock-confusion. "These look like invasion of privacy. Pornography without consent. Extortion, maybe. I'm not sure of all the legal jargon, to be honest. But I bet Maddie is."

Anthony grunts, which is the only indication we get that he's going to make a move. I step forward two paces and step in front of Daphne so he's fully aware of what he's bringing on himself if he dares to come any closer.

"Even if she doesn't know all the legalities or the ways she could sue you, she can afford a good lawyer. Fielding and Dempsey are loaded."

"I-I didn't know. I had no idea—" he stammers.

Daphne takes a little side-step around me so we're standing shoulder to shoulder.

"You're done," she declares. "No more, Anthony. No fucking more. I'll hang on to these as collateral. If you try to contact me, or Fielding, or meddle in our lives in any way ever again, I'll pass these along to Maddie. You'll be *lucky* if all she does is sue you," she threatens.

Anthony blinks twice, nods like a trained baboon, then stalks away without another word.

We stand quietly, relieved but on high alert, as he gets into his car and peels out of the parking lot. Once he's gone, I pull Daphne into a hug and squeeze Winnie between us until she squeals with delight.

"You're so badass," I praise, tilting Daphne's chin with one hand so I can kiss her.

She bats her eyelashes and grins up at me before giving me a bashful look. "I just wanted to take care of him once and for all."

I chuckle as we turn back to the car. "You did good, angel. Standing up for yourself. Standing up for our family. I highly doubt the Adley assholes will be a problem for us ever again."

I open her door for her and wait as she buckles.

"There's just one problem, though." I get Winnie situated in the back seat and double-check her car seat straps before closing the back door.

Daphne's expression falls as she searches my gaze.

I brace myself on the passenger doorframe, leaning in so close our lips brush when I speak.

"Now I've got a raging hard-on from watching you put him in his place," I declare, peppering her with kisses between each word. "Fuck... I wish I would have recorded that so I could play it back later."

Chapter 59

Daphne

Three Weeks Later

I smooth down my dress for the tenth time in as many minutes, watching everyone in the room coo over Elowyn.

Dempsey keeps looking at her in awe. He'll stare at her for a few seconds, then look at Fielding, then quickly glance over at me. His smile is as big as his brother's right now. It's adorable.

Maddie's bouncing on her toes and hasn't stopped gushing. "She's *so* little!"

"Little?" Fielding retorts, pretending to be offended. "Who are you calling little? This kid's already doubled her birth weight, and she's only twelve weeks old! She's a beast!"

He lifts her overhead, and Winnie belly-laughs while he gobbles up her tummy.

I walk over and place a hand on his arm, giving him a pointed look. She just ate, and we can't leave if she throws up and I have to feed her again.

He gives me a sheepish smile, knowing exactly what I'm worried about, and goes into dad mode a moment later—instructing Maddie to sit on the couch so he can explain paced feeding and the best ways to burp her.

Dempsey goes back to reading through the three-page document Fielding wrote out like it's the owner's manual of a new car. I half expect him to pull out a pen and start scribbling in the margins.

Once they're situated and we've confirmed that they're good, they've got this, and they'll call with any questions, Fielding grabs my hand and pulls me back toward our bedroom instead of the garage.

I'm bewildered enough to follow along and not even question his intentions.

As soon as we're alone, he's pushing me against the bedroom door and skimming one hand up my exposed thigh.

Like a man possessed, he ravages my mouth and grips my hips. His intensity awakens something inside me, and suddenly I'm kissing him back with just as much fervor.

I've missed this. I've missed *us*. The care he's shown me over the last few months has been beautiful and heartwarming. But now that I'm healed and starting to remember who I am aside from just being Elowyn's mom, I need him to take care of me in other ways.

"Wait," I pant, placing both hands on his chest to steady myself. "I thought we were going out."

"Oh, we are." He moves his hands to cup my ass as he hauls me into his body. "You look fucking incredible," he murmurs in my ear as he teases the hem of my dress. "I love this, and I'm going to need to see you in it again soon."

I'm wearing a new cornflower blue wrap dress that will flutter open the second he pulls on the ties. I had to go up two sizes to accommodate my boobs and belly, but I feel pretty for the first time in weeks.

"I brought you back here because I think you might want to change into pants. We're taking the bike."

He steps back then, and as if reading my mind, pulls open the belt on my dress.

"Goddamn," he mutters in appreciation, lifting his fist to his mouth as he gives me a thorough once-over.

"I'll wait for you in the kitchen because we literally won't make it out the door if I don't remove myself and let you get changed in peace."

I roll my eyes at his dramatics but can't fight the smile that creeps onto my face. This man makes me feel *so* good. Inside and out. Every single day. I can't wait to spend an afternoon alone with him.

I work my hands under his shirt and feel his taut stomach muscles contract beneath my fingers. I hold on tighter as the wind whips around the hair peeking out from under my helmet.

Pressing my cheek into his back, I revel in how far we've come since the last time I was on his bike. The night we met at The Oak, I would have never in a million years guessed I'd be back on this bike with this man as the mother of his child and the center of his world.

Our lives have changed in so many significant ways.

I've changed in a lot of ways, too.

The differences have evolved almost minutely—these subtle but poignant realizations about who I am and what I've settled for over the years, especially from the people who supposedly love me.

Basking in Fielding's personal brand of adoration has changed how I define love. Creating our own family has elevated everything I thought I wanted and deserved.

I've never felt more settled and at peace—or as excited about what the future holds.

He eases the bike into a parking garage and comes to a slow stop as I take in our surroundings.

We're about half an hour from home, at a swanky shopping and restaurant district. I tickle his stomach to get his attention, nodding toward the sign in front of us.

"It says hotel parking only."

He whips his head around, gives me one of those megawatt smiles, and winks. "Good thing we have a reservation."

My eyes go wide with excitement, but that feeling is quickly replaced with dread.

"Relax," he soothes, dismounting and offering me his hand. "I know you don't want to be away from home for more than one feeding, and I packed your pump. I just wanted to get you alone and let you unwind. We can order room service. Or take a nap. Catch up on those stupid TV shows you like. Whatever you want to do, angel, I'm game."

I bite my lower lip and give him a look—I know *exactly* what I want to do in a hotel room alone with him. And he knows it, too, but it was sweet of him to plan this date without expectation.

I was cleared for sex several weeks ago… and I had an IUD inserted at my postnatal follow up appointment since condoms have let us down once before. But it's hard to even consider getting it in with a baby at home. I'm exhausted all the time. Even when Winnie does sleep, I try to catch up on all the things I can't do when she's awake.

We've fooled around here and there, and we've gotten away with two quickies. But we've also been interrupted more than once. Nothing kills a lady boner faster than a wailing baby and the accompanying surge of milk letting down.

I wouldn't have thought to come to a hotel for a date. But now there's nowhere else I want to be.

Check-in is seamless, and I pounce on Fielding in the elevator, forcing him to drop the overnight bag he's carrying. If there was any question about how I wanted to spend our evening away, my intentions just came through loud in clear.

He groans into my mouth when we get to our room, then curses under his breath when he fumbles to hold the key card to the door.

The door has barely clicked closed when he's pushing me against the wall, dominating my mouth and grinding his pelvis against my core. "How do you want me?" he demands on an exhale.

"Hard and fast," I pant. "Remind me I'm yours."

He bites my neck—hard, just like I asked—before taking my earlobe between his teeth.

"Fuck, angel. That might be the hottest thing you've ever said to me. Take off your pants and get on the bed. Now."

I scurry over and undress, not bothering to make a show of stripping out of my clothes. The day will come where we have time to take things slow. To kiss and touch. To explore and savor. I'm way too desperate for any of that now.

My body literally craves his touch. As I watch him strip, my empty pussy pulses with need. I quickly lick my fingers and graze them against my core, mewling on contact as he stalks toward the bed.

"Look at you, all hot and needy. You can't even wait for me?"

I shake my head mischievously but rise to my knees to kiss him all the same. He works a hand into my hair while the other travels down and interlaces with my fingers.

Fielding lifts our joined hands to my lips, demanding "suck" as he pushes into my mouth and presses down on my tongue.

He uses both our hands to rub my clit, working his fingers in tandem with mine. "You're fucking soaked," he murmurs in my ear, separating our hands to cup my pussy with an appreciative growl. "Fucking soaked and so fucking ready. What do you need, angel? What do you want that only I can give you?"

I thrust against his hand, craving more contact. I want him. He fucking knows it. But I also know he wants to hear me beg.

"Fielding," I whimper, catching his hand and pressing it hard against my clit. I reach for his other hand and guide it to my throat, then peer up at him longingly. "Please."

It's like that one word is his kryptonite. He pushes me back so hard I rebound off the mattress and yelp in surprise. He prowls toward me until I'm scrambling back, but he reaches out and grips my hips before I can get comfortable.

"Flip," he demands, helping me turn over before he braces over me and lines himself up, teasing the tip of his cock at my entrance.

"Just like this?" He angles over me and bites at the pulse point in my neck before turning my head and stealing a bruising kiss that leaves me breathless.

"Just like that," I pant. I wiggle my ass in the air, frantic to feel him slam into me. But it's not his cock that makes contact first. It's his hot, demanding mouth.

He licks my entire slit and both his hands dig into my ass as he spreads me wide. He lets out a string of expletives before probing me with his tongue. "I fucking love the way you taste," he practically moans against my core. I peek over my shoulder and watch as he feasts—it's such a turn-on to hear him moan and feel the ferocity of his lust.

I arch my back and get lost in the ministrations of his mouth, but at this angle, it's just not enough to push me over the edge. I moan and pant, and as if he can read my mind, he instantly pulls back. "You need more, don't you, angel?"

I whimper my assent, trusting that he knows exactly what I want. And I practically squeal in delight when he rises to his knees, leans forward to wrap one hand around my throat, and shoves me face firs- into the bed.

"You like that?" he murmurs. He knows damn well I do. With his cock teasing my entrance, he leans forward again and kisses my shoulder. "You better make a fucking mess on my dick, angel. I'm going to give it to you just how you like it, but you need to be a good girl and come hard. Think you can do that for me?"

My eyes are already glazing over with pleasure, but I nod wordlessly and arch up to meet that first delicious thrust. He doesn't ease into me—he knows better than to take it slow—instead setting a brutal pace as he fucks me from behind.

Fuck. Yes. Just like this.

I purr in satisfaction when his balls slap my clit. Every time our bodies connect and he bottoms out, he squeezes my throat, electrifying every one of my nerves.

He's relentless as he hammers into me—giving me everything I want and all I need. When I'm close, I return the generosity.

"Fielding," I manage to choke out, my voice raw and airy from the way he's gripping my neck.

"Yes, angel?" he teases. He knows what's coming. We both do. That doesn't make it any less thrilling. There's a distinct intimacy in knowing exactly what your partner craves without them even having to ask.

"Harder. Please. I'm close. I need you."

He grunts, bottoms out again, then fucks me even deeper.

"Please don't stop," I cry, bracing my arms against the headboard as he drills into me harder. His hand leaves my throat and shoves between the mattress and my body. When he pinches my clit and doesn't let go, my entire core tightens, and I finally topple over the edge.

He fucks me through the orgasm, only letting himself come once I'm a sated, whimpering mess. Eventually, he slows, his forehead coming to rest in the middle of my back as we savor the aftershocks and waning waves of pleasure.

I love how well he knows me: how he doesn't question my requests, try to temper his pace, or give me anything less than his personal best.

Slow and steady was never going to be enough where this man is concerned. Hard and fast is perfect when it comes to Fielding Haas.

The alarm I insisted on setting vibrates on the nightstand beside us. Fielding groans against my stomach, right near my c-section scar, before he resumes lavishing me with kisses.

After round one, he ordered room service, and we both dozed off just long enough to recover for round two. Now we're somewhere between rounds three and four. I've sort of lost count of our orgasms in my blissed-out state. All I know is that we've been at it for hours. He hasn't stopped touching me. Kissing me. Gathering up our joint release and using it to get me off again.

I hit snooze to silence my phone but rise to my elbows anyway.

"No," he groans in protest, his mouth tickling lower as his tongue brushes over my swollen, sensitive clit. "I'm not done with you. I need more."

"More? More what?" I tease, running one hand through his wild, crazy sex hair.

"Everything," he answers without hesitation. "More kisses. More cuddles. More orgasms." He peers up at me and smirks. "More moments like this." He sweeps two fingers through his cum, massaging it between my folds before pushing it back into my pussy and crooking his fingers. I whimper on instinct, my body betraying the more sensible part of my brain that says we really do have to get going.

"Today was incredible. Thank you," I murmur, pulling him toward me and forcing him to focus on something besides my pussy. "I promise we'll have more everything. I want more with you, too."

He kisses me slowly, trying in vain to deepen the kiss before I pull back and give him a look. "But right now—"

"I know, I know," he groans. "I just can't get enough." He kisses my lips again, then licks down my neck. He grazes both my breasts before kissing my stomach and trying to resituate between my thighs.

"Fielding!" I scold, clamping my legs around his head to stop whatever he thinks he's about to start.

"Ten more seconds," he counters, pressing the flat of his tongue against my core and groaning in pleasure. "Fuck, I love the way you taste when you're filled with my cum."

Arousal courses through me—*again*. I'm such a sucker for his delicious, dirty mouth.

"I can't wait to wife you up and put a dozen more babies in here," he declares, prodding my entrance with his tongue. "Eventually," he adds. "When you're ready."

I don't bother scolding him for getting ahead of himself. I know him well enough now to know there's no point trying to rein him in. Fielding only knows how to love full out.

"I love you so much," I start, shifting away and rolling to my side. "But we really do need to get going. Don't you want to get home and see Winnie before she goes down for the night?"

He's up in an instant, rummaging around for our clothes and ushering me into the shower so we can get going. I fight back a smirk at his reaction to potentially missing bedtime. I can't help but grin as I watch him switch back into dad mode, texting his brother our ETA and retrieving the milk from the mini fridge that I pumped a few hours ago.

He must feel my eyes on him, because eventually he looks up and gives me one of those perfect Fielding grins. "I love you," he tells me simply, locking me in his gaze and making sure I feel the gravity of his words.

"I know," I reply, accepting his affection and feeling his sincerity in my bones. I always did believe in fairy tales. I just had no idea happily ever after could feel like this. "I love you, too."

Chapter 60

Fielding

"I love her. I've only known her for two days and already—I *love* her."

My brother has the goofiest grin on his face as he stares adoringly at my daughter. He's got his feet propped on the coffee table, and she's lying on his thighs while she grips both of his thumbs.

Daphne and Maddie are out back sharing a bottle of wine around the firepit. We told them we were having a Haas family meeting, and since they aren't technically Haases, they weren't invited.

Maddie got sassy, as expected. Daphne just scoffed playfully and smiled. She sees right through all my excuses to carve out little pockets of alone time for her. But she plays along, and I genuinely believe she appreciates it, too. Which works in my favor because I have no plans to stop anytime soon.

I want to provide for her. Give her everything she needs and support her in ways she never experienced before me.

That's my focus now—my purpose. I dicked around for nearly three decades, making selfish, immature choices. If this is my penance—doing all I can for the woman I love, who deserves the world and more—then sign me the fuck up.

Winnie squawks in my direction, and I lean in close to scrunch my nose against hers and kiss her sweet little head. She keeps looking from me to Dempsey, then back to me again.

I can't imagine how confusing it is to stare at two versions of her own dad. But she saves all her gummy smiles for me, so I'm almost positive she can tell the difference between us.

"You made this," he mutters in disbelief. He's taken at least a hundred pictures of her since they got into town, which is ridiculous because we already send them multiple pictures every day.

I've never seen him like this before. Part of me feels a twinge of guilt—I'm going to have to warn Maddie. She's got her five-year plan, and they just moved to NYC. She's starting law school at Columbia in the fall. If my brother's head is where I think it is…

"I want one," he declares, leaning in to make a ridiculous face at Winnie as she coos.

Called it. I'll definitely have to give Little Wheeler the heads-up…

"Gimme my baby before you catch a fever," I insist, lifting Winnie out of his arms, then hugging her to my chest. Her little fist finds its way into the neck of my T-shirt as she turns her head and rests her cheek on my shoulder to stare back at my brother.

I kiss the top of her head, inhaling that delicious baby smell that's quickly become one of my favorite scents in the world.

"I want to smell," Dem grumbles, crowding my space so he can take his own whiff. "Fuck, that's heavenly," he curses, before asking, "Oh shit. Are we still allowed to say fuck?"

"You hear that, little angel? Your Uncle Dumpy has a potty mouth." I smirk at him over her head before adding solemnly, "I figure we've got a year or so to break the habit."

"She's just so perfect," he croons, grinding his hard head against my shoulder so he can get right up in her face.

"I seriously can't believe *you* made this," he gushes.

I give her bum a little pat, then rest my head against his. We regard my daughter as her lagoon-blue eyes stare right back at us as a comfortable silence settles around us.

"What if everything that happened had to happen so we could get here?" I whisper. It's a thought that's nagged me for weeks. Winnie is so amazing, so worthy, so good. It still doesn't make sense that after all the shit I pulled and all the heartache I caused, I get to be her dad.

"Hmm." Dem sighs contemplatively beside me, brushing one finger along her chubby cheek.

"Or what if she's the bright spot you need and deserve after so many shitty years?"

I hadn't thought about it like that. Mostly because I still don't know that I deserve any of this.

Maybe we're both right. I've fucked up enough to know exactly what not to do this time around. I've accepted what I've done and who I once was—but I've also accepted that my life is better than it's ever been, right here in this moment.

It's an overwhelming sensation—to be so needed and so loved by not one but two people. But I'm up for the challenge, and there's no doubt I can handle this beautiful gift I've been given.

I'll make the most of each day. I'll be the best for them because they deserve the best. And when I inevitably fuck up, I won't let it pull me down or deter me for long. I'll learn from my mistakes and move on. It's who I am. It's what I do. I only know how to play full out.

Just can't get enough Fielding and Daphne? <u>Sign up for my email newsletter</u> and receive a FREE eBook that includes an extended epilogue for Field, Daph, and all their kids!

Afterword

Thank you so much for reading *Full Out Fiend*! This is a project that almost didn't happen, simply because of who Fielding is and the atrocities he committed in previous books. But everyone deserves a chance at happily ever after, and writing his story feels very full circle.

If you're new to my books and want to know exactly what happened between Fielding and Maddie's sister-in-law, Tori, check out my Hampton Hearts series (book one is called When You're Home). Jake also has his own prequel novella and full-length novel (his books are titled Rowdy Boy and Mr. Brightside) and Maddie and Dempsey's epic love story unfolds in their book, Fourth Wheel.

If you enjoyed this story, I have a feeling you'll really like what comes next. Hampton Holiday Collective is a collection of four novelettes featuring your favorite couples from my previous books. It's my FREE GIFT to you when you sign up for my email newsletter!

By Abby Millsaps

presented in order of publication

When You're Home
While You're There
When You're Home for the Holidays
When You're Gone
Rowdy Boy
Mr. Brightside
Fourth Wheel
Full Out Fiend
Hampton Holiday Collective

Too Safe: Boys of Lake Chapel Book One
Too Fast: Boys of Lake Chapel Book Two
Too Far: Boys of Lake Chapel Book Three

About The Author

Abby Millsaps is an author and storyteller who's been obsessed with writing romance since middle school. In eighth grade, she failed to qualify for the Power of the Pen State Championships because "all her submissions contained the same theme: young people falling in love." #LookAtHerNow

She's best known for writing unapologetically angsty romance that causes emotional damage for her readers. Creative spicy scenes and consent as foreplay are two hallmarks of her books. Abby prides herself in writing authentic characters while weaving mental health, chronic illness, and neurodiverse representation into the fabric of her stories.

Abby met her husband at a house party the summer before her freshman year of college. He had a secret pizza stashed in the trunk of his car that he was saving for a midnight snack—how was she supposed to resist that level of golden retriever energy and preparedness? When Abby isn't writing, she's reading, traveling, and raising her three daughters.

Connect with Abby
Website: www.authorabbymillsaps.com
Instagram: @abbymillsaps
TikTok: @authorabbymillsaps
Email: authorabbymillsaps@gmail.com
Newsletter: https://geni.us/AuthorAbbyNewsletter
Facebook Reader Group: Abby's Full Out Fiends

www.ingramcontent.com/pod-product-compliance
Lightning Source LLC
LaVergne TN
LVHW030317070526
838199LV00069B/6480